Strategies in
Teaching Anthropology

edited by
Patricia C. Rice
West Virginia University
and
David W. McCurdy
Macalester College

Foreword by Conrad P. Kottak

Introduction by Yolanda T. Moses

PRENTICE HALL, Upper Saddle River, New Jersey 07458

©2000 by PRENTICE-HALL, INC.
Upper Saddle River, New Jersey 07458

ISBN 0-13-025683-8

Printed in the United States of America

CONTENTS

Contributors   v

Annotated Index by Topic, Learning Outcomes, and Student Activity   vi

Foreword by Conrad P. Kottak   xiii

Introduction by Yolanda T. Moses   xv

Part I: General

Participation and Page References: Sharpening the Focus of Class Discussion (Douglas Caulkins and Vicki Bentley-Condit)   1
Web-Based Research Projects in Anthropology: Notes From the Virtual Field (Eric C. Thompson)   6
Discussion Preparation Guides (Charles O. Ellenbaum)   13
A "Class inside the Class" (Patricia C. Rice)   21
New Technology, Library Budget Cuts, and How to Deal with Them All (Dirk Van Tuerenhout)   24

Part II: Biological Anthropology and Archaeology

"First Steps" in Hominid Evolution: A Lesson on Walking (Janet Pollak)   27
A Feline Paternity Suit (Joyce Lucke)   31
The Trouble with the "Race" Concept: It's All in the Cards (Robert Graber)   38
"Excavating" in the Classroom (Julia L. J. Sanchez)   43
An Exercise in Real World Archaeology (Maureen Siewert Meyers)   55

Part III: Cultural

Cultural Anthropology 101: Teaching Cultural Anthropology Scientifically (Beverly Goodman)   63
The Penny Game: An Exercise in Non-Industrial Economics (Cathy A. Small)   71
Value Orientations in the Classroom (Robert C. Harman)   78
Cultural Rights (Suzanne LaFont)   84
Potlatching Classroom Participation: Using "Prestige" and "Shame" to Encourage Student Involvement (Daniel M. Goldstein)   88
"And a Hush Fell Over the Courtroom": Use of a Mock Trial in Cultural Anthropology (David Howard Day)   93
Nacirema Writing (John M. Coggeshall)   99
Dr. Seuss Meets Up with Anthony Giddens (Matthew J. Richard)   102
Quizzing the Kula Way -- With Persuasion (Renee M. Gralewicz)   106
Exploring the Meaning of Family (Matthew Kennedy)   113

iv

Museum Visits in Cultural Anthropology Courses (Serena Nanda)   117

The Political Economy of Socialism (Elizabeth Dunn)   122

Building Student Interest, Input, and Engagement: Organizing Small Group Projects in
        Large Lecture Classes (Marilynne Diggs-Thompson)   128

Mnemonics, Quotations, Cartoons, and a Notebook: "Tricks" for Appreciating Cultural
        Diversity (Charles F. Urbanowicz)   132

Field Trips and Student Involvement: Hands-On Learning Components (Ruth Krulfeld)   141

Growing Up Pink or Blue:Using Childrens' Television Commercials to Analyze Gender
        Enculturation (S. Elizabeth Bird)   145

How to Teach Self Ethnography (John L. Caughey)   149

Pre-Class Fieldwork: Ethnographic Introductions (Dickie Wallace)   157

Familiarizing the Exotic in Ethnographic Film (Sam Pack)   159

Doing Ethnographic Research in the Classroom: A Simple Exercise for Engaging Introductory
        Students (Grace Keyes)   164

Moiety Exogamy, Sibling Exchange, and Cross-Cousin Marriage (Ernest L. Schusky)   167

Short Writing Assignments in Large Classes (David F. Lancy)   171

Interviewing Tricks for Student Ethnographers (David McCurdy)   173

"Sensory Anthropology": A Sensi-ble Way to Teach Anthropology (Ann Christine Frankowski)
    178

v

CONTRIBUTORS

S. Elizabeth Bird (University of South Florida)
John L. Caughey (University of Maryland)
Vicki Bentley-Condit (Grenell College)
Douglas Caulkins (Grenell College)
John M. Coggeshall (Clemson University)
David Howard Day (Monroe Community College)
Marilynne Diggs-Thompson (Hunter College – CUNY)
Elizabeth Dunn (Encyclopedia Britannica)
Charles O. Ellenbaum (College of DuPage)
Ann Christine Frankowski (University of Maryland, Baltimore County)
Daniel M. Goldstein (Miami University)
Beverly Goodman (Pennsylvania State University)
Robert Graber (Truman State University)
Renee M. Gralewicz (University of Wisconsin – Barron County)
Robert C. Harman (California State University, Long Beach)
Matthew Kennedy (City College of San Francisco)
Grace Keyes (Our Lady of the Lake University)
Ruth M. Krulfeld (The George Washington University)
Suzanne LaFont (Kingsborough Community College – CUNY)
David F. Lancy (Utah State University)
Joyce Lucke (IUPU – Columbus)
David McCurdy (Macalester College)
Maureen Siewert Meyers (Louis Berger and Associates)
Serena Nanda (John Jay College – CUNY)
Sam Pack (Temple University)
Janet Pollak (William Paterson University)
Patricia C. Rice (West Virginia University)
Matthew J. Richard (Valdosta State University)
Julia L.J. Sanchez (UCLA Institute of Archaeology)
Ernest L. Schusky (Southern Illinois University)
Cathy A. Small (Northern Arizona University)
Eric C. Thompson (University of Washington)
Charles F. Urbanowicz (California State University, Chico)
Dirk Van Tuerenhout (Middle American Research Institute, Tulane University)
Dickie Wallace (University of Massachusetts)

ANNOTATED INDEX BY TOPIC, LEARNING OUTCOMES, AND STUDENT ACTIVITY

Growing Up Pink or Blue: Using Childrens' Television Commercials to Analyze Gender Enculturation (Bird)

... gender as a cultural construct;
... students learn how TV commercials enculturate children into culturally proper gender roles;
... students watch a prepared video tape of ads aimed at children and then discuss the depicted gender coding. (Additional related exercises are suggested.)

How to Teach Self Ethnography (Caughey)

... ethnography of self;
... students learn how to do field work as well as discovering "hidden truths" about their own culture;
... students choose an informant whose cultural background is significantly different from their own and through "field work" interviewing, compare the resultant life history with their own.

Participation and Page References: Sharpening the Focus of Class Discussions (Caulkins and Bentley-Condit)

... class participation using "page referencing;"
... students learn to read for comprehension, solve problems, and use team discussion of "narrative" readings (rather than informational readings);
... students are prepared to answer open-ended questions (prepared and distributed by the instructor before reading), note the page where the answer occurs, and respond in class in the order of the pages, resulting in contributions from the entire class.

Nacirema Writing (Coggeshall)

... writing about the relationship between assigned readings and a related subject;
... students learn writing skills and how to apply the specifics in a reading assignment to a general theme;
... 12 times a term, students write a10-minute in-class essay on an assigned reading as a prelude to class discussion launched by that reading.

"And a Hush Fell Over the Courtroom:" Use of a Mock Trial in Cultural Anthropology (Day)

... a classroom mock trial concerning Native American medical practices;
... students learn about Native American medical practices as an alternative to American medicine and the legal problems this entails;

... the mock trial allows students to play trial roles: the Native American accused of illegal acts, lawyers, judge, witnesses, jury members, and court stenographer.

Building Student Interest, Input, and Engagement: Organizing Small Group Projects in Large Lecture Classes (Diggs-Thompson)

... term team projects;

... students learn that anthropology is the study of modern, technologically complex people, not just ancient, extinct, "primitive" cultures;

... in teams of 9-10, students make in-class presentations based on one of 60 randomly chosen topics gleaned from articles from *The New York Times*; the presentations can be reports or debates and can include data, slides, or charts.

Teaching the Political Economy of Socialism (Dunn)

... the economics of political socialism;

... students gain an understanding of the principles and implications of state socialist economies;

... following a model and instructions, students attempt to build "houses" from gummi bears and toothpicks, though there are shortages of both; they may resort to stealing, biting bears in half, or trying to work in teams to fulfill their "plan."

Discussion Preparation Guides (Ellenbaum)

... discussion of articles or films;

... students learn how to share information and views on articles or films;

... students sit in groups of 5, use their filled-in Preparation Guides (provided) and discuss the main points of a reading or film.

"Sensory Anthropology:" A Sensi-ble Approach to Teaching Anthropology (Frankowski)

... "sensory anthropology:" sight, hearing, smell, touch, taste;

... students learn how human senses are culturally constructed and how anthropologists use their senses while doing field work;

... through various exercises, students taste, observe, hear, touch, and smell features of cultures other than their own.

Potlatching Classroom Participation: Using "Prestige" and "Shame" to Encourage Student Involvement (Goldstein)

... classroom participation;

... students learn the principles of potlatching, reciprocal gift giving, and their associated shame and prestige;

... students must attempt to answer questions pertaining to recently presented class material on Durkheimian social theory in order to discharge their obligation for a gift given to each.

Cultural Anthropology 101: Teaching Cultural Anthropology Scientifically (Goodman)

... science-based cultural anthropology research project;
... students learn how to develop a science-based research project in cultural anthropology from hypothesis generation to field notes and final report;
... students engage in designing survey questions, getting permission from survey candidates, conducting field interviews, and writing up field notes.

The Trouble With the "Race" Concept: It's All in the Cards (Graber)

... the concept of "race;"
... students learn that the traits used to construct "races" are not concordant and therefore do not produce biological races;
... using two decks of manufactured cards, students sort one deck into two "races," but no matter how hard they try, cannot sort the second deck because more than one trait is used.

Quizzing the Kula Way – With Persuasion (Gralewicz)

... term quizzes using kula concepts;
... students learn the economic and social principles of Kula Ring transactions, i.e., persuasion;
... half of the students "travel" to other groups and half "stay behind" to receive travellers, each group attempting to persuade the other group to give up its "gifts."

Value Orientations in the Classroom (Harman)

... research on "national culture" value orientations;
... students learn the value of anthropology's attempt to understand other cultures, in this case "national cultures;"
... students pick the country (or culture) they wish to investigate for a term-long research project and research the value dimensions and value orientations of their chosen national culture, reporting their results orally and in written form.

Exploring the Meaning of Family (Kennedy)

... personal kin diagram;
... students learn how anthropologists trace descent in "other" cultures by doing their own kin diagram;
... students interview family members to construct a diagram that is at least three generations long and includes at least 10 people in either their mother's or father's line.

Doing Ethnographic Research in the Classroom: A Simple Exercise for Engaging Introductory Students (Keyes)

... in-class ethnographic research;
... students learn how to interview, collect, and interpret data;
... students take turns interviewing each other, first asking two "get acquainted" questions and then a "serious" question about American eating behaviors; implications and meanings are then discussed by the class.

Field Trips and Student Involvement: Hands-On Learning Components (Krulfeld)

... field trips as data bases;
... students have direct experience with a culture different from their own by participating in cultural events;
... students observe, interview, participate in events, and write-up the experience under the guidance of the professional anthropologist-teacher.

Cultural Rights (LaFont)

... cultural rights;
... students learn about the complexity of cultural rights issues;
... after a small amount of preparation, in a one-class session, students discuss a particular cultural rights issue in small groups, with responses noted; the issues are discussed in the full class the next session. (Suggestions are given for cultural rights issues.)

Short Writing Assignments in Large Classes (Lancy)

... research papers in large classes;
... students learn the research process by doing a standardized assignment;
... students use a "critical source library" to research a topic, ending with a 2½ page research paper (that does not take much time to grade).

A Feline Paternity Suit: An Exercise in Anthropological Genetics (Lucke)

... principles of Mendelian genetics;
... students learn basic genetic terms and principles by studying the genetics responsible for cat coats;
... students use the knowledge of cat coat genetics to describe the phenotype and genotype of a "mother cat" and her kittens and then predict the phenotype and genotype of the unknown Tom cat. (More advanced exercises are suggested.)

Interviewing Tricks for Student Ethnographers (McCurdy)

... eliciting cultural knowledge from informants;
... students learn about cultural knowledge and how to elicit knowledge from informants;
... students interview an informant (of choice) for a term; the article gives 7 "tips" for
     interviewing to elicit the most relevant information.

An Exercise in Real World Archaeology (Meyers)

... an exercise in archaeological sampling and research design;
... students learn how to create and carry out a research design and how to apply different
     sampling strategies to different situations;
... in teams of 5 - 7, students receive a research scenario and spend 15 minutes designing a
     research strategy, presenting the strategy to the class as a whole for critique. (A total of
     five different "scenarios" are included.)

Museum Visits in Cultural Anthropology Courses (Nanda)

... effective museum visits;
... students learn to apply in-class abstractions to concrete examples in museums as well as to
     appreciate diverse cultural heritages;
... students visit special or permanent museum exhibits, focusing on a particular topic or
     problem, observe and then describe what they see in short, focused, papers.

Familiarizing the Exotic in Ethnographic Film (Pack)

... viewing ethnographic film;
... students learn how to critically examine the ethnographic films they see;
... with only their brains and eyes being active, students see films of "the primitive" from a non-
     ethnocentric perspective.

"First Steps" in Hominid Evolution: A Lesson on Walking (Pollak)

... critical thinking about bipedalism;
... students learn how to dissect a seemingly easy behavior -- walking -- and thus learn how
     anatomically and physiologically complex the behavior is;
... students write a paragraph for "an owner's manual" for standing/walking by either observing
     others or "practicing" the behavior; after reading a sample of the first-drafts to the class,
     the instructor returns the papers for rewrites.

A "Class inside The Class" (Rice)

... in-class discussion;
... stress-free discussion of written materials;
... 3 - 4 students have a "conversation" with the instructor on a small-group basis with the rest of the class as the "audience."

Dr. Seuss Meets Up With Anthony Giddens (Richard)

... use of Dr. Seuss' "Sneetches" as the "other" to understand cultural relativity;
... students learn about cultural relativism, ethnocentrism, and socially constructed world views;
... no student activity. (The instructor reads portions of the children's book in class, pointing out the parallels to perceptions of "others.")

"Excavating" in the Classroom (Sanchez)

... archaeological survey, "excavation," and interpretation;
... students learn to use a budget, do a survey, "excavate," and interpret a simulated project;
... students do a survey based on map grids of a chosen site, receive a set of survey results (features and artifacts), and decide where to "excavate;" the result is a site report/interpretation.

Moiety Exogamy, Sibling Exchange, and Cross-Cousin Marriage (Schusky)

... three "exotic" rules of behavior: moieties, sibling exchange, and cross-cousin marriage;
... students learn the nature of these sets of rules and under what circumstances the behaviors will occur together;
... students move to one of two "villages," choose "siblings" in that village, choose spouces from the other "village," and then find spouces for their children.

The Penny Game: An Exercise in Non-Industrial Economics (Small)

... the principles of reciprocity;
... students learn that generalized and balanced reciprocity is not a matter of "naive" non-Westerners giving their wealth away but a matter of marketing "savvy" and often necessary to survival;
... each student starts with 12 pennies and following the rules, meets and "exchanges" (or not) with others; after counting pennies at the end of the exchange period, strategies are discussed; a "surprise" at the end alters the fortunes of many.

Web-Based Research Projects in Anthropology: Notes From the Virtual Field (Thompson)

... Web-based research projects;

... students learn to separate fact from opinion and assess the quality of website materials;

... students do two Web-based research projects, chosen to coincide with the themes and intent of the course.

Mnemonics, Quotations, Cartoons, and a Notebook: "Tricks" for Appreciating Cultural Diversity (Urbanowicz)

... a series of ideas to use in teaching cultural anthropology;

... students are aided in their understanding and appreciation of cultural diversity;

... no student activity. (Instructors are shown how to use a number of ideas to teach diversity.)

New Technology, Library Budget Cuts, and How to Deal With Them All (Van Tuerenhout)

... a comparison of "text" from a textbook and a "text" from a website on the same subject;

... students learn how to evaluate what they read, in this case both website materials and textbook materials;

... students investigate a particular topic (the nature of Maya writing) through reading a chapter in a textbook and a specific Web-based article.

Pre-Class Fieldwork: Ethnographic Introductions (Wallace)

... an ethnography of the first day of class;

... students learn about field methods and the ethics of doing field work;

... no student activity. (The instructor sits in the back of the room dressed as a student, takes notes and observes behavioral patterns of students as they come into the classroom the first day of class. This is the basis for an immediate discussion of field work and ethics.)

FOREWORD

Conrad P. Kottak

We all have our teaching tricks and we sometimes share them anecdotally with colleagues. We may do this in meetings, conferences, or over lunch with a fellow faculty member. Usually, however, our focus at national meetings and professional conferences is the more exalted domain of research. As anthropologists, we don't talk about **how to teach** as much as we should. This volume provides a welcome forum for a group of seasoned teaching anthropologists to share their pedagogical techniques, knowledge, and observations with their fellows. And in a sense, it is a sequel to the 1997 *The Teaching of Anthropology: Problems, Issues, and Decisions* that I co-edited with Jane White, Richard Furlow, and Patricia Rice. This new volume is the applied "how to do it" side of the pedagogical nature of teaching our discipline.

Anthropology's breadth supports an array of teaching strategies, and it is useful to have a number of these strategies assembled here in a single volume. A range of articles representing anthropology's sub-fields exposes numerous teaching "tricks." As teachers, we have discovered that some things work while others do not. Some of the strategies we use with undergraduates may not work with graduate students. One strategy that can work at both levels, when used properly, is the team project. In a large class, such projects can also reduce our workload, permitting us, say, to read fifteen papers instead of thirty. Teamwork, a tradition in archaeology and biological anthropology, is featured in several of the strategies discussed in this volume. Such joint work does pose a challenge to the lone ethnographer model that has long, and probably unfortunately, dominated cultural anthropology. But I have found that joint writing projects, especially involving teams of two students who are allowed to choose their own partner, enhances the quality of presentation. Students have to get their points across to each other before trying to explain them to me. Better, clearer writing, and higher grades result, along with a sense that even cultural anthropologists can learn to work in teams.

Often we develop special strategies for parts of the introductory course that our students find particularly challenging, such as genetics and kinship. The papers in this volume offer tricks for making comprehensible several of anthropology's "esoteric" topics. These range from the kula, the potlatch, and economic exchange theory, to cross-cousin marriage and moiety organization. Other contributors describe strategies they use to demonstrate anthropological perspectives that contradict everyday experience and establish social categories, as in teaching about the social construction of race.

The book offers teaching tricks ranging from specific to very general applicability. Strategies involving interviewing, hypothesis testing, field trips, museum visits, ethnographic film viewing, and Internet use can be applied in a variety of courses. Others have more particular goals, such as using cat's coats to teach about genetics or a mock trial to teach about culture clashes. Almost everyone who teaches introductory anthropology has learned the usefulness of using the familiar to illustrate the novel. Students appreciate American culture examples, whether we are teaching about kinship, genetics, race, gender, rituals, or values.

This volume enhances anthropological pedagogy by assembling tricks of the trade from anthropologists working in a variety of teaching settings. For those of us who value teaching, which after all most of us do for a living, this book, once read, should be placed on an easily reachable shelf.

INTRODUCTION

Yolanda T. Moses

Anthropology has often been called the science of the 21st century. It is a wonderful discipline with at least four sub-fields: Cultural-Social, Biological, Archaeology, and Linguistics; and with two dimensions: research and applied studies. One major problem with anthropology in the United States is that it is not usually taught in high schools, so the first time most students are exposed to the subject is at the college or university level. Consequently, the first exposure to anthropology and how it is taught is critical.

Anthropology professors, like most classically trained academicians, do not learn how to teach as a part of their training. We learn our subject matter, often in great detail. In fact, we are often the only experts in our particular subject area in the entire world. There is, therefore, a huge gap between the student who is taking an anthropology class for the first time and faculty members who know their own "dense" subject matter, but do not know how to pitch it to their audience, to "engage" them in anthropological subject matter and its processes. I have found in my many years of teaching students (mostly non-anthropology majors), that they learn anthropology best by "doing it."

This book is the first of its kind as far as I know to focus on the "how" of teaching anthropology across all of its sub-fields, with a wide array of learning outcomes and student activities. For example, in Part I, the general section, the authors recommend tried and true strategies to engage students in all sub-disciplines in learning about anthropology. These strategies are particularly appropriate for students' first exposure to anthropology and college classrooms in general. For example, "Discussion Preparation Guides" by Ellenbaum and "A Class Inside the Class" by Rice give tips on how to create student successes every time.

In Part II, Biological Anthropology and Archaeology, "'First Steps' in Hominid Evolution: A Lesson on Walking" by Pollak provides the opportunity for students to develop critical thinking skills around the deceptively simple art of walking, which actually turns out to be an extremely complex phenomenon. Students then write about standing or walking by observing others or "practicing" themselves. Graber's article "The Trouble with the 'Race' Concept: It's All in the Cards" shows students that the traits used to construct "races" are not concordant and therefore do not actually produce biological "races." By using two decks of cards, the students easily sort one deck into two "races," but no matter how hard they try, they cannot sort the second deck into "races" because more than one trait is used. Both of these examples have the ability to engage students in understanding the complex issues of hominid evolution and "race" through activities and props very familiar to them.

Part III, Cultural Anthropology, has the largest number of examples, ranging from "Value Orientations in the Classroom" by Harman to "Cultural Rights" issues by LaFont, to "Exploring the Meaning of Family" by Kennedy. These authors engage students in a series of activities that challenge the familiar and reveal that which is masked or often covert. Gender differences are explored in a very visual way in Bird's "Growing Up Pink or Blue: Using Childrens' Television Commercials to Analyze Gender Enculturation." Field trips are emphasized in Nanda's "Museum Visits in Cultural Anthropology Courses." She points out that the tried and true visit to the museum can be very effective as students learn to apply in-class abstractions to concrete examples in museums and to appreciate diverse cultural heritages. And, in "Field Trips and Student Involvement: Hands-On Learning Components," Krulfeld treats field trips as data bases with students participating in cultural events of a group different from their own and then writing about the experience.

The hallmark of cultural-social anthropology is ethnography. I am pleased to see that this book contains four articles that directly teach ethnography: Caughey's "How to Teach Self Ethnography," "Pre-Class Fieldwork: Ethnographic Introductions" by Wallace, "Doing Ethnographic Research in the Classroom: A Simple Exercise for Engaging Introductory Students" by Keyes, and "Interviewing Tricks for Student Ethnographers" by McCurdy. Finally, the volume uses technology in several articles to engage students. It is a medium that many of them are already comfortable using. For example, in "New Technology, Library Cuts, and How to Deal with them All" by Van Tuerenhout, students learn to evaluate what they read through both text and related website materials.

My thanks to the editors, Patricia Rice and David McCurdy, for bringing these talented colleagues together to share their best practices with other teachers, anthropologists, and non-anthropologists so that we can finally provide our undergraduate students the best experiences possible in their discovery of the wonder of anthropology.

PARTICIPATION AND PAGE REFERENCES: SHARPENING THE FOCUS OF CLASS DISCUSSIONS

Douglas Caulkins and Vicki Bentley-Condit

As a pedagogical tool, class discussion of assigned readings has the well-known advantage of helping students explore and analyze the readings in a dialog with their peers and instructor. The effectiveness of class discussions, however, can be undermined by a variety of problems, including (1) uneven student participation in which more able or assertive students dominate the discussion while the shy or less articulate students withdraw; (2) uneven student preparation, in which some students master the assigned reading while others barely skim it; (3) lack of focus to the discussion, and (4) inadequate summary of what the discussion has accomplished or failed to accomplish.

In this contribution, we describe a technique that helps to keep discussions focused on the assigned text, creates both an expectation and an opportunity for each student to participate, and gives a visual device for summarizing and evaluating the trajectory of the discussion. The technique works best when the readings are "anthropological narratives" or relatively complex arguments, rather than standard expository textbooks. Anthropological narratives include not only classic fieldwork narratives, such as *Return to Laughter* (Smith 1964) or *The Forest People* (Turnbull 1961), and life stories, such as *Nisa* (Shostak 1983) or *Lakota Woman* (Crow Dog and Erdoes 1990), but also a wide variety of contemporary experimental ethnographies, as well as many chapters of case studies, such as *Life in the Pueblo* (Kamp 1998), *The Dobe Ju/'hoansi* (Lee 1993), or *The Invisible Culture* (Philips 1993). We have also used the technique with such dense and closely-argued readings as Goldsmith's *The Biological Roots of Human Nature.* If the text is worth discussing, then this technique, which we call "page referencing" for short, may be helpful in producing the discussion.

The page referencing technique is suitable for all levels of courses, from introductory level to graduate level, because the aim of getting students evenly involved in discussion sessions is what is important. Class size is the more important variable, with an ideal class size of 20 or so students; in larger classes, students can be formed into teams with each team responding for each discussion and students rotating assignments within teams.

The Page Referencing Paradigm

The paradigm for the technique involves 10 steps. In synopsis form, the instructor (1) distributes a reading assignment and (2) poses a question that requires a response or interpretation from each student. In preparing for class, the students should not only (3) formulate a response or interpretation, but (4) note the page in the text where he or she finds the evidence for the interpretation. In the next class, the instructor (5) asks each student to give the page number for the passage that he or she has identified and (6) writes the page numbers in numerical order in a horizontal line across the board. Then the instructor (7) points to the earliest page number and asks the person who suggested it to give his or her response. The instructor (8) moves from page number to page number, writing key words from each student's response on the chalkboard over the relevant page number. Whenever appropriate, the instructor or students (9) synthesize the points made by the last few students. Also, the instructor or students can draw attention to related points in the pages that have not been noted by discussants thus far. Near the end of the class period, the instructor or students can (10) summarize the discussion, noting the themes, differences of interpretation, and new questions that emerged in the discussion. Notes from steps 9 through 10 can be written on the board, making it a detailed representation of the trajectory of the discussion.

Details and Variations

The page referencing paradigm is affected by different sizes and types of classes. What follows are details and variations:

The reading assignment. The discussion can focus on an article, a chapter, or even a whole book, depending on the level of detail that the instructor wants to achieve. For the first attempt at page referencing, while the class is learning this approach to discussion, it is probably best to focus on a short reading assignment. The page referencing technique is not appropriate for purely informational readings or ones in which the author furnishes an unambiguous interpretation that the instructor has no wish to challenge. Whenever the author presents a complex or controversial argument, however, this technique can be productive.

The questions. The questions should facilitate discussion rather than mere recitation that occurs when there is one unambiguous "right" answer. Instead, we want questions that have a number of possible answers, although some may be better or more insightful than others. Productive questions are intended to open up the possible interpretations of or responses to the readings. The question can be exploratory, particularly when trying to assess students' level of comprehension. For example, one of us asked students reading Goldsmith's *The Biological Roots of Human Nature*, "What do you find either problematic or important in the argument in this chapter? On which page does this occur?"

For courses in which students read brief ethnographic descriptions of a variety of cultures, the following question can be posed about each culture:

Imagine that you are a long-term visitor in this culture. What single feature of the culture would you find most congenial – most to your liking? Note the page number of which this feature is described and be prepared to explain your preference. What single feature of this culture would you find least to your liking? Note the page number and be prepared to talk about your discomfort.

Because this question calls for an individual response, it is unlikely that all or most of the students would select the same features and the same page numbers.

In another course, where we use *Lakota Woman*, one of us asked the students, "In this chapter, what seems to be an important event or occurrence shaping Mary's sense of self?" Note the page number and be prepared to explain your point.

In an advanced course on ethnographic representation, we posed the following: "We have asserted that irony is a popular trope in ethnography. In this chapter, note the page number of a passage in which the author uses irony in a particularly effective or significant manner. Be prepared to discuss your interpretation."

Student formulated responses. The instructor needs to make it clear that this is not intended as an exercise in reading the instructor's mind to find the "right" answer. You can model the kind of analysis that you are trying to foster, but emphasize that each student should develop a response that he or she can explain and discuss in class. We find that students are more likely to prepare for this kind of question than for discussion questions handed out in advance. With discussion questions given to the entire class, some students automatically assume a passive role, relying on others to respond. With page referencing, each student knows that he or she will be called on for a contribution.

Note the Page. This helps to anchor the students' interpretations or responses in the text rather than in vague references ("I think it said somewhere...") or in none at all ("I haven't read the chapter but I think..."). As a consequence, it will be easier to maintain the focus of the discussion.

Start class with each student giving a page number. If the class is relatively small, it takes only a couple of minutes to go around the classroom and get each student's page number either orally or on a slip of paper. The process can be started with early arrivals before class starts, too. For larger classes, students might be required to email their page number to the instructor before class, although the upper limit for the class or discussion section size is probably 20 or fewer students. In larger classes, or for variation, students can be assigned to small teams, each of which has the collective responsibility of formulating a response. The important point is that each student or team must commit themselves to a particular passage before class starts.

The instructor writes the number on the board. If the numbers have been obtained in advance or are delivered on slips of paper, it is easy to sort the numbers before recording them in a horizontal line across the board, with roughly equal spaces between the numbers. Use the whole board so there is plenty of room for notes. If, on the other hand, you go around the room asking for numbers, you need to space the numbers by approximation and trial and error. Alternatively, you might write the notes on overhead transparencies that would have the advantage of preserving the visual representation of the discussion but almost certainly would extend over a series of transparencies.

Point to the first number to start. You don't need to know in advance which student is attached to which number. You might ask each student to remind everyone of their name as they talk about their page. By this point, all the students know when they will be called on and the talk can move fairly steadily, since everyone should be prepared for their contribution. Occasionally, but not every time, the instructor might put in a page number too, particularly if he or she wants to model an analytic approach. To put in a page number for every discussion would, however, invite the students to think that there really was a "right" answer that the instructor was looking for. You might discover that some students invariably pick high page numbers with the consequence that the class either runs out of time before getting to their contribution or gives it only brief attention. In this case, the instructor can occasionally take the page numbers out of order, making notes about them (see step 8) and return to numerical order.

The instructor will make notes on the board. Each student's contribution should be noted by a key word or phrase, stacked or angled over the student's page number. If two students have selected the same page number but have emphasized different points, the notes for one could be written above the line of page numbers and the other below the line.

Periodic Synthesis or evaluation. This is crucial. Without it, all we have are serial reports, not a discussion. This is where the instructor must constantly be alert for connections or lack of connections between the interpretations: "Wait a second. Three of you seem to be saying X and the others are saying Y. Is there some way that we can resolve this?" Or, "We have gone past page 47 and no one seems to have picked up on...." Or, "What is the common feature in the points made by the last three students?" Or, in an upper division course that aims at preparing students for cross-cultural experiences, "Last time we saw that most of you liked the egalitarianism of society X and this time several of you claim to dislike the formalism and hierarchy of society Y. Since some of you are planning to live in hierarchical societies, what kinds of adjustment difficulties can you anticipate?" Notes from these discussions can be stacked on top of the other notes on the board, along with brackets, arrows, and any other diagrammatic features needed to clarify the visual representation of the discussion. The instructor needs to seize every opportunity to encourage students to think about what others have said rather than shutting down after they have said their piece. We try to encourage an attitude of joint problem solving in the classroom.

Summary. Students and teachers can often have the impression that they have had a "good" discussion without quite knowing how they got there or what they concluded. The visual representation of the discussion on the board (reading roughly from left to right with the page numbers) facilitates a rapid, accurate summary, either by the instructor or a volunteer (or nominated) student. This is good for creating a sense of cumulative development or of closure on a topic (if there is one). "So, today we saw X, Y, and Z, which will be a foundation for talking about A, B, and C next time." As a consequence, it is more likely that at the next class meeting, the instructor's question about "What we concluded last time" will be met by more than a bewildered silence.

Conclusions

We find that this technique is particularly useful at the beginning of courses, to get students used to hearing their own voices and to establish a sense of individual responsibility for participating. We find that page referencing allows us to monitor the students' overall and detailed comprehension more immediately so that we can supply explanations and explications as needed, rather than after an exam demonstrates that a number of them don't understand the material. Page referencing is particularly helpful in addressing complex topics and breaking them down into major components. Since the whole class participates in this process, it models one form of group problem solving and analysis. Finally, the product of page referencing is archivable if done on transparencies or recorded by an appointed "scribe." Wherever appropriate, the class can return to these visual artifacts to see how they have progressed or to review their treatment of an earlier reading.

References Cited

Crow Dog, M., and R. Erdoes
    1990 *Lakota Woman*. New York: G. Weidenfeld.

Goldsmith, T.
    1991 *The Biological Roots of Human Nature: Forging Links Between Evolution and Behavior*. New York: Oxford University Press.

Kamp, K.
    1998 *Life in the Pueblo*. Prospect Heights, IL: Waveland.

Lee, Richard
    1993 *The Dobe Ju/'hoansi*, 2nd edition. New York: Harcourt Brace.

Phillips, S.
    1993 *The Invisible Culture: Communication in Classroom and Community on the Warm Springs Indian Reservation*. Prospect Heights IL: Waveland.

Shostak, Marjorie
    1993 *Nisa, the Life and Words of a !Kung Woman*. New York: Vintage Books.

Smith, E.B.
    1964 *Return to Laughter*. New York: Doubleday.

Turnbull, Colin
    1961 *The Forest People*. New York: Simon and Schuster.

WEB-BASED RESEARCH PROJECTS IN ANTHROPOLOGY:
NOTES FROM THE VIRTUAL FIELD

Eric C. Thompson

During the 1998 fall term at the University of Washington, I was involved in the development of Web-based research projects for our department's Introduction to Anthropology course. These projects were the result of a cooperative venture by the instructor and the teaching assistants.[1] Our goal was to incorporate the growing popularity and usability of the Internet and the World Wide Web (WWW) as a technology and forum for communication into the four-field introductory course. But, as with others from academics to business, we were faced with the challenge of inventing and thinking through ways to utilize this powerful new medium. What follows is a report on our approach for instructors who may want to take advantage of Web-based research yet are new to its use as a teaching tool.

Setting Up Web-Based Research Projects

There are a number of things to think about when setting up a Web-based research project. The kind of research project suggested here does not require extensive computer knowledge on the part of the instructor nor the students. In these writing projects, the Web can be envisioned as analogous to a massive library. One lecture should be devoted to a demonstration and explanation of Internet Web searches. We invited a guest lecturer from our university's communications and computer division who was able to introduce students to the Internet and answer questions about access to the Web. An instructor who is well versed in doing Internet searches could do the demonstration without depending on outsiders who know the technology but who are not as familiar with the discipline. The amount of time that can be spent introducing students to the Web will depend on the students and level of the class, but it is likely that most students will have had some previous experience with the Internet. It is a vital conduit of information that students should become familiar with at the college or university level if they have not done so before. A good demonstration of Web searches should be of value to all but the most savvy Web surfers in your class. Even those familiar with the WWW can learn more advanced methods for conducting searches.

Using the Web as a kind of vast library is a useful analogy. First, it is useful in explaining to students about the research project since they may be more comfortable with a library-based research project than with something as "high tech" as a Web-based research project. This may be more true of older students or faculty than with today's undergraduates, who have no memory of a time when personal computers were not a common academic tool.

---

[1] James Green was the instructor in charge of the course, with teaching assistants Eric C. Thompson (lead), Ke Fan, Thomas Murphy, Judith Pine, Mary Shenk, and Clark Speed. The author is very grateful for their help and enthusiasm developing the assignments used in the course.

The Web-as-library also helps to orient those who might think it is an undue burden to "force" students to use the WWW. It is not any more of a burden than "forcing" them to use the library as long as there are a sufficient number of computers on campus and students have free access to the Internet.

However, the Web is not really a library and Web pages are not books, journals, or magazines. The difference should be taken carefully into consideration when setting up any Web-based research project. Perhaps the most important difference is the disappearance of layers of editing, peer review, selection, and censorship traditionally involved in the production of articles or books. The wonder of the WWW is that it provides an amazingly broad forum for divergent views, opinions, and information. But it also demands an even sharper degree of critical thinking on the part of the reader to separate opinion from fact and understand the agenda and background of the author. The research projects we designed for the course encourage students to focus on both the subject matter on Web pages and on the quality of information on the Web.[2]

Although we use this approach in a large 350-student class in introductory four-field anthropology, it is appropriate for both small and large classes and in any anthropology course at the introductory level, i.e., cultural anthropology, world cultures, archaeology, or physical anthropology.

The following section provides examples of the Web-based writing projects that we developed, the objectives of the assignments, and the results. Instructions for the writing projects are in the same form as were given to students and can be found at the end of the narrative of this article. They can be photocopied for student use. In addition, students are given an outline of the criteria for the project and a list of possible websites for the first assignment. These will be discussed in a subsequent section.

Examples of Web-Based Research Projects

As taught at the University of Washington, the introductory course emphasizes biocultural and sociocultural anthropology. In the first part of the course, issues in biocultural anthropology including evolution, human biological variation, and critical subjects such as "race" and gender are discussed. Race and gender issues are used as a bridge to sociocultural anthropology, focusing on the nature of culture, kinship systems, and religion. The two examples of Web-based research projects used here were developed in the context of this

---

[2] The term "Web page" is used to indicate one particular page or file that can be assessed through the WWW. A Web page has one specific URL address. A "website" refers to a group of interrelated Web pages (e.g. the University of Washington's website). The two terms are often used interchangeably and can cause confusion. For example, following this nomenclature, a "personal Web page" would actually be a "personal website." But the former term is more commonly used.

particular course. While instructors will want to develop Web-based projects tailored to their own courses and course content, there are some general principles that should be considered in developing any Web-based research project.

The First Project/Writing Assignment. In each project, students will produce a five to seven page paper based on their critique and analysis of a particular type of Web site. The first project addresses a major theme of the first half of the course, evolution. Both readings and class materials introduce students to the theory of evolution, the specific history of human evolution, and the issue of cultural resistence to evolutionary theory by particular groups in the U.S. The first writing project requires students to compare and contrast Web pages that discuss the theory of evolution. (See the handout that follows on p. 11 for instructions to students.)

The purpose of this assignment is to prompt students to think critically about the information and views available on the WWW. The prototype paper that we envision in writing this assignment would be a comparison of a website written from an evolutionary perspective with one that argues against evolutionary theory such as from a creation science perspective. Although we do not want to overly constrain the parameters of the project, we do want to encourage students to explore the vast diversity of opinions available on the Web. To facilitate this goal, students are provided with an extensive list of possible websites to critique (see handout for possible websites and criteria for evaluation). They are also encouraged to search beyond this list. Since websites unfortunately go out of date, they should be checked out before students are given the handout.

To bring in concepts from the course to the critique, we emphasize the use of evolutionary theory as a basis for contemporary biocultural anthropology and also make a distinction between scientific "truth" and religious or creedal "truth." Most importantly, the assignment emphasizes the necessity of evaluating information such as is found on the Web where the source of the ideas is not necessarily apparent and where a wide variety of opinions appear with little basis for orienting the reader to the agendas behind them.

Evaluating the first paper. In general, the research paper evaluators concluded that the assignment was quite successful. It turned out to be very easy to clearly differentiate good papers from mediocre ones. Students did display a critical stance in their evaluations of the sites, and some students related that the assignment changed their understanding and approach to information on the WWW. The evaluators also concluded that students may have been given too broad a leeway in choosing websites. Specifically, some papers were submitted that critiqued alternative creationist websites. There was some feeling that this may have served to unduly undermine the evolutionary approach to understanding human variation presented in class. In addition, some students tended to find the arguments of creation science particularly seductive and displayed a poor understanding of the hypothesis testing model of scientific method and theory. Finally, some students did not refer to the often simple counter-arguments to creationist objections of evolutionary theory.

The Second Project/Writing Assignment. In the sociocultural segment of the course, students were given more direction in developing a particular kind of argument about presentations of self on the WWW. They were asked to answer more specific questions about the websites they were to write about. The questions directed the students to use terminology and concepts introduced in class, such as reading "subtexts" within "texts." The assignment also leaned on Benedict Anderson's seminal theory of "imagined communities" that had been introduced in class. (See the handout that follows on p.12 for instructions to students.)

One aspect of this project is that it verges on virtual ethnography. The students are encouraged to treat the information provided on personal home pages somewhat as they would use information from ethnographic interviews in analyzing the discourse of personal home pages. Of course, just as the Web is not a library, neither is it a traditional field site. It would be useful to discuss the differences between Web browsing and participant observation or ethnographic interviewing in class.

Conclusions: Issues in Web-Based Research

This project only touches on one approach to Web research. There are many other kinds of Web pages and websites that could be incorporated into Web-based research projects. And the possibilities for using the WWW and Internet expand even further if email, news groups, or chat rooms are considered that allow direct communication between two or more parties. Instructors should attempt to use these technologies as well as the Web in ways that would enhance student learning and expand the bounds of anthropological research.

One issue that may arise regarding the use of Web pages in student research is in regard to copyright. Internet copyright law is still in its infancy. A general rule of thumb is that Internet Web pages should be treated as copyrighted materials in a library. Students should be encouraged to use appropriate citations for Web pages that they use in their research or papers. A simple citation guide that includes citation styles for books, articles, and Web pages can be generated and distributed in class. As part of the assignment, students are also instructed to include a printout of the main page of the websites they critiqued. This is helpful for evaluating student work. Printouts should be covered under fair use copyright law.[3]

A related issue may arise with respect to accessing and critiquing personal home pages. There is an ethical question involved in accessing and critiquing home pages without the knowledge of the author. On the one hand, Web pages are public documents. From this point of view, students and the general public should be free to read and critique them as they would books or articles without the consent or knowledge of the author. It is not generally considered necessary to get the consent of authors of newspaper articles or autobiographies, for example, in order to read and comment on them. However, the WWW is an emerging technology and some authors of Web pages, particularly personal home pages, may not be aware of the implications of

---

[3] This is the lay opinion of the author and should not be taken as legal advice.

Web publishing, that Web publishing involves the creation of a public document that anyone with a computer and modem can access. And they may well put information on the Web that they might withhold if they expected their sites to be widely accessed by people whom they do not know. Here again, the analogies of Web-based research to library research or ethnographic interviewing is pertinent.

In the opinion of the author, Web pages should be treated as public documents and it should not be incumbent upon researchers to receive permission to use these documents in their research. If such a standard were to be established, it would be unduly burdensome to researchers and possibly infringe on standards of academic freedom (the equivalent of requiring the researcher to get permission from authors to review their writings in a public library). Rather, it should be the responsibility of individuals publishing on the Web to edit their own writings and exclude information that they do not want made public. At the same time,

however, the ethical standards of the American Anthropological Association should be taken into account when conducting Web-based research.

As with business, government, entertainment, and communication, anthropology on the Web will be a growing area in the coming decades. The standards and methods for such research will change with the rapidly expanding use of Internet technology. The ideas outlined here are just a start toward thinking about creative and productive uses of the Internet in teaching anthropology. It is hoped that it will encourage teachers to involve their students in the development and critical thinking about this expanding field of cultural interaction.

Reference Cited

Anderson, Benedict
   1991 *Imagined Communities: Reflections on the Origin and Spread of Nationalism* (Revised edition.) London and New York: Verso.

FIRST WRITING PROJECT

The theory of evolution, while generally accepted at present in the scientific community, is still widely debated and not accepted by many people. The most recent and fastest growing forum for expressing opinions on this subject is the Internet. For your first writing project, write a paper comparing, contrasting, and evaluating at least two Internet websites that address the subject of evolution. The sites you choose to critique should express distinct, and in at least some ways, conflicting viewpoints on the subject of evolution. In the paper, use concepts from lectures and text materials to evaluate the website materials. The paper should include a description of the content of the sites, an appraisal of the viewpoint of the creators of the sites, a use of concepts from the course materials (class materials and readings) in evaluating the websites, and your opinion about the validity of the information presented in the sites you choose to critique.

Possible sites to critique include: science, Christian creationism, Islam, Mormonism, pedagogy, homosexuality, and pharmacology. You are encouraged to search the WWW beyond this list:

http://www.ucmp.berkeley.edu/history/evolution.html

http://www.geocities.com/CapeCanaveral/Hanger/2437

http://onramp.ior.com/~kjc/creation.html

http://emporium.turnpike.net/C/cs/index.htm

http://library.advanced.org/19012

http://www.daveyd.com/Boards/Politics/Posts/951.html

http://www.su.ic.uk/clubsocs/scc/islamic/articles/evolution.htm

http://www.usd.edu/anth/cultarch/culttopics.html

http://home.onestop.net/mhh/INDEX.HTM

http://www.druglibrary.org/schaffer/lsd/univch6.htm

http://www.frii.com/~allsop/eyring-l/faq/evolution

http://users.cybercity.dk/~dko12530/qstudies.htm

SECOND WRITING ASSIGNMENT

Cultural anthropologists study many kinds of communities using concepts such as kinship (family), ethnicity, religion, gender, and language. Cultural anthropologists also study identity, or how people understand and express themselves as members of various communities. In the second half of the course, you will read about various aspects of community in your text and see representations of communities in various films. Traditionally, anthropologists have conducted participant-observation looking at what people do, listening to what they say, and reading what they write to understand how people come to think of themselves as members of particular communities and what those communities mean to them.

As discovered in the first writing assignment, the Internet is fast becoming a major forum for people and institutions to express themselves. For the second writing assignment, you will be critiquing two or more personal home pages. Like film, Web pages are texts that include subtexts, defined as implicit messages within a particular text. When analyzing the Web pages, look for the subtexts within the pages that help you answer the following questions; write an essay organized around a central argument.

(1) How do people express their membership in and connection to particular communities through their Web pages?

(2) Are certain communities emphasized more than other kinds of communities in personal home pages? (Readings and class materials will identify types of communities traditionally studied by anthropologists.)

(3) How do the communities with which people align themselves through their Web pages compare to those traditionally studied by anthropologists (such as kinship groups or religious communities)?

(4) Reflect on how you would construct a personal home page.
   a. What would you choose to include or exclude?
   b. Why would you make these choices?
   c. Has your view of personal home pages changed in light of your research for this paper?

If you already have a home page, you may choose to critique it with these questions in mind. But you should not use your own page as one of the two or more home pages you initially critiqued.

DISCUSSION PREPARATION GUIDES

Charles O. Ellenbaum

A Common Teaching Problem

Have you ever had the depressing experience of showing a provocative and exciting film to your students, asking for reactions after the credits have run, and getting virtually no response? Have you ever had large- or small-group discussion on an assigned article become the sharing of ignorance by students? Films and readings are necessary vehicles for teaching our visually exciting discipline, but there appears to be a problem common to all of us and that is getting students to properly discuss the materials.

One Way to Solve the Problem

At a National Institute for Staff and Organizational Development Conference on Excellence in 1992, I heard James Gonzales (El Paso Community College) speak about his problems in running class discussions. Knowing I was not alone was a relief. His solution was based on *Learning Through Discussion: Guide for Leaders and Members of Discussion Groups* by William Fawcett Hill (1982). Gonzales claims to have learned the technique through an earlier presentation by Laura Hodges and Jean Carlisle (Rice), and he modified it to fit certain specific needs.

I made anthropological modifications to the technique and tested them first in my Cultural Anthropology classes and later in Peoples and Cultures of the World. I now use them in my World and Comparative Religion classes as well because it works! I have used the technique in lower division undergraduate classes that range from 30-47 students, and in both honors and regular sections.

Almost any anthropology reader could be used in conjunction with this technique, from basic introductory to more specialized readers. In my Peoples and Cultures of the World course, for example, I use *Distant Mirrors: America as a Foreign Culture* (De Vita and Armstrong 1998); students are assigned readings and fill out a Discussion Preparation Guide for each reading (see Appendix). Although the small-discussion group technique could be used for a small number of films during a term for any course, for my Cultural Anthropology course, I use Karl Heider's *Seeing Anthropology: Cultural Anthropology Through Film* (1996). The students view film clips on their own time that are an integral part of the text. Using my modification of Heider's general questions about films, students meet in their small groups each week and discuss the film clips, having filled out a Film Discussion Preparation Guide during and immediately after seeing each film (see Appendix). The Guides are a basis for the small-group discussion. Given scheduling problems, sometimes an in-class film has to be shown one day and discussed the next day, but by filling out a Guide, the student can recapture some of the immediacy of the film. The following process is used for small discussion groups that focus on either readings or films.

The Discussion Process

Assigning groups. Either divide up the class (e.g., count off by eight to divide a class of forty into groups of five) or have the students divide themselves into groups. In general, the groups maintain their integrity for the term, although individuals are allowed to switch groups every three to four weeks. A packet of Guides should be given to each student, and they must be reminded to carefully read the Instructions on the back of the Guide before the first discussion group session.

Discussion days. There is at least one regularly scheduled discussion every week. Students are required to come to class on those days with their discussion Guides filled out. At the beginning of the session, I check to see that they are completed, and assign a grade of 8 (top) to 0 (bottom) points based on how well their answers pertain to the reading or film; I take off points if the answers are blank, extremely brief or incomplete, or do not deal with the specific materials. Students are seated in their small groups in a circle or around a table. Occasionally, after small groups discuss an article or film, I ask each group to report the main points they discussed to the class as a whole, and the entire group becomes involved in a general discussion.

You need to convince one student in each group to volunteer to serve as discussion leader, a job that earns an additional eight points . Be sure to check to see that the discussion Guides of the volunteers are filled in or they are not likely to be prepared. The leaders do not "play" instructors, but act as moderators to budget the time allotted for the day's discussion and to keep the discussion moving. The leader collects the Guides from the group members at the end of the discussion session and marks the total discussion points each person earned, initialing the score. The leader then returns the Guides to the students before leaving that day. Leaders should not serve again in that capacity until every student in the group has had the job.

Once the discussion begins, the instructor should remain silent and sit away from the students. This is difficult and at first, I felt I was taking a lazy, unprofessional way out. I have since realized how important it is to keep my distance, and I now sit where I can see and be seen, and can listen to what is being said, but in an unobtrusive manner. Occasionally, I walk around the room. I found that once students got used to this format, discussion proceeded well.

Learning is taking place in a variety of styles during the discussions. The leader follows the discussion Guide and calls on those wishing to speak. Since both content/task functions and process/maintenance functions of a group are valuable, points can be gained in several ways: by initiating discussion, giving information, asking for information, raising questions, answering questions, giving a restatement of another's contribution, asking for clarification, giving examples, encouraging others, or relieving group tension. Students are encouraged to make at least eight positive contributions to each discussion. The leader may call on any member of the group to offer an opinion or to ask a question even if the student has not raised his or her hand. The leader should not ask questions and then offer opinions, but rather should concentrate on drawing out contributions from the rest of the group, making sure that each item is adequately considered before moving on to a new item. The group should aim for a dynamic discussion with plenty of interaction among participants, and students should address their questions and remarks to the group rather than to the leader.

Unsupported opinions (e.g., "I didn't like it") do not gain points since they do not serve to illuminate the reading or film. Students may lose points for counter-productive behavior such as trying to dominate the discussion or mocking another group member. Students should use the discussion sheet itself to mark their contributions with stars next to the appropriate items and make additional brief notes to document responses to items not originally noted on the discussion Guide. This identifies what they contributed to the discussion and helps the instructor resolve the rare grade dispute. If a student misses a discussion session, the group will determine the required make-up work, subject to approval by the instructor. Discussion Guides are kept by students, once graded by the instructor and the discussion leader. The discussion Guides can be turned in after each session or as a unit, depending on personal preference.

The points for each discussion Guide and session are as follows: eight possible points for an appropriately filled-in discussion Guide plus eight possible points for discussion equals a possible 16 points. The point and grade ranges are: 16-15 = A; 14-13 = B; 12-11 = C; 10-9 = D; 8-0 = F. At the end of the term, points can be totaled and divided by the number of readings/films, using the grade range, to give a final discussion grade. I always announce in the course outline how much of a student's final grade comes from this grade. How much of a student's grade comes from discussion depends on the relative amount of work done for this segment of the course.

Finally, there were two unintended consequences of this technique. First, unstructured discussion (not announced class discussion) also improved. For example, in one case I passed out copies of "Body Ritual of the Nacirema" for them to read and asked them to discuss two questions: What errors of fact did you find? What interpretations to you disagree with? After discussing these questions in their small groups, they reported to the class as a whole, leading to class-wide discussion. This has changed from groups sitting like lumps making few comments, to lively and probing discussions. After a few small-group discussions, more questions -- in general -- have been asked in class. A second unintended result was that the groups become a focal point for networking and support both inside and outside of class. My college is a commuter college where students come and go, often lacking primary group support while on campus. The people in the discussion groups become important to each other and I encourage the comradery by having the group assign make-up work if a student misses a discussion period.

The two Guides in the Appendix that follow may be photocopied or modified to suit your particular needs. The two Guides can be photocopied back to back on a single sheet.

16

References cited

De Vita, P.R., and J.D. Armstrong
    1998 *Distant Mirrors: America as a Foreign Culture*, 2nd ed. Belmont, CA: West/Wadsworth.

Heider, Karl
    1996 *Seeing Anthropology: Cultural Anthropology Through Film.* (Boston: Allyn and Bacon)

Hill, William Fawcett
    1982 *Learning Through Discussion: Guide for Leaders and Members of Discussion Groups*,
    2nd ed. Walnut Creek, CA: Sage.

DISCUSSION PREPARATION GUIDE

Name _____ Date _____

Article: Title/Author _____

1. What words were unfamiliar to you or seem to have been used in a special manner to create a particular impression? Define the word in the context of the phrase where you found it.

a.

b.

c.

d.

e.

2. What particular items seem especially significant or puzzling to you? Items can be anything – a statement, the setting, a name, the title, the situation, a conflict, an irony – anything of interest. Prepare questions about these items to ask in class. "How..." "Why..." questions are especially good.

a.

b.

c.

d.

3. State in one complete sentence, the theme of this work.

4. Sum up the reading in a motto, a bumper sticker, or in a T-shirt slogan.

5. How would you relate this work to others you have read, to materials you have studied in other courses, or to something you learned outside of school?

6. What is your opinion of this selection? Give a reason for your opinion.

7. What did you learn from the article?

8. What is your personal reaction to the material you read?

INFORMATION

1. You must have your Discussion Preparation Guide completely filled out when you come to class on the day assigned. Your instructor will check to see that it is completed at the beginning of the session. Completed and properly filled in Guides are worth eight points. At most sessions, you will be seated in a circle or at a table in your small group.

2. One of you will volunteer to be the discussion leader for the day; you must have your Guide filled out to play this role. It is worth eight points. As discussion leader, you will not "play" teacher but will act as a moderator to budget the time allotted for the discussion and to move discussion along. After the discussion, you will collect all of the Guides, mark the total discussion points each person earned and initial the score, returning the Guides to the students before you leave. You will not serve again as leader until all in the group have served in this capacity.

3. Once the discussion begins, your instructor will remain silent and will sit away from you. You are entrusted with the responsibility of discussing the selection. The leader will follow the discussion Guide and call on those wishing to speak. Try to make eight positive contributions to each discussion so you can earn eight points: initiate discussion, give information, ask for information, raise questions, answer questions, give a restatement of another's contribution, ask for clarification, give examples, encourage others, or relieve group tension. Be sure to ask your questions or address your comments to the group, not to the leader. The leader may call on any member of the group, even if you have not raised your hand. The leader should not ask questions and offer opinions but rather concentrate on drawing out contributions from the rest of the group, making sure that each item is adequately considered before moving to a new question. The group should aim for a dynamic discussion with plenty of interaction among the participants to help accomplish the primary objective of the discussion.

4. Unsupported opinions (such as "I didn't like it") do not get any points since they do not help illuminate the selection. You can lose points for counter-productive behavior such as trying to dominate the discussion or mocking another group member.

5. Mark your contributions to the discussion by making a star next to the appropriate item on the Guide. You should also make additional brief notes to document responses to items not originally noted on the Guide. If you miss a discussion session, your group will determine your required make-up work, subject to your instructor's approval.

6. The discussion Guides are kept by you, once they are marked by the instructor and the leader. The Guides may be called in by your instructor, so keep them available. The points assigned are: eight potential points for a properly filled in Guide and eight potential points for discussion to total 16 possible points. Point/Grade range: 16-15 = A; 14-13 = B; 12-11 = C; 10-9 = D; under 9 = F.

FILM DISCUSSION PREPARATION GUIDE

Name _____ Date _____

Film Title _____

Culture(s) shown_____

Main subjects _____

1. How ethnographic is it?

2. How much is the people's own view represented?

3. Whose voice or point of view is on the soundtrack?

4. What is the art/science balance?

5. What is the influence of the film crew?

6. Does the film create empathy or disgust?

7. Are film shots given a context?

8. Does the film follow through on important themes?

9. How visual and how wordy is the film?

10. How much distortion of time and space do you see?

11. What did you learn from the film?

12. How did you feel during the viewing of the film and afterward?

13. How is the culture shown in the film similar to your own?

14. How is the culture shown in the film different from your own?

15. What is your personal reaction to the culture you viewed in the film?

INFORMATION

1. You must have your Film Discussion Preparation Guide completely filled out when you come to class on the day assigned to discuss the film. Your instructor will check to see that it is completed at the beginning of the session. Completed and properly filled in Guides are worth eight points. At most sessions, you will be seated in a circle or at a table in your small group.

2. One of you will volunteer to be the discussion leader for the day; you must have your Guide filled out to play this role. It is worth eight points. As discussion leader, you will not "play" teacher but will act as a moderator to budget the time allotted for the discussion and to move discussion along. After the discussion, you will collect all of the Guides, mark the total discussion points each person earned and initial the score, returning the Guides to the students before you leave. You will not serve as leader again until all in the group have served in this capacity.

3. Once the discussion begins, your instructor will remain silent and will sit away from you. You are entrusted with the responsibility of discussing the selection. The leader will follow the discussion Guide and call on those wishing to speak. Try to make eight positive contributions to each discussion so you can earn eight points: initiate discussion, give information, ask for information, raise questions, answer questions, give a restatement of another's contribution, ask for clarification, give examples, encourage others, or relieve group tension. Be sure to ask your questions or address your comments to the group, not to the leader. The leader may call on any member of the group, even if you have not raised your hand. The leader should not ask questions and offer opinions but rather concentrate on drawing out contributions from the rest of the group, making sure that each item is adequately considered before moving to a new question. The group should aim for a dynamic discussion with plenty of interaction among the participants to help accomplish the primary goal of the discussion.

4. Unsupported opinions (such as "I didn't like it") do not get any points since they do not help illuminate the selection. You can lose points for counter-productive behavior such as trying to dominate the discussion or mocking another group member.

5. Mark your contributions to the discussion by making a star next to the appropriate item on the Guide. You should also make additional brief notes to document responses to items not originally noted on the Guide. If you miss a discussion session, your group will determine your required make-up work, subject to your instructor's approval.

6. The discussion Guides are kept by you, once they are marked by the instructor and the leader. The Guides may be called in by your instructor, so keep them available. The points assigned are: eight potential points for a properly filled in Guide and eight potential points for discussion to total 16 possible points. Point/Grade range: 16-15 = A; 14-13 = B; 12=11 = C; 10-9 = D; under 9 = F.

A "CLASS INSIDE THE CLASS"

Patricia C. Rice

Several years ago, I asked one of the best students I have ever taught why she never contributed to any discussions in the five classes she took with me during her undergraduate career. There were plenty of opportunities to do so, including the discussion of fifteen articles that made up the text for half of one class. I knew she had read the materials because occasionally I asked her a question and she always knew the answer so it was not a matter of being unprepared. In answer to my question, she told me that she simply did not like to talk in a classroom situation, though she was fine during our one-on-one conversations. I decided that like many students, she was just "shy." In thinking about it later, I concluded that she is one of many past and present students who are very bright, do very well on exams, express themselves very well in writing and yes, are fine in oral conversations with me. But, when it comes to saying anything in class, they appear to range from reluctant to panic stricken. Because I do not believe it is fair to students's psyches to use force of any kind to get them to talk under circumstances that obviously make them very uncomfortable, I tried to think of a way that would get them involved, yet not feed their obvious reluctance. Even some of the toughest football players have told me they cringe at the thought of having to say something in class beyond "yes" or "no."

It was the large-class environment that seemed to be the stumbling block, not the materials to be discussed, and I eventually "invented" what I call a "class inside the class." The first year was one of trial and error, but after three years of using this technique, I have found it to be successful as a way to get even the most reluctant student to talk in class, and several of the "shy" students even spoke up later under different discussion conditions.

The Set Up

This technique works well in a class of up to 60 students; I suspect it would work in any class where the class size is not over the number of assigned readings times three or four at the most. Classes using readers where there might be 40 or more readings could number well over 100 students. I have assigned four students to a reading, but three works better. After the class roll settles down (or earlier if reading and discussing articles is immediate), use the alphabetical class list and the chronological set of readings and just assign the readings as on the class list; I assign 1-15 down the class list and then 1-15 again for the middle part, and again for the end of the class list rather than assign the first three the first reading, the second three the second reading, and so forth. People whose last names begin with V or W often complain that they get the leftovers at the end of the term but this way seems to even things up better. I then give everyone a printed copy of the class list with the number of the assigned article that matches the number on the reading list. I also give an approximate date for the discussion, though this can be either more or less formalized. As long as students know what chronological order their reading is in, it is not vital to set an absolute date for the discussion.

Students are told the first day and in writing on the course outline that they are expected to not only be one of the discussion leaders for one reading, but that they are expected to read every article before discussion day as well. They are told that the discussions won't mean much if they have not done their reading before class and they are given an opportunity to ask questions of the instructor or the "class inside the class" after the discussion (they seldom do this). Finally, students are told that at least half of the questions on exams that pertain to the reading will be those exact questions posed on the Study Guide for Reading handout.

Students know from the written course outline that their participation in one "class inside the class" discussion is required. If for some reason a student cannot be at the appointed session, he or she is required to get a substitute without involving the instructor. And, the students are told that if they do not come to their discussion and neglect to get a substitute, that they will lose the 10 points (out of 100) slated for discussion. In three years, I have not had to penalize a single student for this. They are told that quality counts as well and that they can earn **up to** 10 points for the discussion, but if they are ill prepared, it can be lower.

A "Class Inside the Class"

I tell the class exactly what will happen on discussion days because I believe if they know what will happen, those who might be nervous at least know what the format is and there is one less thing to worry about. On discussion days, I take three or four chairs and set them up in front of the class, but off to one side. Placement is important, but the actual placement of the chairs depends on the contours of your classroom. It is important, however, NOT to use chairs bolted to the floor in the front row. What is needed is separate chairs that can be moved to the exact position needed. If you have a room with moveable chairs, this is easy; if your chairs are bolted, you will have to find a way to bring in chairs on discussion days. Look around the room and find a space where those students in the "class inside the class" can see you in front of them (and you are in front of the class, but focusing on the small group), see each other out of the corner of their eyes, but are not directly facing the class. I arrange the chairs in a semi-circle, a foot or so apart. The rest of the class needs to see the "class inside the class" from the side rather than face on. As the instructor, you will be facing the "class inside the class," but can walk around a bit and when appropriate, address the entire class.

A "class inside the class" works only if there are prepared questions or topics to discuss. I make the questions specific to the reading; some questions are short and factual, some cover the main points I want students to get out of the reading, and some should be personal opinions about something they read. I try to find at least 10 questions for each reading. I make up a Study Guide for Reading handout, one sheet per reading with the questions for particular readings spaced so there is room for writing answers or notes. Students who are the "class inside the class" members for the day can refer to these sheets as we discuss the points or questions. Since everyone in the class is expected to do their reading before the discussion, they can use the sheets as they read for ease in listening to the class discussion and later for studying for exams.

At the appropriate point during the class, the discussants are asked to come join the semi-circle. After they are settled in, I ask the first question (always a fairly simple one) and I usually ask it of someone in the group I know is not reluctant to speak. I may not know the names of all of the students in the class by the first or second reading, but I know the names of the discussants and call on them by their first names.

The Results

Students have told me that after a few minutes of being a member of this small, almost one-on-one discussion group, that they forget they are even in a large class with a lot of students sitting in the "audience" listening. In addition, those not discussing but in the "audience" have told me that they think of this as good reinforcement of their own answers to the questions. The "class in a class" does not take the place of doing one's own reading because the coverage is too spotty, and several students have told me that this format encouraged them to do their reading before the discussion. Because there are never the same readings any two years in a row, any comparison of exam scores before and after would not be valid, but anecdotally, the exam results appeared to be higher than in previous years. Perhaps the best result is on the class evaluations. Before using this technique, several people every year wrote something about not liking the feeling that they were being forced to contribute to discussions (it was worth 15% of their final grade). Not a single student has commented negatively about discussions since I switched to this technique. It seems to work. One student who was worried about his participation, went through the process and said at the end of the session as he was leaving, "well, that was painless."

NEW TECHNOLOGY, LIBRARY BUDGET CUTS AND HOW TO DEAL WITH THEM ALL

Dirk Van Tuerenhout

Setting the Scene

In the following pages I will outline an approach I have used to deal with two problem areas that beset most of us who teach: cutbacks in library budgets and the inability of most of our students to critically evaluate what they read. I ask my students to read an article available on a website as well as a chapter from a textbook assigned to the course, both on a related subject. Their assignment is to read both "texts," and answer a series of questions. Some of these questions are geared toward retrieval of factual information, while others force students to critically evaluate the materials they have just read. I use this approach in an introductory Mesoamerican archaeology class, where it centers on aspects of Maya culture. However, I believe that the technique, as outlined below, is sufficiently flexible to be applied to any introductory-level anthropology class. Moreover, even though I have used this assignment in a course with about 20 students, I am convinced one could apply the same approach to a much larger-sized class.

Making the Assignment: Goals

First, you should survey the resources and evaluate the contributions of both the Internet and books. Because of the increasing popularity of the Internet and the high degree of accessibility of that medium by students, I want to make students aware that there are good websites available, with information provided by reputed scholars. Moreover, once students reach the Web address, I encourage them to browse around and find out what else is offered. At the same time, I caution against taking everything on the Web at face value and illustrate this by referring to mistakes made by some of their predecessors in other classes.

Next, you should evaluate the contributions made by writers of textbooks. Most often, students do not ask how authors came to their conclusions. This assignment forces them to step back, survey the data available to an author and then come to an independent conclusion about where facts end and reconstruction begins.

The materials covered in the assigned reading are part of the larger context of the class. In other words, when done correctly, this assignment helps students to better understand the information discussed in class. However, since they have to make a more active effort to come to this level of understanding, the rate of their overall comprehension of the materials ultimately depends on the amount of work they are willing to put into the project. I advise the students of this aspect of the assignment.

Preparing the Assignment

I confront the issues mentioned at the beginning by assigning a scholarly article available on a website and a chapter from one of the textbooks we use. Earlier, I had searched the Internet looking for an article that would meet the following requirements: it would have to be written by a known scholar; it would have to be available on a "stable" website, i.e., one that would still be around a month after the assignment was made; and finally, the article would have to be well written and not excessively long. In preparing the course, I had also "set aside" one chapter in a textbook as part of this assignment.

By choosing a website article and a chapter from the textbook used in class, I avoid the problem of availability of these materials in the library, as well as the sometimes cumbersome task of obtaining copyright permission to reproduce these materials.

Conveying the Instructions to Students

At the beginning of the term, the students receive a handout that contains the assignment goals, a reference to the sources they have to use, and a series of questions to be answered using these readings. Since there are two sources involved, I provide them with two sets of questions to answer. These questions are not only geared to elicit factual answers, with material culled from the text, but also encourage students to do some critical thinking of their own. I point out these two approaches and ask students to clearly identify in their essays when they were offering their personal observations, as opposed to answering more fact-oriented questions. The handout also contains information about the format in which I expect the answers to appear, including citation format, as well as a time frame and the weight of the paper toward the final grade.

Case Study: Mesoamerican Archaeology

I apply the project format outlined above to the Maya section of a course in Mesoamerican archaeology. One of the myths I want to dispel is that the Maya were "pre-historic" people, lacking any form of writing. The assignment revolves around the nature of Maya writing, and our current understanding of it. I refer to an article by David Stuart, *Copán in the Decipherment of Maya Hieroglyphic Writing*. (Web address: htttp://www.peabody. harvard.edu/Copan/text.html). This source fulfills all of the requirements of a web-based article as noted above.

Through lectures and reading assignments, the students learn that we have come to understand a substantial portion of Maya texts, and how that knowledge has helped us to reconstruct Maya history beyond what "dirt" archaeology can do for us. However, they also conclude that we may never reach a complete understanding of their past, partly because of the fragmentary nature of the preserved documents and partly because of the destruction of most of the books, the Mayan "codices."

With these insights into the contributions and shortcomings of the Maya source materials, students can then tackle a second set of questions: how can we apply this knowledge to reconstruct the demise of the city of Copan? Students were referred to Chapter 8 (Copán: "The Death of First Dawn on Macaw Mountain" [pp. 306-345] in Linda Schele and David Freidel, 1990 *A Forest of Kings: The Untold Story of the Ancient Maya)*. Answers were also to be found in David Stuart's article. Some of the questions pertaining to these documents are:

(1) Enough texts at Copán have been translated by now. With the exception of the "Hieroglyphic Stairway," what would you say the major theme(s) of the inscriptions are at Copán? What kinds of monuments carry texts?

(2) How can we reconstruct Copán's dynastic sequence? What are some of the problems involved? From where do we get most of our information? What might be the reason(s) for the gaps in the historic record at Copán? What may have been the ancient name of Copán itself?

(3) Reconstruct a list of all the rulers mentioned in the two articles. Start with "Ruler 1" and work your way through as many as you can find. For each of these individuals, include any dates that are associated with them (as carved on monuments during their reign, as well as on monuments of later rulers, when they are referred to). Whenever possible, indicate when these people were born, when they ascended to the throne, and when they died. Also, when possible, include the various names (Maya and "western") that have been associated with each of these rulers.

(4) Can you point to any trends over time with regard to which monuments may have been preferred for text carving, as well as to who is allowed to carve and display texts? With regard to the latter, what have the two authors (Schele and Stuart) to say about this shift (especially within the framework of dissolution of royal power)? Is there a link between this shift and the display of war-related iconography?

Applicability of This Approach

While I have used this approach in my Mesoamerican archaeology class to address aspects of Maya culture, I believe that it can be used in just about any anthropology course. The most appropriate audience is an undergraduate one, especially since this is where we should teach people to start evaluating what they read, rather than wait until they get to graduate school. There are a lot of good websites available, often associated with museums and universities. I can also imagine working with CD-ROM-based data, for example in the sub-fields of archaeology and physical anthropology, where students would have to dig through multiple layers of information to come up with answers.

Flexibility on the part of educators by switching to new media, such as the Internet, is a valuable asset. The approach outlined above is especially productive in introductory courses, where working the data to get essential insights is more important than being able to investigate all the minutiae of the subject. I have seen it at work, and enjoyed realizing how a growing desire on the part of students to get their information served up in a visual format interfaced with the necessity to adjust to the reality of continuous library budget cuts. This allows us, the instructors, to attempt to get our students to absorb and retain factual knowledge and to develop a faculty that can critically appraise the very same data.

"FIRST STEPS" IN HOMINID EVOLUTION: A LESSON ON WALKING

Janet Pollak

Teaching multiple sections of Introduction to Anthropology to mostly non-majors who are fulfilling general education social science requirements not only presents opportunities for innovative pedagogy, it demands creativity. Moreover, since "critical thinking" and "intensive writing" (or writing as a mode of learning) are required at many colleges and universities, instructors have begun to experiment and reconfigure segments of courses and even entire courses. In the mid-1980s, I signed up for a week-long seminar in writing across the curriculum, audited the basic English composition course, and revised my Introduction to Anthropology course as a "writing" course. One of the faculty seminar's instructors then audited my class for a semester to assess the re-visioning. I developed fifteen writing and learning segments in the course that involved various types of writing and writing assessment. The most popular assignment focused on bipedalism in human evolution.[1]

The exercise described here can be adapted to a variety of instructional formats, even those that do not incorporate much writing. You will need a full session (60-75 minutes) and, although class size is not a relevant constraint, it works better in rooms where students can get up and move around a bit. "First Steps" can also be easily used in a physical/ biological anthropology course as an introduction to bipedalism.

Because so many undergraduates continue to be stressed by nearly anything in the curriculum that falls under the general science umbrella, my unit on human evolution and the fossil record begins with an exercise that draws on the students' own knowledge and expertise of a motor activity that they have been acquainted with for nearly two decades: walking. I flip on an overhead transparency and distribute a copy to each student:

> "Bipedalism: Human beings are proficient in the mode of locomotion known as
> bipedalism or striding/walking on two legs. Imagine that you have been hired to
> write copy for an "owner's manual" of the human body. On this sheet of paper,
> provide detailed instructions for standing from a seated position (without using
> the hands) and moving forward for about ten feet using only the legs." (See end
> of article for this statement; it can be copied on a transparency or photocopied
> for individual students.)

This "writing about walking" exercise is very deceptive because it appears to be much easier than it actually is. While it proceeds from students' prior knowledge and experience, it compels them to examine the process critically, and focus on sequential steps in great detail. Expect that none of the students have ever dissected the act of walking before. There is one

---

[1] For information on the other writing exercises I developed for my Introduction to Anthropology course, contact the author at pollak_j@wpc.wilpaterson.edu.

caution about using this particular exercise in every class, however. Sometimes a physically-challenged student is present so it may be a good idea to speak with that individual ahead of time and, perhaps, recast the exercise to address some other distinctly human motor skill that everyone in the room possesses, such as manipulating objects with opposable thumbs.

The bipedalism assignment is completed in class and students are allowed to move around and "practice" in order to review the discrete motions required to accomplish the tasks of standing and walking. Give them a few minutes to think about the exercise and make some preliminary notes. Then give them about twenty minutes to complete the assignment. While you do not have to suggest anything about "acting out" the motions, usually one or more students will begin testing various movements while others watch intently or squirm around in their seats to see what body parts move and in which order. In completing this assignment on paper, some students write lists while others write paragraphs. A small percentage of the group (generally less than 10% of a class) will make drawings.

After everyone is finished, collect the papers, shuffle them, and then ask for a volunteer. Clear the front of the classroom and place a side chair (without arms) in the center where all may observe. A volunteer comes forward and is asked to sit in the chair. Read the directions on the first paper (without revealing the author.) The volunteer is required to follow the directions to the letter, and the results are frequently hilarious. Students become instantly aware of which sets of directions are adequate or inadequate, based on what the volunteer is asked to do. Generally, at this first go-around, there are too few specific directions and not nearly enough precision for the volunteer to get to his/her feet, or, if they get the person standing, a number of key components for moving the legs appropriately are missing. While it is not necessary at this stage to read all the papers aloud, it is advisable to change volunteers after every three or four papers. Reading about a dozen or so of the first drafts should suffice. After each set of directions is read, ask students what they think is missing or what should be changed or eliminated.

Following this front-of-the-classroom segment, hand the papers back to the students for revision. This process should take no more than ten minutes or so and you may find that many more students are standing up and walking around to ensure they not only have the steps in sequence, but that they have included sufficient detail in their descriptions of each step. When the first drafts have been revised, divide the class up into groups of three or four (four should be the maximum) and have them peer-review their newly-configured directions. Students will have written their first drafts on the front of the sheet and their second drafts on the back. During the peer-critique phase, they are asked to note the suggestions they receive in the margins. If the exercised is to be evaluated, the papers are collected. (Instead of letter grades, I assign pluses, checks, or minuses.)

This assignment involves problem-solving skills as well as critical thinking and the need to identify a logical progression of movements in a behavior that most, if not all, students have never given much thought to. In all the semesters that I have assigned this exercise since 1986, less than five percent of a class comes up with a complete set of directions the first time through. For students, it provides a comfortable, yet substantive introduction to the "stones and bones" portion of the introductory course. It provides a very necessary preface to what students tell us is the most difficult area of anthropology with just enough humor and sense of accomplishment to tackle the complexities of hominid evolution.

Finally, the exercise could be expanded to illuminate the impact of culture on basic human motor skills. For instance, the type of footwear worn by young children will impact on the foot fall as they walk. Wearing an inflexible sole on a sandal that requires an individual to grip it with the toes may result in the entire foot hitting the ground at the same time, and not the heel-to-toe movement seen with other types of footwear or bare feet.

Appendix

What follows are two examples of students' unedited first-draft directions for this exercise:

(1) #1. Place your feet on the floor.
    2. Lean forward.
    3. Place the weight of your body on your feet.
    4. Extend your legs at the knees.
    5. Now you're standing.
    6. Take your right foot and place it in front of your body.
    7. Take your left foot and do the same while your right foot is stationary.
    8. Alternate back and forth between the right and left foot.
    9. Now you are walking.

(2) #1. Sit in a chair.
    2. While sitting, stretch your legs straight out. (This is how you want your legs for step 3).
    3. Stand up slowly maintaining your balance. Lock your knees. Your upper body should be straight up.
    4. After standing in place with your knees locked and your body upright and balanced, take your left foot slowly and lean forward a little, bending your knee and step forward about six inches. Remember to stay upright and maintain your balance.
    5. Then take your right foot and place it about 6 inches in front of your left foot, maintaining your balance and leaning forward slightly to maintain your balance.
    6. Continue this motion slowly until you are able to move faster.

BIPEDALISM: Human beings are proficient in the mode of locomotion known as bipedalism or striding/walking on two legs. Imagine that you have been hired to write copy for an "owner's manual" of the human body. On this sheet of paper, provide detailed instructions for standing from a seated position (without using the hands) and moving forward for about ten feet using only the legs.

A FELINE PATERNITY SUIT: AN EXERCISE IN ANTHROPOLOGICAL GENETICS

Joyce Lucke

The Problem

For students who do not have a science background, the genetics section of an introductory physical anthropology course can be daunting. Lessons with a hands-on approach facilitate student learning to a greater degree than strict lecture/textbook approaches. Instructors can increase enjoyment and decrease anxiety by introducing activities into the classroom to demonstrate basic concepts of genetics where students can be active participants. Unfortunately, most colleges and universities do not have the necessary genetics laboratory facilities nor resources for hands-on demonstrations or group work.

One Solution

I have found that using a biological population that most students have an intimate knowledge of, and access to, increases the acquisition, comprehension, and retention of material. Using the genetics of the domesticated cat as an example in lecture, the exercise that is described here makes the complicated and removed world of genetics relevant and accessible to all students. Since many of the traits of a cat's coat are Mendelian, a collection of pictures or a neighborhood feline population can act as the database for genotype/phenotype analysis. By posing a theoretical question to the class, "Your cat has just had kittens; which neighbor owns the father?" numerous concepts of genetics found in most textbooks can be demonstrated.

When searching for an exercise to illustrate genetic concepts, without relying solely on the common garden pea, a number of years ago I turned to the *American Biology Teacher* (Todd 1992). Though geared for high-school educators, several of the labs and demonstrations served my purposes, are quick and easy to prepare and carry out with minimal resources. I modified several for college-level classes. The following exercise is based on an article by Roger Quackenbush (1997).

Step 1: Obtain several cat magazines such as *Cat Fanciers Almanac, Cat Fancy, Cats.* Check if your town has a cat club. There you may find several breeders or exhibitors who have years worth of magazines or posters they may be willing to part with. Usually the front/back and inside/outside covers have large, color pictures of cats that can be easily cut out. I cut around the cats as closely as possible and mount the pictures individually on a piece of white paper.

Step 2: Determine the genotype of each pictured cat. I write the traits I want to illustrate in class on the back of the appropriate picture with the genotype, along with the breed if it happens to be a purebred. A breeder or veterinarian can help you with this, especially if you don't know an American Shorthair from an Exotic Shorthair. It is important to have a cat with the "wild type" coat as described by Quackenbush, as this is the basis for the in-class discussion.

The wild type is a brown and black striped tabby with a fairly long coat. A brown mackerel Maine Coon is a perfect example. American Shorthairs show their stripe patterns well and Abyssinians are great examples of an agouti coat (no stripes). A Siamese or Himalayan show the pointed coat well. Of course, the Manx is the tailless cat, but be careful since Manxes can have long tails! Manx tails come in three lengths: regular (long), what looks like a half tail (stumpy), or no tail (rumpy.) After several years of collecting, I have a good set of pictures that illustrate every coat color and color combination. As long as pictures of the coat types noted on the Genetics of the Domestic Cat chart that follows are available, the in-class part of the exercise can be illustrated.

Step 3: In class, I go through the genetics materials as I normally would, discussing Mendelian traits, genotypes/phenotypes, dominance/recessiveness, Punnett Squares, and sex-linked traits. I also cover epistatis and pliotropy as most students ask questions that lead to these traits anyway.

Step 4: Once I have introduced Mendel, his peas, and the basics of genetics, I pull out the cat pictures. I distribute the handout on feline genetics in class (see Genetics of the Domestic Cat handout that follows). Students respond well as we talk through specific variants of traits, using the pictures as illustrations. Students usually recognize a coat pattern or color reminiscent of a pet or neighborhood stray. Students will start to ask questions about their own cats and various odd markings, such as "my cat has only one white foot." At this point, I introduce mutations that humans have artificially selected in purebred cats, for example the Rex coat type (very short wavy hair), curled ears, bobtail, folded ears, or the munchkin cat, which if you have never seen one, looks like a female dachshund. Cats are also wonderful examples of how coloration pairings can produce a wide variety of colors and patterns, the masking of one trait by another, and linked traits. Beyond the fifteen or so Mendelian traits that are easily observed in a cat on the street, several traits can become very complicated. Again, you may want to consult a vet or breeder. For advanced classes, you may want to go into the Abyssinian or pointed patterns, the dormancy of alleles that result in tortoiseshell or calico colorations, and the link between coat color and other traits such as deafness or eye color. The possibilities are great. And some of the folklore about cat colors is true: tortoiseshell or calico cats are female (a sex-linked trait), while males can be either colorations if they have a XXY sex genotype.

Step 5: At this point, you will want to decide if you will present this exercise as an in-class "lab" project or a take-home assignment. If you use it as an in-class lab, you can give pictures to groups to answer identification questions or work out Punnett Squares, or to determine what the offspring might look like for a single trait or multiple traits given knowledge about the parents. Or this can be a practice exercise or a group quiz. For a formal quiz, you can hold up pictures while students write their answers. Previous to the quiz, you can go through the pictures in class and ask questions on single traits, giving students a chance to use the handout and get used to looking at a "specimen" and then determining the phenotype and genotype.

Step 6: If you use it as a take-home assignment, you can give out the handout with the paternity information (see Feline Paternity handout at the end of the article). Be sure students understand Punnett Squares, as they may not understand that offspring information can be given for placement *inside the square* to find the possible genotypes of one of the parents *outside the square*.

Step 7: When going over the lab or take-home assignment, I have pictures ready of the kittens and parents to show. I emphasize that cats with very different looking coats can yield (or "throw" in cat fancier terms) a wide range of coat colors and patterns. When students turn in a take-home assignment, they often attach photos of their own cats with the genotypes written out.

Want To Do More?

If there is time in an introductory course, or in advanced courses, students can design and carry out an analysis of neighborhood cats. The exercise above can act as a practice session to a field experiment. The Quackenbush article outlines this analysis in greater detail. To do this additional field project, I suggest reading the articles listed below on studies of specific city cat populations. I have had adventurous students do an analysis of the percentage of black cats found in an urban area, for example (see Todd 1969).

You can also use feline genetics as an example of biology being influenced by human activity. Several articles have been written on the connection between cats and human migration. Populations of six-toed cats can be traced using sea routes of 17th through 20th century mariners. Cats were on ships as rodent control devices, and mutations were spread from port to port. East coast port cities have high frequencies of polydactyl cats, for example (Lloyd 1986; Todd 1977). There has been research on the spread of certain colors as well. For advanced classes, the article on the murder suspect being convicted because his pet cat's hair was found at the scene of the crime (Menotti-Raymond et al 1997) is great stuff, but my introductory students would never be able to follow the complications in the article.

Conclusions

I have used these materials on feline genetics successfully for several years and find the level of comprehension and retention of materials to be far better than when the genetic materials were presented as straight lecture/text material. I believe this is because the example is more "real" to students. Somewhere in their lives, there is a cat. Students can walk out of the classroom and apply what they have learned as soon as they see a cat on the street. I becomes useful and/or meaningful to them right away. By using these materials, a goal of my course has been met: students realize they can use and do anthropology in their everyday lives.

34

References Cited

Lloyd, Andrew T.
1986 Pussycat, pussycat, where have you been? *Natural History* 95(7): 46-53.

Menotti-Raymond, Marilyn, V.A. David, and Stephan J. O'Brien
1997 Pet cat hair implicates murder suspect. *Nature* 386 (6627):774.

Quackenbush, Roger E.
1992 Genetics of the domestic cat: A Lab exercise. *American Biology Teacher* 54(1):29-32.

Todd, N.
1969 Cat gene frequencies in Chicago and other populations of the United States. *The Journal of Heredity* 60 (5): 273-277.

Other Useful Reference Materials

Gould, Laura
1997 *Cats are not peas: a calico history of genetics.* New York: Springer-Verlag.

O'Brien, Stephen J.
1997 The family line: the human-cat connection. *National Geographic* 191 (6): 77-85.

Robinson, R.
1997 *Genetics for cat breeders*, 2nd ed. New York: Pergamon Press.

Todd, N.
1966 Gene frequencies in the cat population of New York City. *The Journal of Heredity* 57 (5): 185-187.

GENETICS OF THE DOMESTIC CAT

Just by looking at a cat, more than 15 genetic traits can be distinguished, along with their genotypes. Below is a list of the more common phenotypes, with the appropriate allele, for domesticated cats. We are able to note these because the traits are Mendelian, or discontinuous, meaning they have either/or expressions, not a blending.

WILD TYPE		MUTANTS	
Allele	Phenotype	Allele	Phenotype
A	agouti	a	non-agouti (black)
B	black pigment	b	brown pigment
D	dense pigment	d	dilute pigment
i	wild type pigment	I	inhibits agouti (silver)
L	short hair	l	long hair
m	long tail	M	Manx (stubby) tail
o	non-orange	O	orange
pd	normal toes	Pd	polydactyly (extra toes)
s	no white spots	S	piebald (white spots)
T	mackerel striped	Tb	blotched striped
w	not all white	W	all white

A tabby with parallel black stripes against a gray/tan background is considered the wild type coloration. The black stripe is produced by the dominant allele B, with the recessive b producing a brown color. The gray/tan background or stripe, found in many wild animals, is called agouti (or ticking). The dominant allele A produced the agouti condition. The homozygous recessive condition, aa, masks or prevents the expression of the light colored band. A cat with the genotype aaBB or aaBb would be pure black. A cat with the genotype aabb would be pure brown. Other examples of masking involves the allele W that masks the expression of any other allele for color that may be present. Therefore a genotype of aaBBw_ (a dash '_' indicates the allele could be dominant or recessive) would appear to indicate an all black cat; however, the presence of the W allele masks even the black stripe, making for an all white cat. The orange coloration masks the black or brown stripe making for an orange tabby like Morris. The agouti allele is not affected by the orange allele – aaO_ and would still be a striped cat. In the wild type tabby cat, the allele I inhibits (not masks) the agouti gray/tan color band, but allows the black or brown stripe to appear. The agouti region becomes white or the so-called silver color. The recessive allele i allows the wild type pigmentation.

The alleles for white spotting (called piebald) demonstrates inheritance by incomplete dominance. White spotted cats inherit the alleles independent of any other alleles for color. Thus white spotting can be found in conjunction with any other coloration. White spotting is also independent of the pure white condition caused by the allele W and the two should not be confused. A cat can be WWSS, meaning that it is all white with white spotting. While there is much variation, in general, SS produces cats with extensive spotting (more than half the body), Ss cats are mildly spotted (less than half the body), and cats with the genotype ss exhibit no white spotting. An otherwise black cat with a small patch of white hairs would be classed as Ss.

Dense coloration is the normal condition. Dilute coloration is a muted or softened tone of the color. For example, orange will become "cream" and black will become grayish or what is known in cat fancier circles as "blue."

The pattern of the stripes is either mackerel, the stripes being vertical to the spine, or blotched, meaning the coat has a swirl pattern. Many times, the cat will look as if it has a "bulls eye" on its side.

A FELINE PATERNITY SUIT

Your favorite cat has recently given birth to three kittens. Which of your neighbor's cats is the father? Use the provided phenotypic information, your knowledge of genetics, Mendelian inheritance, and your power of deduction to complete the following steps. In the end you will have a description of the wandering tom.

Step 1: Determine all possible genotypes of the kittens based on their phenotypes:

Kitten #1 is an all black cat.

trait	phenotype	ALL possible genotypes
hair length	short	
tail length	long	
pigmentation	wild type	
ticking	non-agouti	
coat pattern	mackerel	
stripe color	black	
color density	dense	
other coat colors	not white	

Kitten #2 looks almost exactly like its mother.

trait	phenotype	ALL possible genotypes
hair length	short	
tail length	long	
pigmentation	wild type	
ticking	agouti	
coat pattern	mackerel	
stripe color	brown	
color density	dense	
other coat colors	not white	

Kitten #3 is an all white cat.

trait	phenotype	ALL possible genotypes
hair length	short	
tail length	short	
pigmentation	not wild	
ticking	non-agouti	
coat pattern	mackerel	
stripe color	black	
color density	dilute	
other coat colors	white	

Step 2: Answer these questions taking into account the mother's genetic information. This may mean that some of the possible genotypes listed above may not be possible.

The mother's genetic information is:

trait	phenotype	genotype
hair length	long	l l
tail length	long	m m
pigmentation	wild type	I i
ticking	agouti	A a
coat pattern	mackerel	T t
stripe color	black	B b
color density	dense	D d
other coat colors	not white	w w

Why is kitten #1 an all black cat?

How does kitten #2 differ from its mother?

Why is kitten #3 an all white cat?

Step 3: Determine all possible genotypes for the potential father. (To do this, use Punnett Squares.)

trait	ALL possible genotypes
hair length	_____
tail length	_____
pigmentation	_____
ticking	_____
coat pattern	_____
stripe color	_____
color density	_____
other coat colors	_____

Step 4: Write a phenotypic description of the father.

THE TROUBLE WITH THE "RACE" CONCEPT: IT'S ALL IN THE CARDS

Robert Graber

Because the populations of a species ordinarily are connected, at least indirectly, by some degree of gene flow, genes are constantly getting "scrambled" so that at any given time the species as a whole cannot be neatly subdivided into distinct subgroups. Astute zoologists recognized decades ago that this renders quite problematic the whole subspecies concept; biological anthropologists increasingly have recognized it as perhaps the fundamental reason that science could not arrive at a satisfactory enumeration of human "races." How the species breaks down will depend on the variable, or variables, looked at, so any particular set of racial categories is not so much a reflection of something real "out there" in the natural world, as it is the result of arbitrary choices by the racemaker. Statistically, the problem is that of discordant variation. But, as I learned long ago, this important concept is difficult to convey to students verbally. As a result, I invented a hands-on approach by designing two decks of cards and inviting students to try their hands at sorting them. This card game can be used in any introductory-level class that has one or more sessions devoted to the study of race, from four-field introductory anthropology to entire courses devoted to biological anthropology. I will describe the decks themselves, then explain how they are used class to demonstrate the concept of discordant variation.

Figure 1 shows the "c" deck: four 3-by-5-inch note cards, each bearing a stick-person. Card "c1" bears the image of a short, solid, curly-haired individual; "c2" a tall, dotted, straight-haired individual; "c3" a short, solid, curly-haired individual; and "c4" a tall, dotted, strait-haired individual. (Actually, the stick people are not solid and dotted, but purple and orange, with blank ink used only for faces and hair.) Figure 2 shows the "d" deck: card "d1" bears the image of a short, solid, straight-haired individual; "d-2" a tall, solid, curly-haired individual; "d-3" a short, dotted, curly-haired individual; and "d-4" a tall, dotted, straight-haired one. Note that the cards' labels are inconspicuous. Sixteen of these decks (8 of each kind) are sufficient for a class of up to about 50 students. You will need about a third as many decks as you have students, so if the class is really large, you will need many decks and a recruit or two to help pass them out; fortunately decks can be made quickly, and as is obvious from Figures 1 and 2, require no artistic ability. Feel free to photocopy and enlarge Figures 1 and 2 on heavy paper, cutting and pasting on 3 x 5" cards, and coloring orange and purple, or make you own variations.

After introducing the subject of biological variation among modern humans, I assert that with humans, as with animals generally, gene flow between populations (concepts covered earlier in the course) tends to make variation **discordant** rather than **concordant.** I write these terms on the chalkboard without attempting to define them in any detail. This brings up the next point in the lecture outline, "The Trouble with the Race Concept." Students invariably show heightened interest when they are told they will be involved in some "active learning." Teams of two to four will be given a deck of cards showing four individuals, all of the same sex; their assignment is to sort the four people into two races. I assure them that I will be coming around to check their races and that their grade for the term depends entirely on their success at this task. I pass out the decks, one to every two to four students, as seating dictates, to make for a pleasant social experience. The cards are purposely prearranged so that the "c" and "d" decks approximately alternate.

After a few minutes, I wander around examining each group's result. The c-deck sorters are lavishly praised for having made such "good races," while d-deck sorters are questioned very briefly as to why they sorted as they did. "Here, trade decks with this group," I say encouragingly, "as I think you will have better success at making races;" and indeed they do. The other group, meanwhile, having received the "d" deck, gets cold water poured on its enthusiastic racemaking. Occasionally a group declines to sort the "d" deck, having recognized the arbitrariness of whatever they might propose; once, presumably acting on an unusually strong aversion to the very idea of racial classification, a group actually refused to even sort the "c" deck!

When everyone has had a chance to sort both decks (and the general hubbub has subsided), I restore order by asking the class in what variables the stick-people differ. Students quickly volunteer them: height, color, and hair form. "For both decks?" "Yes, for both decks." "What states are possible for each variable?" "Tall/short, orange/purple, and curly/straight." "For both decks?" "Yes, for both decks." "So, how do the decks differ?" Suddenly, silence. "In one deck," I point out, "you get the same cut no matter which variable you use, but in the other deck, **the cut you get depends on the variable you use.** Invariably I get raised eyebrows and nods. (The instructor, on a pedagogical roll, wonders why the whole semester can't be like this.) Only then do I call attention to the little labels in the cards' corners. "Can you guess what the 'c' and 'd' stand for?" I ask, gesturing helpfully toward the chalkboard where the terms **concordant** and **discordant** remain, where I had written them several minutes before. It sinks in, students get the point, and the two terms and their importance to the "race" concept are now understood.

I immediately emphasize that I am not saying biological variation is completely discordant among humans, or any other species; only that it is sufficiently discordant to have confounded all attempts to divide the whole species up into scientifically satisfactory biological subgroups.

The next lecture point is entitled "A Better Approach," in which I talk about the insight that comes from looking at the distribution of single traits throughout the species; here we focus on clinal analysis of single traits. My favorite examples are skin color, nose form, and body build, all of which appear to represent adaptation, through natural selection, to specific environmental features (directness of sun's rays, humidity, and temperature, respectively). I conclude by warning, however, that there is something seriously misleading about such examples and that we must not let them obscure the fact that humans expanded into diverse environments mainly by adapting culturally, not by adapting biologically. I point out that humans didn't inhabit the arctic by evolving thick fur any more than we ventured into space by evolving the ability to do without oxygen. I pick up the decks of cards at the door as students leave.

However you frame the sorting experience, it seems more effective and memorable than a strictly verbal approach to the concept of discordant variation. A former student I bumped into recently actually wanted assurance that I was still using "those cards"! Unusual teaching techniques, in my experience, generally take a while to work, then work for only a while; this one, by contrast, was an immediate and lasting success. When making up decks, use high quality materials because you will probably be using them for years to come.

Figure 1: The "c" deck

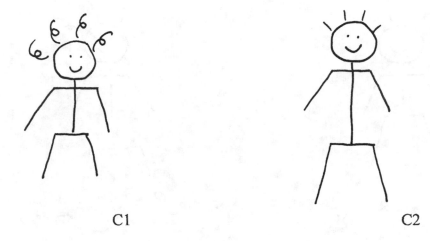

C1   C2

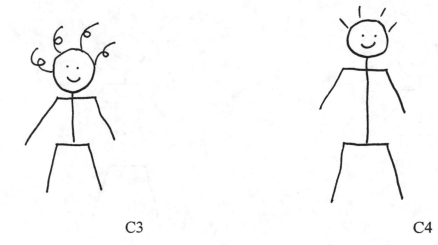

C3   C4

42

Figure 2: The "d" deck

D1   D2

D3   D4

"EXCAVATING" IN THE CLASSROOM

Julia L.J. Sanchez

Students enter introductory archaeology classes expecting to experience heroic, Indiana Jones style adventures. Archaeology is one of the few courses where instructors need not worry about instilling excitement. Students anxiously anticipate exotic cultures, pyramids, and tombs filled with golden treasures, so they come to class with an eager desire to learn. Instead, they are often crushed with lengthy descriptions of surveys and sampling grids. Archaeology is a difficult course to teach because it consists of data collection through survey and excavation, and analysis of artifacts in the laboratory. Without access to a field school, where students can participate in archaeological research, or laboratories with sufficient teaching collections, students must be content to listen to stories of the experiences of the teaching staff.

The "Excavation" Project

When teaching an introductory archaeology class of about 150 students at UCLA, I decided to devise an entire archaeological project in which students could participate without ever leaving the classroom. The project consists of a fictitious archaeological site that students have to survey, excavate, and interpret throughout the course. Students are given budgets and necessary data and are instructed to use material presented in class (lecture and discussion) and reading assignments to complete their investigation. The result is a project that is intellectually stimulating for the students and the teaching staff, adaptable to a variety of classroom sizes and environments, and a favorite part of the course.

In order to keep the project as realistic as possible, actual archaeological data should be used. The data often has to be modified to keep the amateur archaeologists from becoming too frustrated, or to expand the issues beyond what archaeologists may encounter at a single archeological site. I chose Chaco Canyon as the location for the project because my students are familiar with the location and culture, preservation in the region is excellent, a wealth of archaeological data and reports exist, and the types of artifacts associated with the region allow many studies to be conducted. Other well-known and well-researched sites would work equally well.

The project begins with a handout that describes the project and lists the expected goals, including the budget. (See Figure 1.) Students are given a budget and have to decide how to allocate funds for survey and for excavation. Data and laboratory analysis costs are assumed to be included. A map with several archaeological sites and a grid is presented as well. (See Figures 2 and 3.) The budget is designed to prohibit students from making "mistakes," such as conducting a complete survey of the area.

Survey. Just as archeologists must do in actuality, students first have to choose how much survey and excavation would yield the optimum results. Survey has to be conducted in an area before excavation can proceed. The survey is conducted by marking the grids on the map each receives. Maps are turned in to the teaching staff, who use a database to provide each student with a personalized set of results, showing the kind of features and artifacts discovered in each grid. (See Table 1.) The database may be fairly elaborate, but usually a table listing artifacts and features in each grid is sufficient. In each phase of the project, in-class lectures provide students with appropriate information, in this case, on survey techniques and sampling strategies.

"Excavation." Using the survey results, students then decide where to excavate. Again, data are available in areas without architecture, so students who conduct "risky" excavations in those areas will be rewarded with unique information about agricultural fields, turkey pens, or road systems. Students choose areas for excavation by marking the areas on a map, turning maps in to the teaching staff, then receiving their list of data. (See Figure 4.) The teaching staff use a more detailed database that correlates excavations in each grid with the artifacts and features recovered. The database may be elaborate, with different information for each grid on the map, or relatively simple, giving each student similar information. The excavation data includes information on architecture, such as wall foundations, as well as the number of artifacts found in each grid, including ceramic sherds, lithic fragments, animal bones, architectural information, and occasional interesting artifacts such as jade and turquoise effigies.

The database is created to contain information on various temporal phases. Previous to the project, the teaching staff created a history of the area. In this example, artifacts and architecture were assigned to three temporal phases, with some overlap so that the phases would not be too obvious. The first phase was one of relatively small pueblos. The second phase represented a time of population increase, larger construction, and an increased reliance on architecture. Numbers of artifacts increased during this time, more corn cobs were found, and animal bones shifted to include fewer deer and more rabbits and turkeys. During the third temporal phase at Chaco Canyon, the population dropped again, artifact density decreased, and many areas of the pueblos were abandoned.

The architectural and artifactual changes were clues for students. When each student receives a list of excavated material, the difference in architecture and artifacts should be placed in temporal order through the creation of artifact seriations and/or radiocarbon dates. Students then interpret the clues to recreate a history of the area. The clues provided should be obvious to students that there were three phases with different cultural processes. In order to prevent students from having inadequate data, and to make assignments easier for the teaching staff, the excavation data were standardized. Students mainly choose to excavate pueblo rooms, so the first room excavated would always result in data designated as "living quarters," the second room would result in "storage room" data and so on.

Interpretation. The interpretation of data should be assisted by readings and in-class lectures and discussions. At least some class sessions should focus on theory and case studies, demonstrating why archaeologists use particular approaches. Broad topics such as the origins of complex societies or analyses of political systems provide students with information on which to base their final interpretations. If possible, students can "practice" with sample artifacts (or even household items brought to class) to create typologies and seriations. Practice sessions demonstrate the process that students can then apply to their projects. Student interpretations are submitted and graded in three stages to provide feedback and guidance throughout the project (survey, excavation, interpretation).

"Site Reports." The final papers present the entire results as a site report. Many of the final interpretations are speculative, but I have been surprised at the level of sophistication. Not only were the papers an improvement over assignments in the same course in previous years, but the exams were greatly improved as well. By providing students with the challenge of practicing archaeology rather than just reading or hearing about it, the course became an exciting journey for all.

Acknowledgments: Christopher Attarian, Colleen Delaney-Rivera, and Scott Pletka provided valuable insight as teaching assistants for this course. They compiled artifact databases and offered revisions based on their own ideas and on student input.

Chaco Canyon Bibliography

Frazier, Kendrick
    1986 *People of Chaco: A Canyon and its Culture*. New York: Norton.

Hayes, Alden C.
    1981 *Archaeological Surveys of Chaco Canyon, New Mexico*. Washington DC: National Park Service, United States Department of the Interior.

Judge, James W., and John D. Schelberg, eds.
    1984 *Recent Research on Chaco Prehistory*. Albuquerque New Mexico: Division of Cultural Research, United States Department of the Interior, National Park Service, Albuquerque, New Mexico.

Lekson, Stephen H.
    1986 *Great Pueblo Architecture of Chaco Canyon, New Mexico*. Albuquerque, New Mexico: University of New Mexico Press.

Lister, Robert H., and Florence C. Lister
    1981 *Chaco Canyon: Archaeology and Archaeologists*. Albuquerque, New Mexico: University of New Mexico Press.

Noble, David Grant, ed.
    1984 *New Light on Chaco Canyon*. Santa Fe, New Mexico: School of American Research.

46

Sebastian, Lynne
1992 *The Chaco Anasazi: Sociopolitical Evolution in the Prehistoric Southwest.* Cambridge: Cambridge University Press.

Figure 1: Student Handout describing the project and goals

CHACO CANYON PROJECT

You have been asked by the Chaco Canyon Association to survey and excavate part of Chaco Canyon, New Mexico, and analyze the results. Your goal is to excavate at least some pueblos for tourists who visit the area. Your research questions are to understand the area, including how the Native Americans were organized socially and politically, how ideology and ritual are manifested archaeologically, whether or not trade was important, and how all of these aspects of society changed over time.

The CCA has given you a budget of $12,000. It will cost you $100 to survey each unit (see maps), and $500 to excavate a small area within each unit (such as one room of a pueblo). You must survey a unit before you can excavate it. You must decide how to spend your money to best study the area and answer your research questions.

You must submit the results in three reports:

Part 1 (2-3 pages): due date _____
(1) Introduce your research questions and goals (you may add to those listed above);
(2) Describe your survey strategy: the sampling strategy used, where you surveyed and why, and what you found;
(3) Describe your excavation strategy: where you excavated and why;
(4) Give your preliminary interpretations of the area.

Part II (4-6 pages, including Part I): due date _____
(1) Include Part I of your analysis;
(2) Give a preliminary interpretation of the artifacts, ecofacts, and features found through your "excavations." This section should be a revision of your interpretations from Part I.
(3) Do a typology for any artifacts possible and describe the results;
(4) Seriate any artifacts possible and describe the results.

Part III (8-12 pages, including Parts I and II): due date _____
(1) Include Parts I and II;
(2) Analyze dietary information through the ecofacts and other artifacts and features found;
(3) Provide a final interpretation of the area, including information that answers your research questions on social organization, political organization, ideology, trade, and the role of this area within the Southwest.

Table 1. Sample survey results.

Grid	Lithics	Ceramic Jar Sherds	Ceramic Bowl Sherds
A1	2 hoe fragments 1 mano	339 Bruja style 200 Lacona style 335 Ocose style 152 Olec style	223 Chris Creek style 789 Colleen Canyon style 560 Julia Falls style 560 Scott Mountain style
B1	2 hoe fragments 1 mano	65 Bruja style 36 Lacona style 45 Ocose style 12 Olec style	10 Chris Creek style 65 Colleen Canyon style 12 Julia Falls style 55 Scott Mountain style
C1	2 hoe fragments 1 mano	23 Bruja style 40 Lacona style 40 Ocose style 10 Olec style	6 Chris Creek style 79 Colleen Canyon style 10 Julia Falls style 64 Scott Mountain style
D1	2 hoe fragments 1 mano	400 Bruja style 256 Lacona style 465 Ocose style 164 Olec style	123 Chris Creek style 605 Colleen Canyon style 402 Julia Falls style 450 Scott Mountain style
A2	2 hoe fragments 1 mano	60 Bruja style 35 Lacona style 40 Ocose style 40 Olec style	10 Chris Creek style 60 Colleen Canyon style 15 Julia Falls style 50 Scott Mountain style
B2	2 hoe fragments 1 mano	9 Bruja style 19 Lacona style 25 Ocose style 0 Olec style	2 Chris Creek style 17 Colleen Canyon style 12 Julia Falls style 5 Scott Mountain style
C2	2 hoe fragments 1 mano	10 Bruja style 10 Lacona style 10 Ocose style 12 Olec style	0 Chris Creek style 13 Colleen Canyon style 11 Julia Falls style 12 Scott Mountain style

Table 1. Sample Survey Results (cont'd.)   49

Grid	Lithics	Ceramic Jar Sherds	Ceramic Bowl Sherds
D2	2 hoe fragments 1 mano	10 Bruja style 4 Lacona style 12 Ocose style 2 Olec style	3 Chris Creek style 14 Colleen Canyon style 16 Julia Falls style 2 Scott Mountain style
A3	2 projectile points 1 mano	1 Bruja style 0 Lacona style 2 Ocose style 0 Olec style	0 Chris Creek style 0 Colleen Canyon style 0 Julia Falls style 0 Scott Mountain style
B3	2 manos	1 Bruja style 3 Lacona style 2 Ocose style 10 Olec style	16 Chris Creek style 2 Colleen Canyon style 15 Julia Falls style 2 Scott Mountain style
C3	2 projectile points	2 Bruja style 0 Lacona style 0 Ocose style 0 Olec style	0 Chris Creek style 14 Colleen Canyon style 0 Julia Falls style 0 Scott Mountain style
D3	2 manos	0 Bruja style 0 Lacona style 0 Ocose style 0 Olec style	0 Chris Creek style 0 Colleen Canyon style 2 Julia Falls style 0 Scott Mountain style
A4	2 projectile points 1 mano	10 Bruja style 2 Lacona style 15 Ocose style 25 Olec style	25 Chris Creek style 0 Colleen Canyon style 14 Julia Falls style 2 Scott Mountain style
B4	2 hoe fragments 1 mano	25 Bruja style 2 Lacona style 12 Ocose style 50 Olec style	65 Chris Creek style 5 Colleen Canyon style 13 Julia Falls style 1 Scott Mountain style
C4	2 hoe fragments 1 mano	7 Bruja style 1 Lacona style 5 Ocose style 9 Olec style	9 Chris Creek style 2 Colleen Canyon style 1 Julia Falls style 2 Scott Mountain style

Table 1. Sample Survey Results (cont'd.)

Grid	Lithics	Ceramic Jar Sherds	Ceramic Bowl Sherds
D4	2 projectile points 1 mano	0 Bruja style 2 Lacona style 0 Ocose style 2 Olec style	16 Chris Creek style 0 Colleen Canyon style 5 Julia Falls style 0 Scott Mountain style
A5	2 projectile points 1 mano	16 Bruja style 0 Lacona style 12 Ocose style 6 Olec style	16 Chris Creek style 2 Colleen Canyon style 24 Julia Falls style 0 Scott Mountain style
B5	2 hoe fragments 1 mano	150 Bruja style 0 Lacona style 165 Ocose style 2 Olec style	0 Chris Creek style 146 Colleen Canyon style 127 Julia Falls style 1 Scott Mountain style
C5	2 hoe fragments 1 mano	135 Bruja style 2 Lacona style 145 Ocose style 5 Olec style	2 Chris Creek style 138 Colleen Canyon style 125 Julia Falls style 5 Scott Mountain style
D5	2 projectile points	25 Bruja style 0 Lacona style 5 Ocose style 2 Olec style	0 Chris Creek style 14 Colleen Canyon style 53 Julia Falls style 0 Scott Mountain style

Figure 2. Map of Chaco Canyon area, showing location of grids.

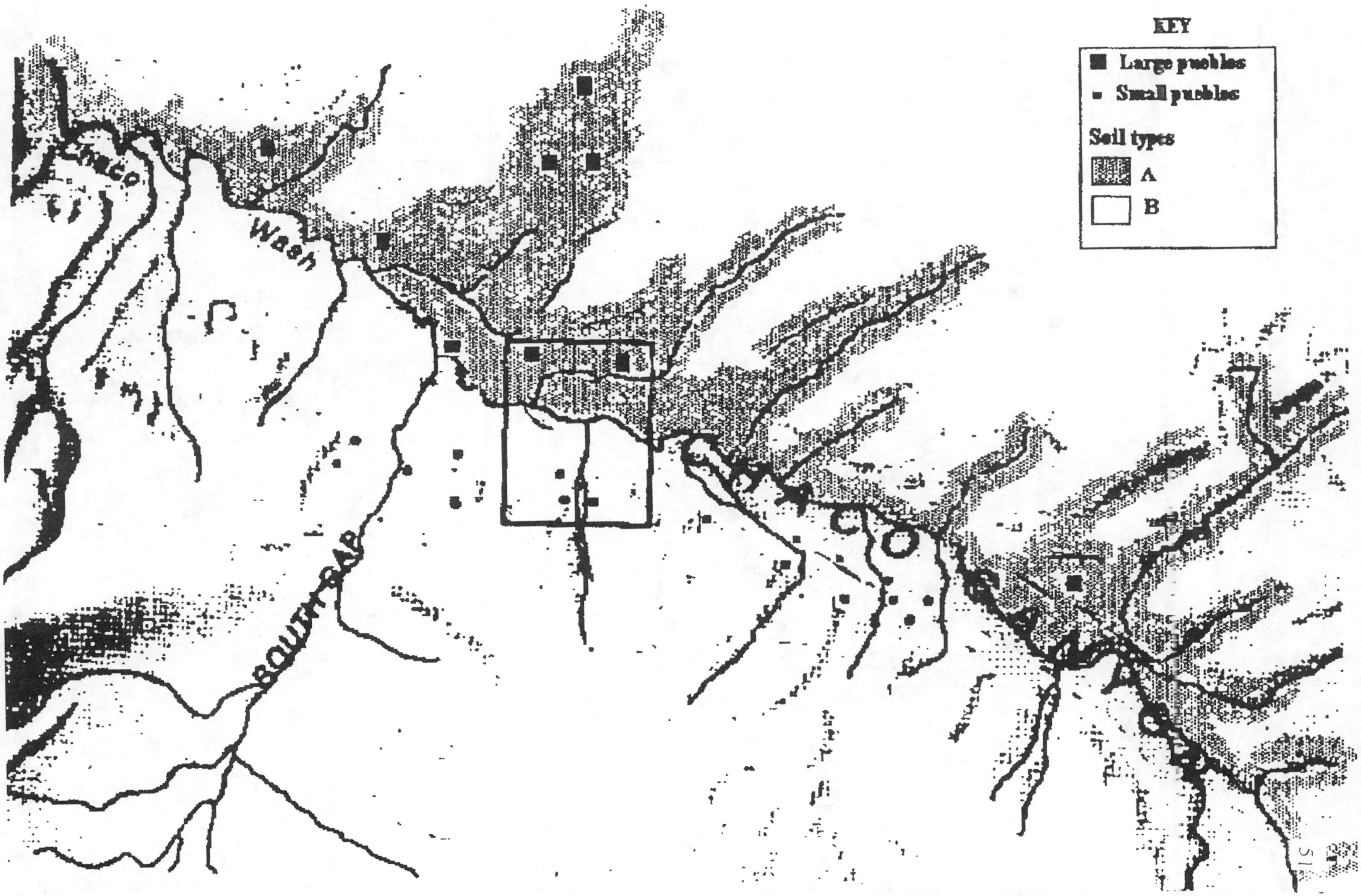

Figure 3. Map of grids, showing the location of the river and large and small pueblos.

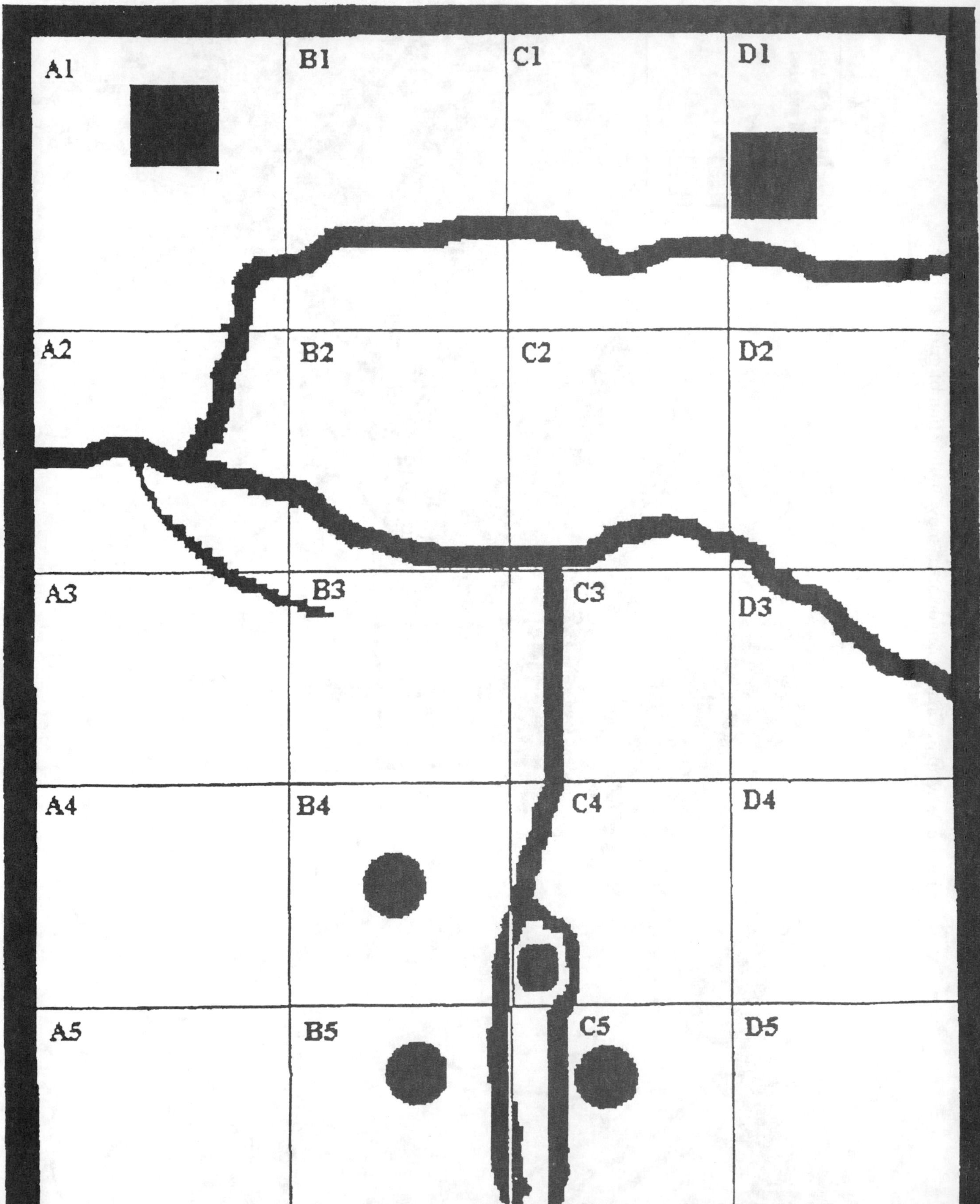

52

Figure 4. Map of the large pueblo in Grid A1. Students choose which rooms to excavate.

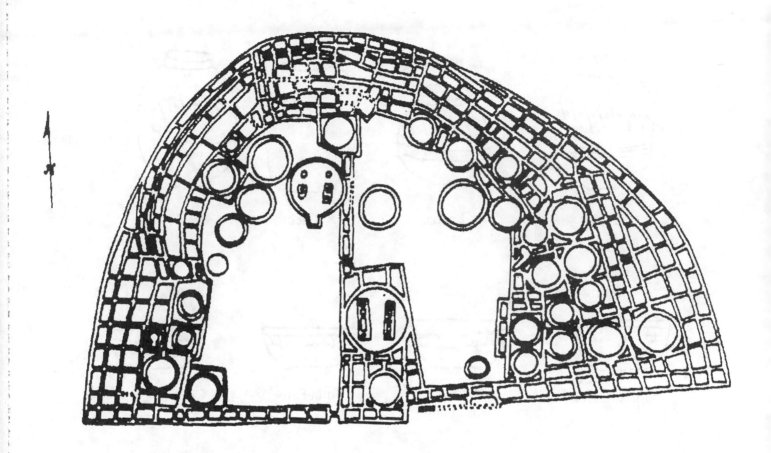

0   50   100 ft.

30 m

54

Figure 5. Student handout showing types of ceramic vessels and projectile points.

Storage jars

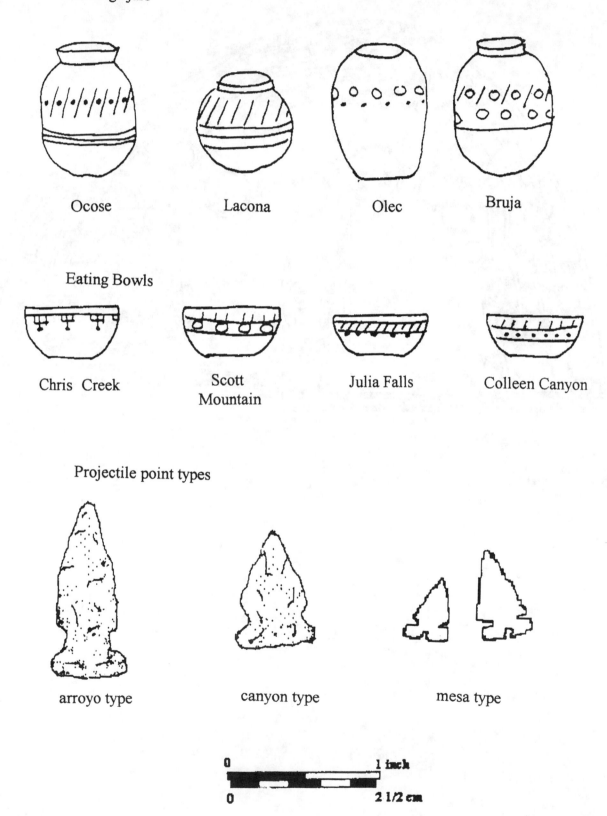

Ocose   Lacona   Olec   Bruja

Eating Bowls

Chris Creek Scott   Julia Falls Colleen Canyon
      Mountain

Projectile point types

arroyo type   canyon type   mesa type

0   1 inch

0   2 1/2 cm

AN EXERCISE IN REAL WORLD ARCHAEOLOGY

Maureen Siewert Meyers

Introduction

As an archaeologist who has worked in various capacities with archaeological field crew members just out of college, I often hear them complain that they were not exposed to "real world" archaeology during their undergraduate training. I know how they feel. Although reasonably well-versed in the theory of archaeology after six years of education, I did not have much practical experience in the field. Specifically, I lacked the practical knowledge of creating proposals, research designs, and budgets for cultural resource assessments, essentials for doing business in archaeology. In addition, the fast pace of cultural resource management was quite an adjustment after doing university-sponsored projects with flexible deadlines. Today, many students want to do field archaeology when they graduate with a B.A., yet are ill-equipped to do the work because field school work differs greatly from CRM. Although there may be proportionately fewer research and teaching jobs for archaeologists in the 21st century, there are still many opportunities for cultural resource managers, an area where good field skills are mandatory.

Taking these factors into consideration, I created an exercise for students in an introductory archaeology class. The exercise pushes students to utilize what they have just learned in recent lectures, that is, how to create and carry out a research design, and more specifically, how to apply different sampling strategies to different archaeological situations. The exercise should, therefore, be timed to coincide with in-class lectures and materials on research design and sampling. Although the exercise gives students only a brief introduction to real world archaeology, it does expose them to the types of situations they will face as archaeologists, either as field crew or as supervisors. By discussing the options students create, the class as a whole evaluates their decisions in an atmosphere of constructive criticism.

The exercise is most suitable for small to medium sized college-level introductory archaeology classes that range from 30-50 students. It would also be useful for specialized courses dealing with sampling and research design, or might work for a rain-day exercise for a field school or field methods class. Large lecture classes could use the exercise if the class is divided into smaller groups that meet outside of class; then the class could spend an entire period, or parts of each period over a week, discussing the results.

The entire exercise takes approximately 45 minutes. In classes that can accommodate the entire group at once (no more than 50 students), twenty minutes are used for students to come up with a research and sampling design, and twenty minutes are spent discussing each group's specific situation and solution. If the class is larger than 100, other accommodations would have to be made. An alternative strategy is to have groups meet outside of class, regardless of size, and thereby cut the in-class time for discussion to about 20 minutes. For larger classes, the exercise could be turned into a take-home short paper, in which both long and short discussion questions are addressed. The instructor, after reading the papers, would use 20 minutes to share highlights of good (and bad) research designs.

Because the length of time the lesson will take can be tailored from a minimum of one class session (or 20 minutes of it) to many, the questions posed to the students presented at the end of each scenario are divided into short discussion and long discussion formats. For the short discussion, only one or two questions are asked. These are ideal if you are using the exercise for one class session or part of one; the long questions are ideal if you assign the exercise as a take-home lesson, either for a group or individually. The long format is perhaps more appropriate for a more specialized course with fewer students.

Beginning the Exercise

To begin the exercise, split the class into groups of 5-7 individuals. More than 7 is too many. Make copies of the 5 "scenarios" that follow, adjusting for the size of the class. Five scenarios times 7 students each is fine for a class of 35 students; if there are more than 35 students, some scenarios will have to be used twice by different groups, but keep the groups to the 5-7 size. Additional scenarios can be written by instructors, based on the principles in the five that are provided. Give each member of each group the appropriate scenario. If the class is using the entire class period for the exercise, allow about 15 minutes for the groups to develop a research strategy. Make sure each group picks a spokesperson to present the group's research design to the class. After calling the class back to order, it is helpful to get the discussion started by the instructor describing each group's scenario and then calling on the spokesperson to describe the strategy. If two groups are working with the same scenario, the second group can give its report that will either be similar or different from the first group's report. After the spokesperson is finished, ask the rest of the class to critique the strategy. Does it seem feasible? Why or why not? What are the strong points of the strategy? What could be improved? Was anything overlooked? Be prepared for discussions that take longer than 20 minutes, because often the students feel they are applying knowledge they have learned, and the instructor can share his or her own archaeological experiences with the class. This is especially true if the class is larger than 35 students and if there are multiple groups doing a single scenario.

Usually, I create another scenario, or use an unused one, as the basis for a short essay question on the next exam. This allows me to gauge individual student's abilities to develop research plans, and it reinforces what was learned.

Conclusions

With this exercise, I have attempted to introduce archaeology students to many of the varied types of archaeological situations and challenges they may experience in the field. Each scenario is located in a different part of the country and each is tailored to the cultural resources of that particular area. Although these scenarios are quite specific, they can be modified to more closely reflect cultural resources in your particular state or region. Perhaps you are located near a state archaeological park or a Native American reservation. Using more local details in the exercises will likely increase student interest. You may also be able to pull current stories from newspapers or journals and ask the students how they would handle the situation. The ultimate goal is for students to realize that there is no one correct research design for every archaeological situation, and their strategies in the field should be flexible to the needs of the cultural resources.

Further Reading

DePratter, Chester B., and Stanley South
 1995 *Discovery at Santa Elena: Boundary Survey.* South Carolina Institute of Archaeology and Anthropology Research Manuscript Series 221. Columbia, South Carolina: The University of South Carolina.

Glassie, Henry
 1975 *Folk Housing in Middle Virginia.* Knoxville, Tennessee: The University of Tennessee Press.

Kerber, Jordan E., ed
 1994 *Cultural Research Management.* Westport, CT: Bergin and Garvey.

Longacre, William A., ed.
 1970 *Reconstructing Prehistoric Pueblo Societies.* Albuquerque, New Mexico: University of New Mexico Press.

Thomas, David Hurst
 1989 *Archaeology,* 2nd edition. Fort Worth, Texas: Holt, Rinehart and Winston, Inc.

58

Scenario #1

You and your four/six colleagues, second and third-year graduate students, have been hired as field supervisors for a University of Virginia field school. Your archaeology instructor is in charge of the field school, but she has turned over the research design to your group. Your interest is mid-eighteenth century archaeology of colonial settlers in the Piedmont of Virginia. The purpose of this summer's field school is to find the home of Louisa County's earliest settler, John Madison Ford, and his family. Through historical research, including deed and land plot searches, you know that Ford came from England and settled in the county in 1739, at which time he purchased 200 acres of prime agricultural land. In 1742, he built a two-room house typical of that period. In 1744, he added three rooms to the house and built a barn and two smaller outbuildings. Ford lived in his house until his death in 1759. His descendants still own fifty of the original acres. No original buildings exist today and the land is presently in pasture. The current owners have given you permission to excavate on the land. Based on land deeds, you believe that Ford's house is located somewhere in these fifty acres. Using the book *Folk Housing in Middle Virginia* (Glassie 1975) as a guide, you have a good idea of the size of the house. It probably had windows, a stone foundation and stone fireplace, kitchen, and two rooms. You have eight weeks and a crew of 12 undergraduates to find and begin preliminary excavations on the house.

Short Discussion: How would you go about finding the house? What type of field methods would you use?

Long Discussion: Based on your time frame of 8 weeks, 5 field supervisors, and 12 field crew, what is your field strategy and time schedule for finding the house? If using shovel tests to find the house remains (hint), what interval would you space them at? How would you use the data from the shovel tests to determine where to place your test units? Check out Glassie's book from the library. Based on Glassie's data, what would you expect Ford's house to look like? What would the remains look like in the ground? How would you catalog the artifacts, and where will they ultimately be curated for the long term?

Scenario #2

You and your cohorts are employees of the National Park Service (NPS) in upstate New York. You work at a preserved Iroquois village site, Three Sisters National Park. The site was first excavated in the 1950s, and the village remains were uncovered. Specifically, evidence of five houses and hearths were uncovered. Good notes and maps still exist on this work. In 1967, the site was bought by the NPS and made into a national historic park. Once a large attraction in the 1970s, its interpretation is now rather dated and the park as a whole fails to draw many tourists. You and your colleagues are the park archaeologists/historians. You have been charged with making the park more interesting to tourists through archaeology. Recent historical research has found French missionary documentation about the site that mentions an impressive longhouse used as the council house for the Five Nations. The previous excavations did not locate this longhouse. Your goal is to locate the longhouse, combine your data with the old data, and develop a new interpretation of the site. This will be used to create a new interpretative center and increase visitation to the park. Without increased visitation, the park will close within a year and you will all lose your jobs.

You have site layouts of other, similar Iroquois villages and you know the average size of an Iroquois longhouse. In addition, you have the 1950s site map for the park.

Short Discussion: How would you go about finding the longhouse, in a timely manner?

Long Discussion: What type of information and displays would you use in the interpretative center to draw tourists? What other ways would you use archaeology to increase interest in the park? How could you incorporate ethnographic methods and ethnoarchaeology into your work?

Scenario #3

You work for a medium-sized cultural resource management firm, Dygers, Inc., in Sacramento, California. Your firm has just been awarded a contract to survey a 30-mile-long strip of coast near Pt. Arena. The area is going to be developed as a public beach, some two miles wide and with a 100-foot-long dock. Previously privately-owned land, the beach has undergone almost no development since historic times. You have been assigned as Principal Investigator for this job. As part of your preliminary research, you have studied aerial photos of the beach, and shell midden remains are apparent. At least two shell middens still exist, and remains of other, smaller middens may be present. In addition, the coastline has altered over time, so sites could be located underwater. However, one of your firm's specialties is underwater archaeology, and you are certified in scuba diving; in fact, your master's degree had a concentration in underwater archaeology. You have a crew of six, of which three are certified scuba divers with some experience in underwater archaeological survey. You have three weeks to survey both land and water for sites.

Short Discussion: What research strategy would you employ to effectively utilize your personnel and time?

Long Discussion: Do some library research. What types of sites would you expect to find in this area? Specifically, what time period and what cultural affiliation would you expect? What would be your underwater survey technique? How would it differ from your land survey technique? What, if any, laws pertain to artifacts salvaged underwater? What type of long-term curation would be needed for these artifacts? What type of long-term research design would incorporate the existing shell middens into the public beach, allowing tourists to see them but not destroy them?

Scenario #4

During your summer break from graduate school, you have been hired to survey fifty acres of National Forest Land in Shawnee National Forest, Illinois. The fifty acres are slated for a timber cut and must be surveyed first to determine if any archaeological sites on the property are eligible for listing on the National Register of Historic Places. The area is heavily forested, and is located in the southern part of the state. You are in charge of a five-person crew. All six of you have been hired to survey the fifty acres over a two-month period. You will write the report during the last month of summer.

The fifty acres are located near Lake Barkley, formerly the location of the headwaters of the Cumberland River, now dammed. A similar survey was completed near your survey area three years ago and found over sixty sites encompassing all cultural periods, from Paleoindian through early twentieth-century.

Short Discussion: How would you go about surveying this area? How many shovel tests would you expect to excavate per day, and how far apart would you place your shovel tests to ensure adequate coverage of the area?

Long Discussion: What type of background information would you gather before going into the field? What types of information would you need for your report? What specific National Forest archaeology mandates would you need to know before beginning fieldwork? What criteria would you use to determine if sites may be eligible for listing on the National Register? What criteria are used across the country to make this determination? What are the merits and drawbacks to these criteria?

Scenario #5

You are trying to establish your own cultural resource management firm in Sante Fe, New Mexico. You have just landed your first contract with the Zuni Tribe. As a graduate student, you conducted surveys on the reservation as part of your dissertation research. In doing so, you established good relationships with the Tribal Historic Preservation Office (THPO) and some of the tribal leaders. The tribe is currently trying to increase its revenues through tourism efforts, and sharing the data from your dissertation with the tribe helped the leaders persuade other tribal members to build a history center on the reservation. They have hired you to conduct further archaeological surveys to gather more information for this history center. Within two and a half months, you need to survey one hundred acres. You know from your previous work on the reservation that remains of both pits and pueblos are visible, but that other sites are buried. You have secured an eight-person field crew, mostly graduate students on summer break.

Short Discussion: How would you survey this area, considering the topography, climate, previous archaeology, and crew size? Would you utilize multiple types of survey methods for this job? If so, which ones, and why?

Long Discussion: How would you involve tribal members and leaders to aid your study? What steps would you take so as not to alienate or offend them? Are there examples where archaeology has been used successfully to aid Native Americans? If so, why have these programs succeeded or failed? What types of state, tribal and federal laws would you need to comply with?

CULTURAL ANTHROPOLOGY 101:
TEACHING CULTURAL ANTHROPOLOGY SCIENTIFICALLY

Beverly Goodman

An important part of teaching cultural anthropology is emphasizing the holistic, comparative, and ethnographic nature of anthropology; these topics should be covered in lectures, readings, and discussions. In addition, the ethnographic aspect can be experienced through active student learning, an application of the learning by doing principle.

Can Cultural Anthropology be Scientific? (Or what is "scientific" anyway?)

There are specific qualities that scientific research must address: science is empirical, systematic, explicit, logical, theoretical, explanatory, predictive, self-critical, and public; it limits bias and is based on testing (Kuznar 1997). Since scientists must define their variables and since culture eludes simple definition, the difficulties cultural anthropologists encounter with the scientific method begin at the very core. An additional difficulty is the inability to restest hypotheses. Cultural anthropological research is often done in remote areas over extensive periods of time; this is costly and time-demanding. Finally, a cultural anthropologist does not have the luxury of experimenting with objects in test tubes that occupy a square foot of space that can be easily put away in a drawer. A course titled Introduction to Cultural Anthropology was devised to overcome these challenges by integrating a hands-on, scientifically-based cultural anthropology research project into the course. Although over 200 students take our course with one instructor and four graduate assistants, one instructor alone should be able to handle a class of 50 students doing this project.

The student research project focuses on: (1) how to develop a cultural anthropology research project based on the scientific method; (2) how to account for the current issues and debates regarding scientific anthropology; (3) good hypothesis development; (4) the legal steps needed for permission to do human research; (5) how to develop and conduct a survey (collect data); and (6) how to write field notes and a final report based on the data.

"The Love Project"

"The Love Project" was designed to help students experience the entire process of scientific ethnographic research. To accommodate students, the research had to be local, inexpensive (cost-free), and require a minimal amount of time to complete. "The Love Project" fit these requirements and is based on the earlier research of Richard Center's study "Marital Selection and Occupational Status" (1949) that compared the relationship between the occupation of a woman's husband and her father. Based on this model, "The Love Project" researched students who self-defined themselves as being "in love," comparing the socio-economic status of each subject's family to that of the subject's "paramour." The resultant data were then processed and used to test the hypothesis that people who come from similar socio-economic backgrounds are more likely to fall in love than those from different socio-economic backgrounds.

How to conduct the activity: The following steps are provided in order of activity, with a time-frame suggested after each step.

Step 1: Scientific Method and Background. The instructor should present an overview of the scientific method, reviewing the general steps and promoting discussion among students. Center's study is presented as a replicable model for a scientific, cultural anthropology research project. (50-60 min)

Step 2: Dialoging and Developing a Research Instrument (Survey). The instructor should work with the students to create a study that investigates the following hypothesis: People fall in love with people who come from similar socio-economic backgrounds. The instructor should engage the students in a discussion on what variables can be measured relative to the concept of socio-economic status. Students are given the homework assignment of designing questions that will generate appropriate responses on socio-economic status. (50-60 min)

Student-generated questions are collected and discussed for their validity as survey questions. The most valid question(s) are compiled into the final Sample Survey. The most likely given question is "what is the individual's job?" (A model of our Sample Survey follows.) It is important for students to be involved in creating their own survey. (50-60 min)

Step 3: Human Subjects Consent Forms and Field Notes. The instructor should explain to students the process of gaining permission to do human subject research and obtaining consent from the participants. The necessary forms should be shown to students, as they will be using copies in their field project. Students are then shown how to approach and gain permission from likely survey candidates and how to write field notes that describe each survey interview. The field notes should include all responses that do not clearly fit the survey tool, extraneous information about the person being interviewed or the interview itself, reflections of the interviewer, and outside comments made by the interviewee. Directions describing the protocol for conducting fieldwork are given to each student to minimize confusion and make the survey process as consistent as possible. (A model of our directions follows.) (50-60 min)

Step 4: Conducting Three Field Interviews. Students then conduct three field interviews. They are given a packet containing a set of directions, 6 Consent Forms, and 3 Survey Forms. They are given a written deadline for turning in the filled-in Survey Forms, complete with field notes, and Consent Forms. (Approximately 60 minutes, with 20 minutes per field interview)

Step 5: Reflection and Feedback. A key part of the project is the student's reflection on the data collecting process. After completing the fieldwork and turning the materials in, the instructor should open a discussion about this particular research. Students should feel free to discuss any thoughts or comments on the project. (50-60 min)

Step 6: Data Analysis and Report. The instructor must see that the data are analyzed and then report the results back to the student researchers. Prior arrangements can be made with a graduate assistant versed in doing data analysis or with an appropriately trained undergraduate doing a special course in data analysis. (Approximately 10-20 hours for 100 surveys)

Hints and Problem Solving

To make this project successful, it is important that the instructor have prior experience or training in ethnographic research. This is especially important for defining appropriate variables and determining the validity of survey materials. If a team approach to the course is used (instructor and graduate assistants, for example), the team should meet regularly to ensure that consistent instructions and training is provided to the students.

Doing an ethnographic research study of this depth requires a lot of time. Ideally, the project should be introduced early in the semester to provide ample time for data analysis. It is an important part of the process to report the results to the class so students are exposed to the entirety of the research process.

It is best to keep the number of variables on the survey tool to a minimum. The survey should address the research question (hypothesis) as precisely as possible. A brief survey tool decreases the training necessary for students, reduces the potential for mistakes, and may quicken the time necessary to complete data analysis.

In Step 5, students are asked to reflect on their experience as a researcher. It is a good idea to record their responses as this will contribute to improvement and change the next time the activity is performed.

One potential problem when working with students in an introductory class is the possibility of students falsifying data. The falsification of data, when conducting survey work means destroying the validity of the research project and students must be made aware of this. The following are ways to minimize the possibility of cheating:

(1) explain the ethical as well as the legal manifestations of falsifying data;
(2) give students who do not complete the survey project an opportunity to complete an alternative assignment (which they can even help design) without penalty;
(3) read the field notes that accompany the Survey sheets; the field notes should describe the interview and include personal comments by the interviewer;
(4) check the signatures on the Consent Forms. Any suspicious signatures or unsatisfactory field notes can be followed up with an interview with the student to ensure that the survey was properly conducted. The Survey Sheets can be discussed with students at random, as well.

66

Conclusions

The limitations endemic to doing scientific cultural anthropology research in a hands-on format can be conquered via a local research study. Students who successfully complete the Introduction to Cultural Anthropology course gain valuable insights into the process of doing anthropological field work/research by being involved directly in data collection and creating the survey materials. In short, students are engaged actively in the learning process designed to teach them how to design an ethnographic study based on the scientific method, create a measuring instrument, collect empirical data, and write field notes.

References Cited and Other Helpful Sources

Centers, Richard
  1949 "Marital Selection and Occupational Strata." *American Journal of Sociology* 54:530-535.

Goodman, Beverly
  1997 "Creating Scientific Cultural Anthropologists." Unpublished paper presented to Dr. E. Paul Durrenberger in his Seminar in Cultural Anthropology Theory and Method, Pennsylvania State University.

Koszalka, T.A.
  In progress "Learning by Doing: Active Learning using eHRAF in an Undergraduate Introductory Cultural Anthropology Course."

Kuznar, Lawrence A.
  1997 *Reclaiming a Scientific Anthropology.* (London: Altamira Press).

Wittrock, M.
  1990 "Generative Processes of Comprehension." *Educational Psychologist* 27 (4): 531-541.

Fieldwork Guidelines for "The Love Project" Investigators

(1) **Approaching the Subject.** Unfamiliar subjects should be approached in areas permitted by your institution. Usually, these are dorms, student unions, or activity centers. Inquire at one of the university's legal offices to find out where surveys are usually conducted. Preferably, to account for bias, the subject should not have a close relationship to the interviewer. This does not apply to people you are familiar with or interviews arranged as referrals. For each interview, begin by saying "Hello, I am a student of cultural anthropology and we are conducting a survey for a research project. Do you have 10 minutes to answer a few simple questions?" (Yes/No)

If no, say "Thank you for your time."
If yes, say "Thank you" and continue by asking "Are you a student?" (Yes/No) and "Are you currently in a romantic relationship?"

If no for either, say "Thank you for your time, but the study concerns only students in love."
If yes for both, ask "Would you say that you are in love?"

If no, say "Thank you for your time but the study is only interviewing people in love."
If yes, say "Please read and sign this Informed Consent Form. It will explain the purpose of the study. Please feel free to ask any questions once you have completed reading the form."

Once the subject has read and signed the form, keep one copy for the study's records and give the other copy to the participant.

If the participant has questions, answer them, but do not explain the hypothesis of the study. You might say that we are comparing the patterns in which people fall in love, but you do not need to give any more detail. The reason why you should not discuss the specifics is because participants may change their answers in order to fit or conflict with the hypothesis.

(2) **Begin the interview.** Ask the questions directly from the Survey Sheet; do not vary the questions unless absolutely necessary. Complete the Survey in clear view of the participant. If your subject gives you variations that do not fit the Survey, write them on the Survey Sheet. Keep these variations in mind as you will need to discuss these issues in your field notes later. If the participant does not answer a question, go to the next question and leave the answer blank.

(3) **Complete the Survey.** After you have finished the questions, thank your subject for participating in the study.

(4) **Complete the Assignment.** After the interviews are completed (or between each, if you prefer), write a description of each interview. It is best to write your field notes immediately after each interview because the interview will be fresh in your mind. Please record where the interview was conducted, any personal reactions, interesting comments, observations, or feelings. Finally, turn in your Survey Sheets complete with field notes, and Consent Forms.

Survey Sheet for "The Love Project"*

(1) Are you in love? Yes ___ No ___

(2) How long have you known the person you are in love with? _____

(3) How old are you? _____

(4) What is the social class of your parents? Lower ___ Upper Lower ___ Middle ___
Upper Middle ___ Lower Upper ___ Upper ___

(5) What is the social class of the parents of the person you are in love with?
Lower ___ Upper Lower ___ Middle ___
Upper Middle ___ Lower Upper ___ Upper ___

(6) What is your mother's occupation? _____
What is your father's occupation? _____

(7) What is the occupation of the mother of the person you are in love with? _____
What is the occupation of the father of the person you are in love with? _____

(8) How strongly do you agree with the following statement: "Love is the most important criterion for marriage."?
Strongly agree ___ Agree ___ Somewhat agree ___
Somewhat disagree ___ Disagree ___ Strongly disagree ___

Participant's Comments:

Field Notes:

Where was the interview conducted? _____

Note: Feel free to adapt or adopt the following consent form, or write your own.

INFORMED CONSENT FORM FOR BEHAVIORAL RESEARCH STUDY

Title of Project: "The Love Project: Study of With Whom do People Fall in Love?"
Person in charge: _____

1. This section provides an explanation of the study in which you will be participating:

    A. The study in which you will be participating is part of research intended to study whom people "fall in love with." By conducting this study, we hope to compare our results with those of Strauss and Romney in "Log-linear Multiplicative Models for the Analysis of Endogamy."

    B. If you agree to take part in this research, you will be asked to answer a number of questions in an interview situation and complete a questionnaire.

    C. Your participation in this research will take a total of about 10 minutes.

    D. In participating in this research, you will be asked to answer personal information regarding economic and social issues related to you and your family. Some of these questions could cause minor embarrassment, but should pose no more risk than everyday activities.

2. This section describes your rights as a research participant:

    A. You may ask any questions about the research procedures and these questions will be answered.

    B. Your participation in this research is **confidential.** There will be no information recorded that can be associated with your identity.

    C. Your participation is voluntary. You are free to stop participating at any time, or decline to answer any specific question without penalty.

    D. This study involves minimal risk; that is, no risks to your physical or mental health beyond those encountered in the normal course of everyday life.

    E. After you have finished participating, you may ask any additional questions and they will be answered.

3. This section indicates that you are giving your informed consent to participate in the research:

Participant:

    I, _____, agree to participate in a scientific investigation of falling in love patterns, as authorized as part of an education and research program.

    I understand the information given to me, and I have received answers to any questions I may have had about the research procedure. I understand and agree to the conditions of this study as described.

    To the best of my knowledge and belief, I have no physical or mental illness or difficulties that would increase the risk to me of participating in this study.

I understand that I will receive no compensation for participating.

I understand that my participation in this research is voluntary and that I may withdraw from the study at any time by notifying the person in charge.

I am 18 years or older and/or a full time student of _____.

I understand that I will receive a signed copy of this consent form.

_____ (name printed)

_____ (signature)   _____ (date)

Researcher:

I certify that the informed consent procedure has been followed, and that I have answered any questions from the participant above as fully as possible.

_____ (signature)   _____ (date)

THE PENNY GAME: AN EXERCISE IN NON-INDUSTRIAL ECONOMICS

Cathy A. Small

When I discuss the economics of kinship-based societies in class, "reciprocity" is always a key concept in the unit. I often illustrate reciprocity with stories from my own fieldwork in Tonga (South Pacific) that involve the generalized or balanced reciprocal exchanges that occurred within daily village life.

Invariably, my students reduce reciprocity in economics to psychology. People there, say my students, are "different" psychologically: they are kind, generous, child-like, and naive. They live simply, and are therefore unconcerned with material goods, leading them to give things away and to engage in reciprocity rather than market exchange. In my mind, their accounts are the contemporary version of the "noble savage" view.

I developed "The Penny Game" to show the material advantages of generalized and balanced reciprocity in economic systems. I wanted students to see that non-industrialized peoples can be astute, shrewd, smart, and interested in material goods just as my students are and yet may still decide to engage in reciprocity. The game is designed to show why, under certain conditions, reciprocity in economics is not only kind and supportive but also extremely "smart" and a real necessity for survival. The game is suitable for up to 50 students in any introductory-level course (or an advanced course in Economic Anthropology) where reciprocity rules and examples are discussed.

The Game: An Overview

Using pennies as units of wealth, I have students engage in a simple exchange game with other students -- one exchange at a time until time is up. There are different choices in the game: one can give pennies away, exchange for equal amounts, or bilk others out of their pennies. (Full rules and details follow in the next section.) I tell students that the object of the game is to have as comfortable and secure a life as they can get. Each exchange action is recorded on a card that each student carries and on which the economic loss or gain and the name of the trading partner is recorded. (Each economic action then also creates a "relationship.") In practice, participants usually reenact an exchange type many times with different people to create an economic strategy. Some students choose to hoard their money, others to accumulate more wealth through bilking others, and others still to give wealth away.

When the time limit has been reached (15-20 minutes), exchange stops, and students will have accumulated a different number of pennies. Everyone counts their pennies and I record the names of the five highest and lowest wealth figures on the chalkboard. The players who have tried to accumulate wealth obviously have big stacks of pennies and think they have won. But, the game isn't over. There is one more thing that I introduce before we determine who won. A cyclone has just hit our community and it has wiped out the wealth of every third person. Students count off by threes. Every third person must turn in all of his or her wealth.

Now who won? Students now refer to their cards. If they "created a relationship" with anyone through balanced reciprocity (an even exchange) or generalized (a gift with no return given), then they may ask that person for help and the person will respond. (See next section for additional rules for what is given back.) If someone has no relationships on their card, they obviously cannot ask anyone for help. We now recount pennies. Almost always, the result is: "the last shall be first." Those who created relationships, rather than stockpiled, come out on top and many of the accumulators are now in dire straits.

The exercise is quite powerful. Students really come to understand that, under the same conditions, they would do the same thing as the "exotic people" they read about and that other economic systems and people can be quite savvy -- just like themselves.

The Rules and Conduct of the Game

The game works best:
... with 50 or less students;
... in a class setting where there is some clear space for moving around;
... in a class of at least 50 minutes (75 with discussion).

Equipment needs (for each student):
... a name tag (students write first name and first letter of last name on tag and wear them in a conspicuous place);
... a large (4 x 6 or larger) index card with three columns headed as below:
(students can fill in the cards if you do not care to do so in advance).

I gave (lost) to:	Even exchange with:	I won (received) from:

... a stockpile of wealth for each student (12 pennies each);
... a pail/can to hold the 600+ pennies.

Instructions to Students: "This is a game about wealth. The object of the game is to live as comfortable and secure a life as is possible. The winners of this game will be considered those with the most pennies at the end of the game. Each of you will start with 12 pennies.

To play the game, you stand and walk until you meet someone. That person is your first exchange partner and you should begin an exchange with him or her. Here is how an exchange works: **without** your exchange partner seeing, put either 0, 1, or 2 pennies into your hand and close your fist. Your partner will do the same. Now, face each other and pump your closed hand two times in unison as if you were playing "odds and evens." Open your hand on the third pump to reveal your gift. The only limitation on betting is that you cannot offer your last penny as a gift; you need that penny to live.

Exchange the "gifts" you have "given" and record them on the card. If Ann P. had 1 penny in her hand and Bob S. -- her exchange partner -- had 2 pennies, then Ann should take Bob's gift and record it on the card as follows: using the card referred to above, Ann should put "Bob S." under "I won (received) from," while Bob should put "Ann P." under "I gave (lost) to." After the person's name, each person should put the number of how much they won or lost after their gift. The "won" or "loss" should be the difference between what was given and received. In Bob and Ann's case, the difference between Bob's gift and Ann's gift was 1 because Bob gave 2 and Ann gave 1 back. If Ann had no pennies in her hand, then the difference would be 2. Record the number lost or won after the name.

Bob's card would look like this:

I gave (lost) to:	Even exchange with:	I won (received) from:
Ann P. (1)		

Ann's card would look like this:

I gave (lost) to:	Even exchange with:	I won (received) from:
		Bob S. (1)

Bob and Ann should move on to new exchange partners and do the same thing. In the case of an even exchange (1 penny for 1 penny or 2 for 2), put the name of the person exchanged within the "Even Exchange" column and the number of pennies exchanged. If you give 0 pennies and your partner gives 0 pennies, then put nothing on the cards. No exchange occurred between the two and each should move on to another partner. If an individual does not want to exchange, avoiding eye contact will suffice.

Exchangers should keep exchanging until the end of the time period. The cards will continue to fill up and every completed exchange must be recorded. OK, get your cards and pennies ready and begin exchanging."

Directing the Game: About 15-20 minutes into the exercise (make sure that students have at least 10-15 exchanges minimum on their cards), call time. Give no warning to alert students that time is going to be running out. Stop all exchanges as soon as time is called and ask students to return to their seats and count their pennies.

You now need a dramatic way to point out who has done "well," and has many pennies and who has not. If the class is small, every student can record their name and number of pennies on the chalkboard. Then the class together can pick out the richest and poorest names. In a class of 40, I tend to single out the richest 6 and the poorest 6. If the class is larger, or coming to the board is too cumbersome, I ask students to stand if they have 18 or more pennies and keep upping the ante ("stand if you have more than 20") until I get about 6 names or the number that seems proportional to the class size. I do the same with the students with the fewest pennies.

(Note that 6 is an estimate. If you use 6 be sure that the 6 highest and lowest really are high and low in relation to others. If there are only 4 students who are really rich and 2 others who are richer than most but close to their starting value of 12 pennies, then pick only the 4.)

Next, you want the students to realize what kind of a strategy got them into the richest or poorest categories. Suggest that most people developed a **strategy of exchange**. Ask students to count the names on each of their 3 lists. Which list is longest? Suggest to the students that "if your 'I won from' category is longest by far, then you probably used a 'Get What I Can' economic strategy;" "if you were a 'Gift Giver,' then you will probably find that column 1 and column 2 have long lists of names. If the overall number of names you have on your card is small (less than __; this depends on the time given), then you probably used a 'Keep What I Have Strategy.' "

Then tell the students, "So let's see what strategies were used by our richest and poorest people." Ask the 6 richest people to stand and ask them to describe their strategies. Ask the 6 poorest people to stand and describe theirs.

Now announce: "But the game isn't over yet. There is one more thing that has happened in our society. A cyclone has just passed through the village, and 1 out of 3 people in our village was completely wiped out, financially." Then have them count off by 3's and write the appropriate number on their card. Pick one of the numbers to be the "wiped out" group and announce it: "If your count off number is 2, I have bad news for you. Your home and your wealth stockpile was completely devastated. Please turn in all of your wealth now."

Students will have to return their penny stockpiles to the penny pail held by the instructor. Collect **all** pennies held by individuals who were hit by the storm except the one they need to live on.

You can continue by saying "Sorry you lost everything, but remember you have friends and relationships you have built over the years. Look on your cards for the relationships you have." (Everyone should look at their cards.)

"First, look at the names under your 'even exchange' column. These are people with whom you have given and gotten things in equal exchange (balanced reciprocity). With these people you had a friendly relationship, and they will respond to you when you ask them for help." A typical card might look like this:

I gave (lost) to:	Even exchange with:	I won (received) from:
Ann P. (1)	Stephen. C (2)	Laurie S. (1)
Audrey F. (2)	Margaret L. (1)	
Seth W. (1)		

Explain: "Look in the column 'I won (received) from.' Sorry, but these are people who have already given you things and to whom you have given nothing. You have no positive relationship with these people and you cannot ask them for help. Turn next to the column 'I gave (lost) to.' These are people to whom you have given things, and yet have never received anything back. These are people who will feel obligated to you for what you have given them in the past.

"So, look at your relationships now. Your 'even exchange' partners will give you again as much as they have ever given you before (1 or 2) because you are a friend and they have seen that you will give an even amount back when you are able to. Those to whom you have given (and not received) owe you much and know they stand in your debt. You may ask anyone in column 1 for double what you gave to them, and they will give it."

(Note: based on the chart above, Stephen will give 2 and Margaret 1. Laurie is not a friend and cannot be sought for help. Ann and Seth will give 2; Audrey will give 4.)

"Go find your friends now. Remember that your friends can only give what they themselves have. If they were wiped out in the storm, they cannot help you now. If they have only one penny left, they cannot give it to you because they need it to live. Go to someone else. When you have contacted all your friends for help and they have given what they should, then sit down."

Now is the time to **really** end the game and tally pennies. There are a number of questions that can be asked of the students to drive home the economic logic of the game. Here are two inquiries that usually work well:

76

(1) Who is rich and poor now?
How many of the (6) richest are still rich?
How many of the (6) poorest are still poor?
or
Who are our (6) poorest people now? What strategies did they use?
Who are our (6) richest people now? What strategies did they use?

(2) How did the cyclone victims fare? (Ask all cyclone victims to stand).
How many of the cyclone victims are surviving well (have 10 or more pennies?)
How many are barely surviving (4 or fewer pennies)?
What strategies did these two groups use?

It will usually turn out (but, not in the case of **every** individual) that students who used a "Gift-Giving" strategy will do better than those who did not. Many of the students who had stockpiles of wealth before the cyclone (that they got through bilking others out of pennies) are those who end up barely surviving. This convincingly makes the point that under certain conditions, "gift-giving" (or generalized and balanced reciprocity) is a very adaptive and advantageous custom. From the point of view of the society, it ensures survival of the social group; from the individual standpoint, it provides a safety net for all who participate and that is why it becomes "smart" to give wealth away rather than hoard wealth or take it from others. Students should understand that it is not that people don't want well-being; it is just that material well-being depends on other things in other societies, like "creating relationships" rather than accumulating things (see discussion item #2 below).

Items for Further Discussion

Lively discussions can proceed from this exercise. Here are a few ideas to start discussion or focus the class after the exercise:

(1) This system of "gift-giving" works best under certain conditions. The condition here that seemed to make a difference was the weather (a cyclone). What if a society did not have cyclones or other natural disasters? Why do you think kinship-based societies all over the world tend to develop a similar dependence on reciprocity?

(2) What if someone told you that people in non-industrial societies are uninterested in material well-being because that is not important to them? How would you respond to them?

(3) Can you see why someone from an industrial capitalist society might look "stupid," "petty," or "childish" to people in a kinship-based society when they attempt to "win" in economic exchanges?

A Story

When I was in Tonga, I used to go to the beach with the local women who sold woven baskets and purses to tourists (tourists came in for the day once per month on tour boats from Australia and New Zealand). Tourists often try to bargain with the craftswomen and talk them down, even though their tour leaders are supposed to tell them that this behavior is not appropriate in Tonga. One day, a tourist was particularly aggressive about the price of a woven purse, probably a gift for a grandchild. The maker had given a price of $5. The tourist responded with a counter offer of $2. The Tongan woman selling the purse was a little shocked and said to me later that she thought maybe this man didn't have enough money to buy all the gifts he needed. So, despite the fact that the purse maker knew the item had taken her a full day to make, she told the man that he could have it for $4. Instead of buying the purse, the tourist shouted back "two-fifty," and started taking out his money. The Tongan woman, embarrassed by the entire experience, said "here, he just take it for nothing." The tourist, now flabbergasted and embarrassed himself, just walked away.

VALUE ORIENTATIONS IN THE CLASSROOM

Robert C. Harman

The course Culture and Communication fulfills an interdisciplinary requirement for undergraduates at California State University, Long Beach. Students write a term paper on a culture or a country of choice. I suggest that each student select a country about which he or she already has a special interest. Students have told me how personal choice of a particular country, for example, came about because partners or relatives raised there have personality traits they hoped to understand better. Most of those same students report that they developed an appreciation for the traits and the culture after engaging in research for the paper.

Nearly all the students who take my class are not anthropology majors and they have limited exposure at the beginning of the semester to non-western cultures. On the other hand, most of the students have some knowledge of other countries, so a large majority of them pick a country, rather than a culture, for the assignment. I encourage students to work on a country because of the greater amount of literature available at that level and because young citizens of the world today need to know about the behavior and beliefs of the "majority people" of other nations. In keeping with that concern, my lectures are largely directed at national cultures.

While "Culture and Communication" is designed for upper division students, it is still an introductory anthropology course for most who are in the class. The procedures described here might also be used in other upper division courses on people of the world, or even lower division introduction to cultural anthropology and general four-field anthropology courses. Optimal class size for using this approach is less than 50 students, although I have done it with classes as large as 70.

Students seeking a grade of A or B on the paper assignment have to use a minimum of ten working sources. Most of those sources must be in the form of books and journal articles. Websites and informants can be used to satisfy part of the required bibliography.

As students are selecting a topic (country or culture), I provide a term paper assignment sheet that lists nine **value dimensions.** In parentheses to the right of each dimension are the theoretically possible **value orientations**. I devote several weeks of classroom time to value dimensions and value orientations, following the value orientations model, in which every culture has a value orientation on each dimension (F. Kluckhohn & Strodtbeck 1961).

Value Dimensions and Value Orientations

(1) Relationship to Environment (Control, Harmony, Subjugation)

(2) Activity mode (Doing, Being-in-becoming, Being)

(3) Time (Past, Present, Future)

(4) Human Nature (Good, Neutral or Good and Evil, Evil)

(5) Power Distance (High, Medium, Low)

(6) Uncertainty Avoidance (High, Medium, Low)

(7) Individualism-Collectivism (Individualism, Collectivism)

(8) "Masculinity-Feminity" (Masculine, Feminine)

(9) Context (High, Medium, Low)

The first four value dimensions and their possible value orientations were developed in the 1940s and 1950s by participants in the Harvard Values Study (F. Kluckhohn and Strodtbeck 1961; Vogt and Albert 1970). The fifth through eighth dimensions are derived from the findings of the Dutch psychologist Geert Hofstede (1980). The ninth dimension came from the work of Edward Hall (1976).

The Harvard Values Study involved faculty from anthropology, psychology, sociology, linguistics and philosophy. They worked under the assumption that differences in values mark the distinctiveness of every culture. Participants developed a theoretical framework consisting of universal value dimensions and specific value orientations, which are the guidelines to thought and behavior that are actually found in societies.

Each dimension addresses a problem area for all cultures, and a value orientation is the solution employed in a specific culture. The first dimension deals with the problem of how people of a culture are expected to address the relationship between the individual and nature (and supernatural). Three alternative value orientations were proposed as solutions by the Harvard participants. One orientation should be dominant among the possibilities on each dimension.

I present some of the Harvard procedures and results of research on the American Southwest in class. On the first dimension, for example, the Harvard participants found that Anglo-American Mormons have a dominant orientation of contol-over-nature. The Mormons, like other Anglo-Americans, learn from an early age that it is culturally appropriate to assume a position of mastery-over-nature. In class I present numerous indicators of the control or mastery-over-nature value orientation in Anglo-American culture. Among these are the enthusiasm with which Anglos alter the course of rivers, dig into the earth to extract minerals, combat disease and explore space. The Harvard anthropologists found that another Southwest people, the Navajo, have a harmony-with-nature value orientation. Indicators of the predominant Navajo concern with harmony are the equal positions they accord humans and nature in their cosmology, a deep respect for and personification of nature and the belief that sickness is a manifestation of disharmony. Spanish-Americans of the Southwest have a value orientation on the first dimension of subjugation-to-nature. Indicators of that Spanish-American orientation revolve around fatalism and submission, and membership in the Catholic Church.

While Harvard participants were optimistic that the value orientation approach held great promise as a research model for anthropology, and several publications appeared in the 1950s, the approach soon disappeared from anthropological inquiry. As the value orientation concept was being abandoned by anthropologists, however, cross-cultural communication specialists from other disciplines rediscovered its utility as a pedagogical device. Edward Stewart (1972), a psychologist, modified the Harvard value orientations and called them "patterns" of mainstream North American culture. John Condon and Fathi Yousef (1975) wrote the first intercultural communication textbook, in which three of their chapters were devoted to value orientations. Larry Samover, Richard Porter and Nemi Jain allocated two of eight textbook chapters to value orientations. Fred Jandt (1998) wrote three chapters on value orientations in his intercultural communication text.

Geert Hofstede (1980), meanwhile, attracted considerable international attention with the publication of a volume on values in the work place. Hofstede's interests were cross-cultural, and he knew about much of the existing anthropological literature, even though he did not appear to be familiar with, or interested in, the Harvard Values Study. Hofstede (1984:46) was chief research psychologist for IBM, when he surveyed 88,000 IBM employees in 66 countries about many issues of culture that included values. He ran factor analyses that yielded four dimensions on which all cultures could be differentiated: power distance, uncertainty avoidance, individualism and masculinity (Hofstede 1984: 63). Each national culture was ranked on the four dimensions, thus providing comparability of countries.

I introduce the Hofstede dimensions to students alongside the Harvard Values Study dimensions for the term paper assignment. Despite conceptual weaknesses in both approaches, they provide thought-provoking ideas for cross-cultural comparisons of values. In order to have the Hofstede dimensions operate consistently with those of the Harvard Values Study, I suggest two to three categories of value orientations for each Hofstede dimension. On the power distance dimension, for example, students select from the orientations of low, medium or high for the particular culture they are researching.

Students catch on quickly to the value orientations model. All my students are able to analyze national cultures using the dimensions of the Harvard Values Study and Hofstede, and that of context as defined by Hall. Students cite historians and political scientists with the highest frequency in their papers because comparatively little has been written on national cultures by anthropologists. Students who are slow at first in comprehending the process of how to make inferences from the literature about the value orientations of a culture, are able to write analyses by the end of the semester. After addressing nine dimensions of values in the paper, students are required to write a concluding section that recapitulates the value orientations of their selected country and then makes comparisons with the value orientations found in other countries studied during the semester. A copy of the values dimensions and value orientations assignment sheet follows, which the interested reader can photocopy and hand out to classes.

A class period, during the last week of classes, is devoted to a sharing by students of their value orientations research results. On that day, we sit in a large circle around the perimeter of the classroom, and each student is allocated two minutes to describe the culture content indicators that led to inferring that certain value orientations are representative of a particular country. Due to time constraints, each student is limited to coverage in class of only two or three value orientations from the nine covered for the term paper. Most students perform quite well on the task, and their fellow students are, invariably, an interested audience.

Student feedback convinces me that using the value orientations model to learn systematically about the customs and beliefs dominant in another country provides a lasting benefit. Most students, especially the non-majors, may never have a similar opportunity. Students taking their one anthropology class usually leave with an impression that the discipline is relevant for understanding real human problems and adaptation in the contemporary world. Students gain an appreciation for the regularity of patterns they discover for a national culture, and they learn about the influence of recent world affairs on that country. The term paper assignment stimulates an appreciation of how anthropology is concerned with systematic inquiry into the way people actually live within the limitations of their society and culture.

References cited

Condon, John C. and Fathi Yousef
   1975 *An Introduction to Intercultural Communication*. Indianapolis: Bobbs-Merrill.

Hall, Edward T.
   1976 *Beyond Culture*. New York: Anchor.

Hofstede, Geert
   1980 *Culture's Consequences: International Differences in Work-related Values*. Beverly Hills, CA: Sage.

Hofstede, Geert
   1984 *Culture's Consequences: International Differences in Work-related Values* (abridged ed.). Beverly Hills, CA: Sage.

Jandt, Fred E.
   1998 *Intercultural Communication: An Introduction*, 2nd ed. Thousand Oaks, CA: Sage.

82

Kluckhohn, Florence R. and Fred L. Strodtbeck
   1961 *Variations in Value-Orientations: A Theory Tested in Five Cultures.* Evanston, IL:
   Row, Peterson & Co.

Stewart, Edward C.
   1972 *American Cultural Patterns: A Cross-Cultural Perspective.* Chicago: Intercultural
   Press.

Vogt, Evon Z. and Ethel M. Albert, eds.
   1970 *People of Rimrock: A Study of Values in Five Cultures.* New York: Atheneum.

VALUE DIMENSIONS AND VALUE ORIENTATIONS

(1) Relationship to Environment (Control, Harmony, Subjugation)

(2) Activity mode (Doing, Being-in-becoming, Being)

(3) Time (Past, Present, Future)

(4) Human Nature (Good, Neutral or Good and Evil, Evil)

(5) Power Distance (High, Medium, Low)

(6) Uncertainty Avoidance   (High, Medium, Low)

(7) Individualism-Collectivism   (Individualism, Collectivism)

(8) "Masculinity-Femininity" (Masculine, Feminine)

(9) Context   (High, Medium, Low)

CULTURAL RIGHTS

Suzanne LaFont

About Cultural Rights

Cultural rights can be defined as the right of ethnic and religious minorities to practice and preserve their religious or cultural customs and way of life. The idea of cultural rights is in many ways a controversial and ambiguous concept. It is, however, an important issue that is being addressed in schools, courtrooms, and the media. Despite this, cultural rights does not seem to be explored in many introductory anthropology textbooks. The project described here can help to fill this gap while adding a lively session to anthropology courses at the introductory level.

The topic of cultural rights can be presented early in the semester along with the introduction of cultural relativity and ethnocentrism, or it may be presented at the end of the semester in more advanced discussions about human rights, indigenous people today and cultural survival.

Discussion can be started by noting that cultural rights are protected in the United Nations Charter under the Covenant on Economic, Social, and Cultural Rights, which is one of the three primary texts that comprise the Universal Declaration of Human Rights. Article 15 of the Covenant on Economic, Social, and Cultural Rights states that:

> "1. The States Parties to the present Covenant recognize the right of everyone:
>   (a) To take part in cultural life;..."

Yet even the United Nations recognizes the potential conflict in such an idea when it states:

> "Cultural attributes can often be attacked or derided by States in attempts to
> favor one national, racial or ethnic group over another, to cite but one example
> of how important the rights in question are. Moreover, these rights include the
> right to participate in the life of society, giving a wide reading to the term
> "culture"." (www.unhchr/html/menu6/fs16.htm) (Article 15)

In-class Group Project

To encourage students to think critically about the complexity of cultural rights, I have developed an in-class group project to promote student-centered discussions of the topic. Although many instructors that I have spoken to have never done group work in their classes, I have been using it for a few years and have had some wonderful moments watching students engage in student-driven debates.

Either all groups can work on a single issue or each group can work on a different issue; in either case, an appointed person from each group will share the group's discussion with the entire class after the discussion session is completed.

(1) The best discussions come from debates on cultural rights and drug use. Having drug use as a topic of cultural rights combines both issues and makes for lively debate among students. It should be noted in class that drug use by indigenous peoples for religious purposes differs significantly from "modern" drug use. Many Native American groups, for example, use peyote to enter into a spiritual state while practicing their Peyote Religion. This is the opposite of drug abuse in many modern societies that often centers on escapism -- so-called "recreational drugs." The entire discussion should be prefaced by the warning that the project is not about supporting drug use per se, but rather in using the issue to explore the complexity of cultural rights.

In 1994, the United States government adopted a law that gave Native Americans the right to practice the Peyote Religion. About 250,000 people practice this religion that embraces peyote as a sacrament and a spirit. Peyote as a natural hallucinogenic drug is outlawed to those who do not participate in this religion.

Note: there is an excellent short article called "On the Peyote Road" by Mike Kiyaani, as told to Thomas J. Csordas in *Natural History*, 3/97, (Pp. 48-49). Another article that addresses the issue of cultural rights is "Throughout the Americas, Natives Invoke the Law of the Land," published in the *New York Times*, August 30, 1998. This article discusses the rights of Native Americans in regard to land, and more importantly, if Native Americans are entitled to engage in activities that are illegal in their "host" countries. It is suggested that students read these materials before the discussions begin.

(2) Another good group discussion can come from the idea of a cultural legal defense. The cultural legal defense debate is outlined in "Immigrant Crime and the Cultural Defense" by Doriane Lambelet Coleman, found at www.law.duke.edu/alumni/news/for 971mm.htm. (This is about two pages of text.)

Two important cases include:

(a) In 1989 a Chinese immigrant in New York City bludgeoned his wife to death after she confessed to marital infidelity. He was sentenced to only five years probation because of "cultural considerations."

(b) In 1996 two male Arab immigrants in their late twenties married two sisters aged 13 and 14 with the consent of their father. The marriage that would be culturally appropriate in their home country was illegal in Nebraska.

Either of the above topics should promote interesting debate. If you choose to have each group deal with a different issue, you can expand your discussion to child-rearing practices, language, and marriage customs.

Group Project Questions

Regardless of the topic(s) chosen, students can be asked to answer the following questions in their debate:

(1) Should indigenous people be granted rights not available to other citizens in this country? Why or why not?

(2) By granting special cultural rights to some groups based on ethnic or religious affiliation, are we not, in essence, discriminating against those who do not belong to those groups?

(3) Can we allow our criminal code to change so as to accommodate different cultural beliefs and behavior?

(4) Should the cultural rights of indigenous people be treated the same as the cultural rights of immigrants?

(5) If we accept the premise of cultural rights under certain circumstances, who should have the power to decide which cultural rights should be honored?

      (a) the national government?
      (b) an independent panel?
      (c) the indigenous or ethnic leaders?
      (d) the United Nations? (enforced by whom?)
      (e) any other unit?

Students should be allotted about 30 minutes to complete the discussion based on the above questions. You should continually remind them of the time constraints by suggesting where they should be in the answering process: allow about five minutes to get into groups, introduce themselves, and read the questions; suggest they spend about five minutes on each question. The written answers should be turned in to you.

About 15 minutes of the next class should be spent sharing the answers of the different groups with the entire class. I usually choose the most interesting answer to each question, read it aloud in class, and then open up the topic for general discussion. This often takes up the remaining class period. I think you will find, as I have, that students have a lot of engaging ideas about cultural rights.

Tips for Group Work

(1) Students work well in groups of five. To form groups of five, first count the number of students, then calculate X (# of students divided by X should equal 5), and have students count off by X, i.e., 35 students will make 7 groups. Be sure to have them count across the classroom horizontally. This fosters interaction between students not sitting together.

(2) Have students move into their groups and form circles with their chairs. You can adapt to permanent seating by encouraging students to break seating conventions and sit on desk tops.

(3) Students should be allowed a few minutes to rearrange and settle into groups. You may have to prompt students to form "neat" circles to encourage full participation. You should provide each group with a hard copy of the questions to be answered. Have everyone in the group introduce him or herself, then read the questions aloud and begin to discuss the answers. Be sure to explain that the topic under discussion may not have a "right" answer. Students within the groups do not have to agree on an answer; they can agree to disagree as long as they explain why.

(4) For convenience purposes, ask for a volunteer "secretary" to record the group's answers.

(5) It is up to you to arrange the environment and then (importantly) step back and let the students take over. Once the groups are formed, you can circulate from group to group and offer guidance and encouragement.

POTLATCHING CLASSROOM PARTICIPATION: USING "PRESTIGE" AND "SHAME" TO ENCOURAGE STUDENT INVOLVEMENT

Daniel M. Goldstein

The Problem

"How can I get my students to participate in class?" I had been teaching anthropology for only a few months, but I had found myself voicing this question on more than one occasion. In my first forays into the college classroom, I was shocked to encounter what one colleague referred to as "the wall of silence," the refusal by students to participate in classroom discussion. When I tried to engage students, they would only stare mutely, lips pursed, blinking at me like fish inside a glass tank. I wondered if there was a conspiracy of silence among the members of the group. Most students steadfastly rejected every invitation to participate in a dialogue about the course material, with only a few individuals willing to verbalize their ideas in the classroom.

Despite assurances from other instructors that this was a common problem in middle-sized undergraduate classes, I immediately blamed myself for the problem: perhaps I was not sufficiently firing the interest of my students, and so they remained mute. A better teacher could surely get some reaction from them. My second inclination was to blame the material: perhaps the ins and outs of Boasian historical particularism or Durkheimian conceptions of social solidarity were just too inherently dry to instigate much conversation. Finally, I blamed the students: maybe they were just too "dumb," or too unprepared, or so apathetic that I could not possibly hope they would respond to my urgings to participate in classroom discussions.

Ultimately, I rejected all of these hypotheses, and began to look for the solution to this problem in the complexity of classroom dynamics: perhaps there is something about public speaking that freezes the undergraduate tongue, such that only the bravest and most self-assured among them feel comfortable in voicing ideas or venturing questions. In conversations with students outside of the classroom, my suspicions were confirmed. It was not that I was an uninspiring teacher, or that the material on the history of theory in anthropology was inherently boring. Rather for many of them, the experience of voicing their ideas (as opposed to their opinions) was completely unprecedented. For undergraduates with limited experience discussing (or even thinking about) ideas and theories, speaking publicly on such topics can be a daunting prospect. Even students who have done the assigned readings for a particular class session and who have definite opinions about the material covered may hesitate to participate in classroom discussion out of a quite understandable disinclination to make fools of themselves before their teacher and fellow students. Embarrassment-avoidance behavior is practiced to ensure that situations do not arise in which they might be exposed to ridicule. In the particular class discussed here, this was compounded by the fact that classroom participation had not been explicitly factored into the semester grade, and many of the students were loath to speak in the absence of a tangible incentive. As a result, the majority of the class preferred to sit silently, allowing those braver, more articulate, and more experienced public speakers in the group to represent the majority when the classroom activity turned to discussion.

Student reluctance to participate in the classroom can have significant repercussions for student learning. The reluctance to speak impacts students' willingness not only to contribute comments in discussion, but also to ask questions on points of the lecture or reading that they find confusing or particularly interesting. Not wanting to ask a question that might appear "stupid" can be paralyzing, and many students would rather not risk seeming foolish even if it means they remain confused on a particular subject. Guarantees from the instructor that "There are no stupid questions" do not seem to help, nor do assurances that "if you are confused about something, many others in the class probably are as well." As questions go unanswered, the instructor, assuming that all is well with student comprehension, proceeds on to new material. Meanwhile, previous failure to understand goes uncorrected, impacting the student's ability to follow subsequent lectures, resulting in poorer test scores. Frustrated, the student "checks out," becoming even more reticent to voice an idea in an arena in which he or she "obviously" knows nothing, contributing to a downward spiral of incomprehension and resentment. The student may even retaliate on the instructor evaluation form at the conclusion of the course, giving the instructor low marks for, ironically, failing to encourage student participation or engage student interest.

For the instructor who wants to get away from a pure lecture format by incorporating classroom discussion and debate of issues into the lesson plan, the refusal on the part of many students to participate can be extremely frustrating as well. Though we recognize that student learning occurs via multiple avenues, of which passive absorption through lecture is but one, we are often at a loss as to how to encourage classroom participation so as to broaden our pedagogical effectiveness. Faced with student silence, it is quite tempting simply to blame the students, and to lapse back into pure lecture mode. This seems to be what students expect, after all, and it seems to require less effort on everyone's part.

A Solution

However, classroom participation can be encouraged and promoted through a simple trick that I call "potlatching" student participation in the classroom. It is a technique that I invented off the cuff, in response to this problem of engaging student voices. The beauty of this trick is that it is easy, effective, and need only be done once or twice in a semester. Potlatching provides a brief but powerful impetus to students to participate in class, requiring each of them to offer at least one comment or question in the course of a class period (or two, depending on the size of the class). As a result, each student has the experience of speaking publicly on a topic in anthropology, of having taken the risk of actually venturing a thought or posing a question before peers and instructor. The outcome is that, at least for a few of them, this experience mitigates their personal reluctance enough that on future occasions they are more willing to speak in class. For particularly reticent classes, the potlatch game can be repeated many times during a term. The activity is most effective with classes of around 20 to 25 students, though a group as large as 40 could realistically benefit from it.

Potlatching student participation is based on the classic studies of the potlatch institution of the tribes of the northwest coast of North America, described in the work of such scholars as Franz Boas and Marcel Mauss. It is a particularly effective trick to use in courses such as the History of Theory in Cultural Anthropology, or in an advanced course in cultural anthropology, because the form of the method so neatly fits the content under discussion. In the description that follows, I will make reference to using the trick in courses I teach, but the technique can be applied to many other course situations. For example, since all introductory level courses (four-field or cultural) are apt to have a section on potlatching, it would not be out of line to have students read the "four pages" in the text that describe the classic potlatch at the beginning of the term with subsequent in-class use of the potlatch idea for discussion rewards. Just because potlatching is usually discussed as a topic under economics does not mean it can't be used earlier.

I begin the potlatch game by lecturing on Mauss (1954) and his analysis of the great feast of the potlatch (based in part on Boas's [1897] original fieldwork) as a "total social phenomenon," one in which many different "spheres" of the social world come together (e.g., the economic, the political, the religious, etc.). Mauss uses the potlatch as a central example of his theory of the gift. According to Mauss, though gifts purport to demonstrate the spontaneous generosity of the giver, they in fact must be understood as reciprocations of previous gifts, where the return is given under duress and extreme social obligation. Failure to reciprocate a gift (such as a potlatch feast and its attendant material and symbolic exchanges) leads to shame on the part of the individual or group unable to pay back the original gift. I also lecture on the creation of prestige through potlatching, that is, the ways in which individual and group status differentials are produced by means of ever-increasing potlatches. In the next class session, students see the film *Ongka's Big Moka* (Granada Television International 1990), that depicts the efforts of a "big man" among the Kawelka people of New Guinea to organize a big feast of reciprocity (*moka*) to avoid shame and curry personal prestige. Viewing this film juxtaposed with the readings on the potlatch provides some cross-cultural comparisons on the subjects of gift-giving and the maintenance of reciprocal obligations.

The third day begins the classroom potlatch. The trick here is that the instructor gives students an individual proxy "gift," and then requires that they pay it back in the form of classroom participation. Before class I print each student's name on a 3" x 5" note card. I then hand these cards out to the students in the class, each receiving the card bearing his or her name. (Many instructors begin the semester by having students fill out personal data cards, which could also be used effectively for this purpose.) Once these cards are given to each student, I inform them that they have just been "gifted," i.e., I explain they have received a gift from me, and now they are under obligation to pay me back. The only way they can pay back this gift is by returning the card to me, and the only way to do that is by attempting to answer a question posed to them. (In this way, their gift to me would be greater than my gift had been to them, a classic element of the potlatch obligation to always reciprocate with a larger amount than originally given.) After the gift giving, I review terms and ideas from the preceding few class periods, during which I had lectured on issues related to gifts and to the Durkheimian social theory at their foundation. Each student who answers a question pertaining to these terms and ideas can return his or her card to me, thus completing their potlatch obligation. As a result, I inform them, they receive "prestige." (Although some instructors may wish to reinforce this prestige graphically with a gold star applied to the student's forehead or with a piece of candy, I am partial to maintaining the immateriality of prestige.) Inability or refusal on the part of some students to answer a question results in their being left holding their card, a marker of "shame" for having failed to reciprocate. Further, a student who makes a correct response then has the power to select the next student to have the opportunity to answer a question and thus discharge their potlatch obligation. This little twist injects an element of politics into the game, as students immediately begin trying to solicit the attention of successful question respondents. A dimension of nepotism also enters at this point, with students passing the favor of answering a question (how quickly it ceases to be a burden!) to their buddies in the class.

After this brief question-and-answer review period (lasting perhaps ten minutes, but depending on class size), I inform the students that we will now proceed with the day's lecture, wrapping up the analysis of the gift and beginning on other varieties of functionalism to have emerged from the Durkheimian foundation. Those students who have not yet been able to discharge their potlatch obligation are not permanently shamed, however, as I inform the students that they can still pay back their debt by participating in class in some way, either by asking a question, answering a question, or offering a comment. Then I begin my lecture for the day.

The effectiveness of this technique is immediately apparent. Students who previously sat stone-faced for the entire semester suddenly begin actively looking for opportunities to participate in the class. Students race to answer questions that I pose during the course of the lecture; this intensifies as the period nears its close and those who are still holding their cards begin to feel the weight of "shame" bearing down on them. Others raise their hands to offer comments on the material being discussed, or to ask questions from the readings they had done the night before. It really is amazing: Previously, these same students had remained silent, refusing to pose what turned out to be really excellent questions. Throughout the class, a level of humor and high spirits is maintained, as those who have already achieved "prestige" laugh along with those still struggling with their "shame," sometimes stepping in to answer questions, gratuitously robbing those unfortunates of their waning opportunities. By the end of the class, all but a few students manage to discharge their potlatch obligation, and leave feeling relieved and rewarded. The positive emotion registers visibly on their faces. As for those unfortunate few left holding their cards at the end of the activity, I playfully wag my finger and pronounce shame upon them. They seem to take it in stride. I have repeated the game on other occasions and have found it to be effective in increasing student involvement in class even when the topic is not specifically the potlatch or the gift.

Potlatching student participation, it must be pointed out, is very overt and entertaining. From the outset, students recognize that it is a blatant attempt to force them to participate in class. Nevertheless, this recognition does not in any way hinder their willingness to get involved and play along. In fact, they do so with abandon: many of them seem to have been craving just such an excuse to put aside their inhibitions and express themselves; others vent their confusion over and frustration with the difficult material. An additional benefit of the activity is that it drives home for students the principles of the ethnographic potlatch and the experiences of shame and prestige that accompany it.

References Cited

Boas, Franz
    1897. *The Social Organization and the Secret Societies of the Kwakiutl Indians*. Washington, DC: Report of the U.S. National Museum, 1895.

Granada Television International
    1990 (1976) *Ongka's Big Moka*. Chicago: Films Incorporated.

Mauss, Marcel
    1954 *The Gift*. London: The Free Press.

"AND A HUSH FELL OVER THE COURTROOM:"
USE OF A MOCK TRIAL IN CULTURAL ANTHROPOLOGY

David Howard Day

"And, your Honor, the Prosecution wishes to submit 'Exhibit A': Sanapia's sucking horn, for the jury's inspection. We will also be entering additional material...." The attorney for the prosecution turned to his witness, a U.S. Park Service Ranger, who claimed to have seen the accused, an elderly Comanche medicine woman, trespassing on Park property and resumed his questioning.

Eavesdropping on a real court case? It might be, but in this case, it is a mock trial being held in an introductory Cultural Anthropology class at Monroe Community College in upstate New York. The participants are all college undergraduates.

Issues of medical pluralism, folk psychotherapy, minorities and the law, and college student "passivity" surface dramatically in this description of a mock trial of a Native American traditional healer. Adaptable for courses in Cultural Anthropology, Native American Peoples, Medical Anthropology, Legal or Political Anthropology, and Ethnic Minorities, the mock trial, as a teaching device, mobilizes virtually the entire classroom as students assume roles as "attorneys," "witnesses," "judge," "jury," "court stenographer," and even "videotechnician." The background ethnography they have been assigned relative to this traditional healer is literally brought to life in the space of a week or so.

Anthropology and Law

Law -- formal or informal -- and the system of social control, what we in America commonly refer to as the legal system, are an integral part of every society and are embedded in them. Millions of us over the years have watched popular TV series like "L.A. Law," "Law and Order," "Equal Justice," or the current "The Practice" or have listened to Judge Wapner's rulings on "The People's Court." Cable channels offer round-the-clock trial coverage to viewers nationwide. "Blockbuster" trials rivet millions to their TV sets.

Three major disciplines have traditionally dealt with the subject of law: jurisprudence, philosophy of law, and the sociology of law. But anthropologists, too, have been keenly interested in law, examining the processes of dispute settlement and conflict-resolution in broader, cross-cultural comparative perspective (see for example Gibbs 1988; Hoebel 1974, and Pospisil 1972). Large numbers of people in the developing world, such as Guatemalans, Tibetans, and Ethiopians, live much of their lives relatively free of any substantial contact with the **official** legal system, which often applies more forcefully in urban areas, losing its grip in the hinterlands where "legal" affairs are submerged within the complex structures of kinship, politics, and religion.

An important exception to this, however, lies with Native Americans, who have become perhaps even more familiar than non-Native Americans with the United States Constitution and Federal and State laws because of their unique treaty relationships, their headline-grabbing land-claims and their religious beliefs and practices. The latter, especially, often raise thorny First Amendment issues. Use of peyote and the Native American Graves Protection and Repatriation Act (NAGPRA) are only the more prominent examples of Native peoples' reliance upon -- or confrontation with -- the U.S. legal system. Indians and non-Indian observers argue that as long as the special status of Indian people is upheld, there will be those who seek to redefine, or take away, their rights.

Assertions of tribal sovereignty make many elements in the majority society uncomfortable; while most segments of our society have been largely supportive of redressing Indian grievances, some states are challenging Indian tax prerogatives, judges question the tribes' judicial authority, off-reservation non-Indians oppose tribal hunting, fishing, and water rights and environmentalists oppose tribal economic development efforts. Churches and fraternal organizations, moreover, have opposed mammoth tribal bingo games and the surging popularity of reservation casino gaming.

Historically, Congress has vacillated between respecting Indians' special status and treating them like other American citizens. Pursuit of traditional, tribal, or folk medical and/or religious beliefs may in fact bring the minority culture smack up against the legal system of the dominant society that surrounds it.

Anthropology students at Monroe Community College have learned to turn their understanding of one particular Native American culture into a kind of *script* for a mock trial where issues of religious freedom, folk-psychotherapy, medical pluralism, and Native American ethnicity may be allowed to surface dramatically in the college classroom, far from where the typical college student expects to encounter a courtroom trial.

Background

Anthropology courses currently being offered on our campus include a one-semester introduction to Archaeology and Paleoanthropology, a cultural anthropology course, Native American Peoples, Anthropology of Religion, and the Anthropology of Tourism. Classes at the upper division level typically run at 40-45 students.

Years ago I became interested in ways to rehydrate turgid ethnographic material, infusing it with more drama, making it more participatory and "fun." I had read a short piece by Peter Brown (1980) about his use of a mock trial with university-level medical anthropology **graduate** students, to whom he had assigned the slim ethnography *Sanapia: Comanche Medicine Woman* (Jones 1972). I wanted a similar "energizer" for my cultural anthropology sections and proceeded to adapt his idea for my **undergraduates**. It has worked like a charm and I acknowledge my debt to him.

Who IS this Woman, Sanapia?

Jones's small monograph incorporates an ethnohistory of the Comanche people and highlights the fiercely independent character of a *Yapai* band northern Comanche healer, who was born in 1895 and died in 1968. It beautifully illustrates the development of an anthropologist's rapport with his informant, involving a lengthy apprenticeship. Illustrated with many early 20th century photos, the text deals with Comanche ethnomedicine, the physical context of healing, the supernaturalistic etiology of disease, especially the culture-specific disorder called "twisted face," shamanic curing, gathering of plant medicines, and the Comanche reservation milieu. Implicit is the role of the anthropologist in documenting fast-changing lifeways and a specific healing tradition on the verge of oblivion.

Students in my Cultural Anthropology classes read the ethnography, then write a paper of no more than five pages comparing and contrasting Sanapia **with their own medical doctor.** The comparison/contrasting assignment is based on the following important "domains:" sources of power in each tradition, training required of each healer, how each healer is viewed by his or her society, types of medicines used, medical specializations, the nature of the doctor-patient relationship, "bedside manner" and culture-specific diseases. I do **not** tell the students in advance that there is to be a trial until I have collected all of their contrast papers, as this immediately colors or prejudices their write-ups.

The "Trial" Begins

Once papers are submitted, I announce the mock trial and the "action"-- the mobilization -- begins. I use Brown's original idea of leveling two "charges" brought (for dramatic effect) by the State of Oklahoma (where Sanapia lives) against Sanapia: practicing medicine without a license and use of an illegal substance (peyote).

After running a ten-minute videotape I have made of a "collage" of trial scenes from previous semesters, I immediately review the requisites of a full-fledged trial, though most students are way ahead of me on this point. Then I announce the "cast of characters" and roles essential for running **this** particular trial. Students usually eagerly volunteer for most roles without any prompting from me.

I bring in my academic commencement robe for the judge to wear and we borrow a gavel from our Student Senate. Someone produces a Bible. I am never fussy about the number of attorneys for both the prosecution and the defense; these key roles allow the most vocal students to really shine. The lawyers, especially, need to know that attendance at each class is essential. Each team is responsible for deciding on appropriate witnesses to summon and these are elicited from the ranks of their respective prosecution or defense teams.

Students are also eager to play the roles of the bailiff(s) who never fail to scarf up some handcuffs, a courtroom artist (great for art majors or closet doodlers), and courtroom stenographer. The latter will review orally at the beginning of each class the previous session's trial proceedings. Another key role exists for a student who wishes to videotape the entire trial.

Probably, there are many students -- the reticent, the shy, the fence-sitters, the "slackers" -- who will opt to be on the jury. I try to control this by adhering to the legal number for a criminal trial, but often permit a larger jury while requiring each student to take notes on the trial which they submit to me. This specific instruction aims at giving jury members something to do besides just sitting in their seats letting their more venturesome classmates entertain them.

As instructor and trial "coach," my demeanor throughout, despite frequent moments of hilarity, is quite serious. I distribute "secret legal briefs" to each team that contain hints for arguing their respective cases, making their case livelier and make suggestions for specific witnesses. I urge them to be creative in summoning witnesses (including "expert" witnesses) and bringing in exhibits. The entire class, of course, benefits from a clear overview by the instructor of the order of the trial; the judge often calls upon my very meager courtroom experience, especially when trying to decide on overruling or sustaining a lawyer's argument and use of sidebars. I, in turn, rely on a handy lawyer colleague.

Instructors must be prepared for this mock trial to last at least one week and often two. I do not flinch at this because of the extremely high level of student involvement, indeed their complete absorption in the issues raised by the trial and the sheer energy in the classroom. As in real life, closing arguments must be well considered and addressed **to the members of the jury, not the instructor.** The judge must remind the jury, as it recesses for its deliberations, that it must address each of the two charges against Sanapia. Students sitting in their chairs awaiting the final verdict often ask what the trial outcomes have been in previous semesters. I prefer to defer any discussion on this until the entire class is back together after the trial.

At times, a "hush" really does fall over the courtroom, as it did one time when the defendant, Sanapia, decided to take the witness stand herself. On another occasion, I had to overrule an overzealous bailiff whose power had gone to his head. At the judge's request, he had expelled a student from the classroom who had created an outburst. Other students noticed the young woman sitting out in the hall on the verge of tears!

Post-Trial Discussion

Use of the mock-trial format, with its focus in this case on medical anthropology, highlights in an absorbing and emotional way, the problem of diverse medical systems in a pluralistic society. The existence and viability of alternative healing systems right under the students' very noses are brought into prominence. This is especially effective in today's multiethnic classrooms where there may be students from India who are familiar with *ayurvedic* traditions seated next to African Caribbeans, and where there may be Latinos, Jehovah's Witness or Christian Scientist students with their own very divergent beliefs. Everyone in class, after all, can lay some claim to some sort of medical experience. And even headaches can be springboards for heated repartee.

At the completion of the trial, class time should be spent discussing the underlying attitudes of both the prosecution and the defense. How **do** we define medicine in a complex society? Is Sanapia an adequate window into Comanche culture? As we approach the millennium and try to look beyond it, what options for health care are open to us?

Students have absolutely no trouble evaluating their own performances, and general feedback on the trial is invariably outstanding. Without trying to make too much of a "federal case" out of it, I orally evaluate the defense and prosecution teams on their command of Jones's ethnography. Their contrast papers receive letter grades. In almost all cases, juries render verdicts favorable to Sanapia. I am impressed with the original research done by the student legal teams at the college library; they dredge up the Federal Controlled Substances Act (1970), the Native American Religious Freedom Act (1978), and various definitions of "doctor," "Native American Church," and "peyote." The American Medical Association and, of course our own cumbersome, complex, medico-legal system come in for some good bashing.

As time allows, I try to display the often striking drawings or cartoons of the classroom "artists." In one case, a student created a "Sanapia crossword puzzle" on her computer that I distributed to the class. Videotapes from the growing corpus of recent ethnographic film on ethnobotany or on Yanomamo shamanism may be shown for comparative context. See especially Mark Plotkin's *20th Century Medicine Man* video (New Explorers) and NOVA's *Warriors of the Amazon*.

References cited

Brown, Peter
   1980 *Medical Anthropology Newsletter* (August)

Chagnon, Napoleon
   1983 *The Fierce People*, 3rd ed. NY: Holt, Rinehart, and Winston.

Gibbs, James L., Jr.
   1988 The Kpelle Moot: A Therapeutic Model for the Informal Settlement of Disputes. *In Anthropology for the Nineties*. J.B. Cole, ed., Pp 347-359. New York: The Free Press.

Hoebel, E. Adamson
   1974 *The Law of Primitive Man*. New York: Atheneum.

Jones, David E.
   1984 *Sanapia: Comanche Medicine Woman*. Prospect Heights, IL: Waveland Press.

98

NOVA
1996 *Warriors of the Amazon* (video). South Burlington, VT.

Plotkin, Mark
1991 *20ᵗʰ Century Medicine Man* (video) New Explorers Series. Chicago, IL: Lincoln Park
Zoo.

Pospisil, Leopold
1972. *The Ethnology of Law*. Module in Anthropology #12. Reading, MA: Addison-Wesley.

NACIREMA WRITING

John M. Coggeshall

"OK -- everybody take out a piece of paper and put your name and social security number on it." Twelve times a semester, these words stimulate first a groan and then a rush of creative thinking in undergraduate students enrolled in my introduction to anthropology course because the command signals a forthcoming essay on an article due to be discussed that day. Those who have read the assignment listen carefully for the imminent question they will have to answer, pens in hand, prepared to start writing. Those unprepared nervously search the faces of their classmates for some clue as to the content of the reading they now regret "blowing off." After 10 minutes, the students pass in their answers and class formally begins -- with a discussion of the article assigned for the day.

The purpose of these in-class essays is to fulfill several important pedagogical purposes: to supplement text assignments, to improve student writing, to enliven class discussions, and to guarantee student compliance. While many students may not consciously recognize an improvement in writing skills during the semester, students receive ample practice in summarizing complex information within a concise and coherent paragraph or two. Secondly, the essays enliven and enrich in-class discussion. It is often difficult to get students to talk, particularly in large classes, and the essays guarantee that they will have ideas to share. Finally, the writing assignments help guarantee that students will have actually read the article and the instructor can be relatively assured of a base level of knowledge for the entire class, providing a springboard for launching additional lecture or discussion material. Most students, anticipating a potential essay with every reading, will have read each article before class. This assumption is theoretical, of course, but it seems to work.

Through trial and error, I have learned to address the essays in the course outline and to offer hints to students for reading. In the "course mechanics," I write: "Note: appropriate article preparation requires that you read carefully the assigned article well before class begins. Hints: (1) take notes on the main ideas of the article; (2) summarize the main points; and (3) think about how those points relate to class information. Do not substitute highlighting for note-taking. Remember that I am not interested in, nor will I test you on, definitions and/or terms from the readings; rather I am interested in your ability to relate what you are reading to a larger context." Students typically highlight what they consider to be important points from articles. Note-taking, on the other hand, requires that students not only read but translate the important points into their own words, reinforcing the learning process even more by the act of recopying.

The articles that students read for these timed writings are taken from *Practicing Anthropology* (Podolefsky and Brown 1997), but could as well be taken from any typical undergraduate collection or from articles gathered from instructor-selected sources. The questions I ask are not summaries; rather, students must draw upon information from the article in order to answer a related question. After the essays are turned in, we have a class discussion in order to answer a related question. After the essays are turned in, we have a class discussion on the question upon which they had just finished writing.

At the next class session, I often read an essay example (anonymously) to the class to illustrate what a well-reasoned argument sounds like. This is an oral follow-up to a statement in the course outline that clearly tells students how their essays are to be evaluated. Under "grades and assignments," I write, "Essays -- in order to enhance analytical and writing skills, brief essays will be assigned in class, usually based on the assigned articles in the reader. At the beginning of class, you will be asked to write for about 10 minutes on a question relating to the assigned reading or video for that day. Notes cannot be used as memory aides. Thus it is imperative to have done the readings carefully before coming to class. Essays will be evaluated on a 10-point scale as follows:

      10 pts = clear and detailed; insightful
       9 pts = clear and detailed
       8 pts = details need elaborating but generally answered question
       7 pts = too much unnecessary information
       6 pts = too vague
       4 pts = absent for essay."

Writing experts often argue that in-class writings should not be graded because to do so might inhibit free expression; students can get overanxious about spelling to the point of missing the point of the essay. I tell students that I do not evaluate their essays in terms of grammar or spelling but evaluate them solely for their content. This allows students who have carefully read the articles and have carefully thought through their answers to be rewarded. In turn, students need not worry about grammar and free-write instead.

Here is a specific example: for Horace Miner's classic "Nacirema" article, I ask students to explain what the basic Nacirema value or attitude is and whether or not it differs from our own. Those students who have not read the article generally either admit their lack of preparation or guess at an answer. Those who have glanced at the article generally write about the Nacirema concern for health as their answer to the basic value question, while those who have read it more carefully recall the Nacirema concern about the body. Even better students make the connection that the Nacirema consider the body to be unclean and degenerating, and thus undergo painful rituals. I award the maximum amount of points for original thought or good organization, regardless of whether the writer actually recognized themselves as Nacirema.

Similar essay assignments could be given in any upper-division anthropology class, even those that might at first not appear structured enough to utilize a collection of articles. Students in methods classes, for example, could read and critique the methodology from journal articles. They could also develop their own research project using the same or an alternative methodology. Likewise, students in a theory class could explain the underlying assumptions by the author of an article, and perhaps critique those ideas against another theory already mastered in class. Regardless of the topic, students can be asked to write and to think critically, and can do so effectively. And, as a bonus, the instructor has a class that is prepared to discuss the day's topic.

DR. SEUSS MEETS UP WITH ANTHONY GIDDENS

Matthew J. Richard

In the early part of my Introductory Anthropology class, I employ an unusual approach to pique students' interest in the subject. My goal is to entice students, and at the same time, to demonstrate the relevance of the discipline. To me, this means cultural relativism, plain and simple; if students can view the world from cultural perspectives other than their own, and learn how such world views come about (or are socially constructed) in the first place by way of myths and rituals, norms and taboos, a more just social order free of discrimination and prejudice is more likely to become a reality.

I must admit at the outset that I am not a fan of standard anthropology textbooks, especially at the introductory level; their clinical tone and ponderous narratives, not to mention their sheer bulk that symbolizes drudgery, quickly create emotional and intellectual distance, thereby forfeiting the allure that is intrinsic to the discipline. We are just another "ology" then, which has failed to make a lasting impression on our undergraduates. ("It's time to kill a goat," quips one of my colleagues right around midterm in reference to losing student interest and the only way to get it back.) In my opinion, textbooks provide exactly the wrong formula with which to begin the long semester; by formalizing or "freeze-drying" the material, they render a subject to be unlike that which we practice and love. I favor starting from simplicity, from proximity, from familiarity. Over the succeeding 15 weeks, there will be ample opportunity for detailing and abstracting. In reinterpreting the familiar, there are numerous and profound lessons to be learned.

I use Dr. Seuss's story of "The Sneetches" to set the stage in the course. It's a familiar tale to many of the students, although none of them remembers it as a sociology primer. This, of course, is precisely why it is effective; students are both surprised and delighted by its sociological content; moreover, mastery of history and philosophy, often a deterrent to the analysis of "real life," is not a prerequisite to their understanding of Star-Belly hegemony. Once these barriers are removed, students are in an analytical mood, right where I want them. They are pleased to discover the message that eluded them in their childhood, and what's more, Seuss's allegory provides a model that we will return to again and again during the term when, for example, we consider race, class, and gender: Why is there discrimination in the world and how is it perpetuated? And just why are those Star-Belly Sneetches so cruel and arrogant? In other words, students quickly recognize patterned behavior and its not-so-mystical cause; truly, this is a breakthrough for many young minds, and many of my students profess an excitement in anthropology early on. They are also pleased to see how quickly some of the concepts we have defined in class, such as otherness, socialization, and the prescriptive aspect of culture, allow them to penetrate what they previously had deemed obscure situations.

The Lesson

I begin the class by telling students "We're going into the field today." I show them a slide of a shepherd boy on horseback from Lesotho, up in the Drakensberg Mountains. I tell the students this is a picture of a Lesotho boy and ask if anyone knows where it is. Usually no one does. Then I say, "but we're not going to Lesotho anyhow; we are going to Sneetchland." I pass around the 4 or 5 Sneetch books I own and students share them. I begin reading the story in class and I point out the gestures, the language, the recursive/discursive practices as I go:

(1)   Now, the Star-Belly Sneetches
(2)   Had bellies with stars.
(3)   The Plain-Belly Sneetches
(4)   Had none upon thars.
(5)   Those stars weren't so big. They were really so small
(6)   You might think such a thing wouldn't matter at all.

"The Sneetches," for those who don't know the story, or who have forgotten it, is the story of a society bitterly divided between Sneetches with stars on their bellies and those whose bellies have no stars. The Star-Belly Sneetches are confident and proud; they have frankfurter roasts and marshmallow toasts, and their kids regularly play ball. The Plain-Belly Sneetches, on the other hand, are meek and disheveled, and they are forever on the sidelines, "moping and doping alone on the beaches." They have little choice but to endure the taunts of the Star-Bellies who like to brag, "We're the best kind of Sneetches on the Beaches;" and "We'll have nothing to do with the Plain-Belly sort." The only consolation the Plain-Bellies can muster is to demean the Star-Bellies as "snooty old smarties," but it makes no difference; the Star-Bellies remain unmoved and on top.

The story continues:

(7)   But, because they had stars, all the Star-Belly Sneetches
(8)   Would brag, "We're the best kind of Sneetch on the beaches."
(9)   With their snoots in the air, they would sniff and they'd snort
(10)   "We'll have nothing to do with the Plain-Belly sort!"
(11)   And whenever they met some, when they were out walking,
(12)   They'd hike right on past them without even talking.
(13)   When the Star-Belly children went out to play ball,
(14)   Could a Plain-Belly get in the game...? Not at all.
(15)   You only could play if your bellies had stars
(16)   And the Plain-Belly children had none upon thars.

The story continues with its many wonderful scenes, numerous settings, and exquisite dialogue. The rhymes are accompanied by wonderful illustrations that depict the tortured facial expressions of the Plain-Bellies and triumphant body language of the Star-Bellies. Posture, discourse, and attitude are all significant; each contributes to basic group identity, which Isaacs (1989:38) points out "consists of the ready made set of endowments and identifications that every individual shares with others from the moment of birth by the chance of the family into which he is born at that given time in that given place." Elsewhere (ibid.:117), he adds, "the shared past enters into the making of every individual life in every culture, whether in archaic times or in our own; [i]t does so whether it appears in the guise of 'myths' . . . or as 'history' that purports to relate the 'facts' of 'real' or chronological time."

As can be seen above, I use this little tale as a vehicle to introduce a host of theoretical concepts, both for present and future consideration. I am "planting seeds" to "harvest" later in the term as well as in upper level courses as I proceed through the introductory course. In addition to those concepts already mentioned (social constructionism, myths, rituals, norms, taboos, hegemony, otherness [race/class/gender], socialization, culture, cultural relativity, discourse, and identity), the class gains insight into power, social structure/organization, and stratification, as well as an appreciation of ethnography itself. In short, "The Sneetches" provides an instant context that allows students to build more than their vocabulary; I believe it is instrumental in forging practical consciousness, or praxis. Students learn from the experience because, in a sense, they participate in it; they "live" it. And all in only 15 minutes.

(17)   *When the Star-Belly Sneetches had frankfurter roasts,*
(18)   *Or picnics or parties or marshmallow toasts,*
(19)   *They never invited the Plain-Belly Sneetches.*
(20)   *They left them out cold, in the dark of the beaches.*
(21)   *They kept them away. Never let them come near.*
(22)   *And that's how they treated them year after year.*

The story subsequently takes some interesting and amusing twists and turns; in other words, there's plenty of Sneetch history to come. I prep the class by reprising the critical questions once posed by Auguste Comte: How and why does society stay the same (i.e., the question of social statics)? And how and why does it change (i.e., social dynamics)? These are interesting questions to students; they seem to touch an idealistic nerve. Using a structuration theoretical perspective formulated by Anthony Giddens (1979), I introduce the notions of practice (both recursive and discursive), structure, and agency. That is, the normal, meaningful, or quotidian practices of a society's members, reproduced day in and day out, year after year, keep the social order intact (lines 13-16, and 17-22 for example). The same applies to a society's speech acts (lines 8 and 10); unless a novel, intentional or conscious departure from the norm is made, i.e., an assertion of agency, or what Giddens refers to as a generative action, the norm is upheld, and with it, a culture's structure. To drive home the importance of discourse, I have students surf the World Wide Web in search of examples of hate speech; they always report back with appalling results.

In short, "The Sneetches" helps students to see that a culture's reality is made and remade by people's deeds and words, their customs and speech acts. Our social life is neither inevitable nor is it natural; rather, our residual practices build and rebuild a culture's structure which in turn supports the status quo. This entire paradigm is reinforced by viewing the PBS documentary, "A Class Divided," which shows how a third grade teacher in Iowa resocialized her pupils on the basis of eye color.

There's something hopeful (dare I say liberating?) about this newfound "sneetch knowledge," and once established, we build on our model by holding "Generative Action Day" during one class period; this is the day that students come to class prepared to change the world, or at least things they don't like, just as Rosa Parks, Ghandi, Picasso, and Galileo did, by announcing in front of everyone a generative action of their own that they hope will become recursive, that is, the new norm. Sometimes I encourage them to read the op-ed page of the local newspaper and think for a couple of days about what they would like to change. I yield the podium to them. Students pledge to stop eating meat, or to stop dropping cigarette butts on the ground, or to give some of their business to minority businessmen and women in town. All are proud of their revolutionary status and class is particularly lively that day and the best generative actions are applauded.

In summary, I strive to impart an "anthropological way of thinking" in my introductory course. In order for the course to start out being lively and intelligible, it needs to be fun. In addition, an enduring analytical framework, a model that will serve us for the rest of the semester and even beyond, needs to be established as quickly as possible. Dr. Seuss, meet Anthony Giddens.

References Cited

Dr. Seuss
  1961 *The Sneetches and Other Stories*. New York: Random House.

Giddens, Anthony
  1979 *Central Problems in Social Theory. Action, Structure and Contradiction in Social Analysis*. Berkeley, CA: University of California Press.

Isaacs, Harold
  1989 *Idols of the Tribe. Group Identity and Political Change*. Cambridge, MA: Harvard University Press.

QUIZZING THE KULA WAY – WITH PERSUASION

Renee M. Gralewicz

Face-to-face, teacher-learner courses are being challenged to develop new techniques in order to compete with non-class, impersonal, instructional methods such as "asynchronous" Internet and video-based courses. These courses that allow students to "learn at their own pace" and "when they want to" are gaining academic approval and learner acceptance. In-person teachers are being asked to be as "engaging" and "lively" as professional videos and Internet courses while ensuring a quality education. In addition to creating a dynamic, student-centered class, we must continue to assess both our successes as teachers and our student's successes as learners. Within this environment, I have begun to use and incorporate the Trobriand Islander's kula as a focus for the teaching/learning process.

Assessing classroom learning and keeping student attention are both difficult and important for the learning process. One means of assessment that I and many others use is "the quiz." Quizzes consume only a small amount of class time and help gauge the class pace of learning, yet the standard quiz format has become boring and predictable. Over time, I have developed a quizzing method that utilizes the learners as teachers and gets everyone out of their seats. I use a simplified and extremely modified version of the Trobriand Islander's kula that both the students and I find rewarding.

Briefly, kula exchanges involve cultivating trading partners from each island within the Massim area of Melanesia in order to eventually possess items of high value such as armshells and necklaces. The trick is to establish and nurture these relationships across a number of islands by only meeting, persuading, and seducing those on one's immediately adjacent islands. Most trading partners in a single kula ring never physically meet. Every individual's goal is to exchange "an armshell *[mwali]* to which cowrie pendants, beads, and string have been attached for an equally valued necklace *[soulava]*, from which gold-lipped oyster shells and other trinkets hang from either end" (Weiner 1988:139). While cultivating relationships in hopes of acquiring the *mwali* and *soulava*, partners trade various items falling into categories: ceremonial; elaborately decorated carved weapons; stone implements; and "articles of domestic and industrial nature, too well decorated and too clumsy for use" (Malinowski 1961:89). Even though some items of utility are traded, most trade centers around items that have overgrown their use through elaborate decoration. However, the primary focus of trade remains one of persuasion, persuading partners to trade the *mwali* and *soulava* when they have the means to do so. Each and every exchange throughout the years is made in this effort. It may take a lifetime to persuade others to release the unique shells and many do not succeed. Because offering real wealth to persuade others in our society is called "bribery," I provide candies representing various levels of wealth and university bookstore coupons representing the armshell, *mwali*, and the necklace, *soulava*, for classroom exchange purposes.

Kula Quizzes

The following discusses how I use the kula for class quizzes; it is suitable for either of the introductory courses, cultural or four field general. Due to its complexity, the exercise needs to be read through completely in order to grasp its instructions and value. I incorporate the Trobriand Islanders into lectures within the first month of the course and from there, discuss the kula when appropriate. Since many general anthropology introductory texts do not contain very much information on the kula or the Trobriand Islanders, I interject the subject under discussion of material wealth. Annette Weiner's *The Trobrianders of Papua New Guinea* (1988) Chapter 9 "Kula and the Search for Fame" provides the foundation of discussion that I supplement with segments of Chapter III, "The Essentials of the Kula" from Malinowski's *Argonauts of the Western Pacific* (1961). The depth of information provided by the kula allows instructors a variety of foci. For example, although I discuss the kula as innovative means of acquiring material wealth without permanent accumulation or inheritance, kula can also be used as a modem for discussing the notion of "gift giving" with intent of increased returns (see Mauss *The Gift* 1990).

Once attendance is stabilized, the class is divided into four groups. After the students appear to have a grasp on the concept of "exchange" and future rewards, I give them in-class time for each group to create its own "clan name," to select a chief, and claim "island territory." Chiefs are responsible for ensuring participation and monitoring its clan's "wealth" during the quizzes.

In the process of a kula quiz, students get a chance to get out of their seats, socialize with, and evaluate others. During the quiz, half of a clan journeys to its kula partner in search of wealth given to them because of their correct responses to quiz questions. The other half of the clan stays behind to greet visiting trading partners to their island and administer them a quiz. Prior to administering the quiz, gifts (candy) and pleasantries are exchanged. Students quickly learn the arts of persuasion (i.e., being personable, agreeable, sharing candy and information). One positive outcome of the kula quiz is that students learn about each other and develop friendships that extend beyond the classroom. This activity takes an entire 50-minute class period the first time. After the groups become familiar with the procedure, the activity takes only about 15 minutes. In order to emphasize the concepts of exchange and retribution, there should be at least four kula quizzes during the term.

Getting Started: Group Organization

As with most new techniques, the advance preparation seems daunting, but it is not much more work than creating quiz questions themselves. Once set up, there is little additional work. The four large groups, each with a chief, are already established. The chiefs act as my assistants by keeping attendance, participation, and clan wealth records. At this point, each group must be divided into two groups: one will journey and one will stay behind. For the purposes of this exercise, the two groups will be referred to as the "Travelers" and the "Stay-behinds." Each group should alternate "Traveling" and "Staying-behind" roles for each quiz; this ensures that everyone gets a chance at receiving individual quiz grades in addition to their group grades (see below for details on this point). The clan chiefs and I both keep records of how many individual quizzes each member takes. My goal is to have each student end up with one individual grade for every two group grades. Students are relieved to know that they can succeed even when their group fails to meet their standards.

If the class is larger than 50, the four clans can be divided into three -- rather than two – smaller groups with two Traveling (one clockwise and one counterclockwise) and one Staying behind. My experience has shown that if subgroups have more than five individuals, it becomes too easy for some individuals to not participate in the quiz, relying on their **peers** for their grades.

Quizzes

I prepare a number of quizzes (about 5-7 questions each), ensuring I have a different quiz for each Stay-behind group. This means preparing at least four quizzes for a small class and eight if the clans have been divided into three groups. All lectures and readings, not just kula information, are fair game for quizzes. Only the Stay-behinds receive individual quiz grades as well as the group grade their Traveling clan members receive. I usually fold the four or eight quizzes in half and let each group select their own at random.

Quiz questions vary depending upon how much time I want to spend on the quiz. Questions range from definitions and listings (i.e. list the levels of social organizations, list three of the kinship systems) to explaining key components of theoretical perspectives. My quizzes include information from videos, lectures, readings, and discussion from the first day of class. These types of quizzes reinforce integrated knowledge and act as refreshers for exams.

Wealth

As in real kula situations, students need something with which to trade. Trade items are used as welcoming gifts to visitors and as persuasive incentives to encourage the Stay-behinds to offer hints for answers to questions. To represent clan wealth, I purchase three large bags of small candies that are used to "persuade" or reward other groups. I give each clan about five pieces for clan wealth (held by the chief) and each individual receives two. The chief decides where to best distribute the wealth, either with the Travelers who confess they did not read the assignment for the day and may need to offer a lot of persuasion, or to the Stay-behinds to mend or build a relationship with the Travelers they receive. For example, on one kula quiz day, the GoGetter Clan traveled to meet the Shell Diggers over perceived poor quality hints based on the amount of candies the GoGetters offered. Needless to say, the Shell Diggers would no longer be persuaded to offer any further hints throughout the quiz. The next kula day, the chief of the GoGetters gathered all of the wealth, setting aside two-thirds for the Shell Diggers who were to visit. It took a few more kula quizzes before the incident was forgotten.

As in real kula, the goal is increasing returns for gifts given. Quality matters more than quantity. This is one reason behind the elaborate decorations on everyday items such as the stone axes, jewelry, and baskets. Candies given during a kula quiz need a shared value; hence, each type of candy is to be rank ordered for exchange purposes, and I let the students as a whole determine the ranking. For example, one class cherished peanut butter cups that then outranked the plain chocolate candies that outranked the hard candies. In addition to the small wealth (candies), I have convinced the university bookstore to provide discount coupons that I use to represent the famed necklace and armshell. Since the prizes (the big wealth) need to start somewhere, I place the coupons in two of the folded quiz sheets and it becomes the luck of the draw as to who gets the necklace-coupon and who gets the armshell-coupon first. As with real kula valuables, one coupon travels clockwise (the necklace-coupon) and one travels counterclockwise (the armshell-coupon).

At the end of the quiz, all wealth is recorded for each clan by the chief. If the class is small and my budget adequate, I encourage students to eat their wealth after the exercise is complete. Either way, their wealth will be restored for the next quiz reflecting their current amount of wealth.

At the conclusion of the entire term's quizzes, or the last kula exercise, I finalize individual and group grades (see grades below). Group wealth (amount of candy or coupons) does not effect their grades. Those who ended up with the discount coupons can keep them. If the candy was collected and "stored" throughout the term, students can finally eat their wealth.

Rotation system

The rotation system consists of the four "clans" all rotating clockwise to their nearest "island" partners (or each clan sending groups both ways if there are three groups in a clan). After they "trade" clockwise for the first quiz, they then must trade counterclockwise for the next. Clans claim their territory (in the classroom or adjacent hallway) on the first kula day. They then occupy the same territory for each quiz. I display a graphic representation on the chalkboard or overhead during the quizzes. The concepts of "retribution," "persuasion" and "obligations" become painfully clear after the third quiz because "what goes around, comes around." If one group is greedy with its wealth (not offering each other gifts of candy) or ignores the persuasion of others (refusing to offer clues to the answers), other trading partners find out and respond accordingly.

Kula Day

The first kula exercise day is a bit hectic. First, the clan chiefs decide who is in what group. All of the Stay-behinds come to one area and each chief picks the quiz his or her **group** (clan) will have. Stay-behinds are given five or so minutes to complete their quiz on an individual basis. I evaluate the quiz, award points and make sure they understand the correct answers. I keep the quiz they completed and give them the same quiz question sheet (without

110

answers) that they will use to evaluate their kula partners when they are subsequently visited. At the same time, the Traveling groups review their lecture notes and reading for the day because the same quiz questions already given to the Stay-behinds will be asked of them. After the Stay-behinds are done (and I have recorded their grades), a recording of a conch shell sounds and the Travelers journey to their kula partners. In turn, the Stay-behinds receive a group of Travelers from a neighboring "island;" in both situations, a few moments are given to exchange pleasantries and small gifts (candy).

Using the blank quiz sheet, the Stay-behinds ask the questions and record all the responses from their trading partners (the Travelers). If the answer to the question is incorrect, the Travelers may try to "persuade" the Stay-behinds to give hints. Persuasion comes in the form of "wealth" (candy) and promises that extend into the future (to trade the necklace or armshell once received). If the trading partner group (Travelers) improves on their response, it is also recorded on the quiz sheet. In many instances, the appropriate response is never reached and, if the answer has to be given by the Stay-behinds, the grade is lower. For example, the Stay-behinds may ask their trading partners to list and describe the components of culture and the first response from the trading partners may only include language and symbols. The Travelers may offer more candy in exchange for hints to the other components. Each time a hint is offered, the trading partner's **group** grade is lowered. It is through this interaction that students become teachers and mentors to their peers. Because there is a time limit, many times a correct response is never reached, but partial credit is awarded for partial answers.

Evaluation: Grades

Individual grades are recorded for the Stay-behinds (i.e., the grade they got on the quiz). I try to ensure at least one individual grade for every two group grades. If there are four kula days, each student should have 6 quiz grades, 2 individual and 4 group grades. Many students appreciate the fact that their grade does not solely rest on peer knowledge (or lack thereof). The notion of sharing knowledge and helping other learners does not come easy to some. This exercise introduces "peers as teachers and helpers" rather than "peers as competitors" without too much threat to any one's individual grade.

Group grades for the entire clan (both Stay behinds and Travelers) are somewhat trickier. If a response is correct the first time, full credit is given. Each time a hint is offered, the grade lowers until no credit is received. (I have them use 5,4,3,2,1 points.) The entire group (clan) receives this grade and in the case of the Stay behinds, it is added to their individual grade for the quiz. So for every kula day, some students receive two grades, individual and group. It is personal choice as to the weight of the two types of grade. A 2:1 ratio works well, with the individual grade being twice as important as the group grade. Those group (clan) members who are absent receive zero for the quiz, regardless of the group grade.

Sometimes the Stay-behinds intentionally refuse to be persuaded, thus lowering the score of their trading partners (the Travelers). Should a Stay-behind group not be persuaded to assist (determined by the number of responses recorded before an appropriate response is made or given), they lose points from their accumulated wealth (as determined by me). This lowers the group's trading ability. Additionally, they will eventually be evaluated and have to persuade the group that they failed -- retribution and obligation.

Wealth

Evaluating wealth and what to do with the wealth has lots of possibilities. Wealth must be shared and used as bargaining tools of persuasion so every group ought to have different wealth at the end of the term. When I have sixteen groups being evaluated, I distribute more wealth such as coupons worth a bag of apples, oranges, or a liter of juice. The coupons must circulate; otherwise the main effort is lost as with original kula wealth. After the third exercise, most groups understand this through peer pressure and persuasion.

Most of the time, it is easier to allow students to consume all earned candy wealth at the end of each exercise. Their totals are recorded and I can redistribute the correct amount next time. Those clans that "own" coupon wealth at the end of the semester decide how to distribute it, and that usually means a small in-class party.

During the process of the quiz, the group that has possession of the armshell or necklace is required to pass it along or suffer the consequences of retribution from their peers. If a Traveling group responds correctly to **all** the questions, they must be rewarded by receiving the highest amount of wealth the Stay-behind group has in its possession (i.e., armshell, necklace, other "coupons"). One requirement I have about the armshells and necklaces is that the receiving group has to have **at least** 90% on the quiz. This keeps the value high.

Conclusions

At the end of the term, I have conducted seven or more kula exercises and hence that many quizzes. The students are more involved in the learning process and it is really much more fun than sitting and taking a quiz; it is also more fun for me than grading a pile of quizzes. We all get to visit, become more familiar with, and learn from each other.

References Cited

Malinowski, Bronislaw
 1961 [1922] *Argonauts of the Western Pacific.* New York: E.P. Dutton and Company.

Mauss, Marcel
 1990 *The Gift.* New York: W.W. Norton and Company.

112

Weiner, Annette
1988 *The Trobrianders of Papua New Guinea*. Orlando: Harcourt Brace Jovanovich College Publishers.

EXPLORING THE MEANING OF FAMILY

Matthew Kennedy

Students of introductory cultural anthropology often "hit the wall" with kinship. The terms are alien, abundant, and mystifying. Bilateral cognatic descent? Maternal cross-cousin marriage with patrilocal residence rules? Unpacking the complexities of kinship was vexing to students until I introduced an assignment that continues to be greeted with great enthusiasm.

Students in my classes have the opportunity to write their own kinship diagrams using the standards and methods employed by genealogists and anthropologists. They trace ancestry, noting important dates (birth, death, marriage, divorce) and confirming anything unusual (twins, same sex marriage, step-children) with footnotes. Students must be accurate and unambiguous in the depiction of their family and must include information on residence and rules of endogamy and exogamy.

The assignment allows students to better understand their own families and the social dynamics that build families all over the world. For each student, kin are brought into a larger context, making this a valuable assignment in social science objectivity.

The assignment is appropriate for introduction to social and cultural anthropology or in introductory four-field anthropology. I use it in classes that range from 12-50, but the only size restriction is instructor time to review and grade the assignment. There are variable lessons on many fronts here: students may interview a grandparent on family history that might otherwise be lost or forgotten; they may complete the assignment using computer graphics; they evaluate systems and relationships that define generations and extended families; and they render it all in an artful and readable presentation.

The kinship diagram assignment should accompany the text/lecture/class section on kinship. Ideally, it should be due after students have been exposed to the basic terms and concepts of kinship. A follow up class session, after the diagrams are turned in and reviewed, can point out lessons to be learned about kindred. Be sure you get permission from any student whose diagram you wish to use in class.

Options, Exceptions, and Alternatives

The assignment is presented as a option among three essay assignments. Acknowledging that some students don't have families, or would just as soon not associate with them, they may opt to write a more standard question on kinship. Or, they have the option to interview someone else about kinship cross-culturally. For example, a student whose family has been in the United States for generations may interview a newly arrived student from Cambodia for information on marriage patterns and relations and illustrate that student's family in a diagram. Otherwise, they complete the assignment in the same way as those doing their own families. Students who know they are adopted use their adoptive family.

The Assignment

At least three generations must be included on the diagram and there should be at least 10 individuals to make it worthwhile. Students are asked to trace only their father or their mother's line, since doing both could get messy. Each individual is rendered with the traditional circles for females and triangles for males. Each individual must be listed by a first and last name if the name is newly introduced into the family by marriage (i.e., surname of a groom taken by the bride and their children). Birth, death, marriage, and divorce dates must be included. Birth and death dates are listed under the individual's symbol and name. Marriage and divorce dates are listed above or below the marriage "equals" sign, respectively.

As in any formal kinship diagram, clean and clear representation is important. Footnotes are encouraged to clarify anything unusual in the family. Members of the same generation must be on the same longitude so that cousins aren't stacked unevenly on the page. Students use 8 ½ x 11 inch paper taped together or use butcher/wrapping paper; the diagram can then be folded to 8 ½ x 11 inch size. I discourage using rolled poster paper as it is cumbersome to transport. Lines must be straight, symbols consistent, and any unknown date or name noted with a question mark.

The assignment does not end with a diagram. Students are given a set of questions that help them plug their families into the larger concept of kinship. Questions include "identify your cross and parallel cousins on this diagram," "explain your family's formal and/or informal rules of endogamy and exogamy," and "where would you live today if your family lived in a culture with strict patrilocal or matrilocal residence rules?" (It is remarkable how many students respond to the endogamy/exogamy question with "We don't have any rules," while the surnames on the diagram bespeak a particular ethnic and cultural background.)

Grading

Grading decisions are made on the basis of accuracy and presentation. Can an outsider read this diagram and understand the important facts of this family? Is everything and (hopefully) everyone accounted for? How well presented is the diagram? Was there obvious care taken in layout and design?

Using the Student Handout

Be prepared to spend some time discussing this assignment in class. Students will have many questions and it is important to establish a willingness to solve some of mysteries of the assignment. Someone will ask "What about my father's brother's wife who was married three times before and has two children from each marriage and where does this all go on the diagram?" You can photocopy the handout that follows for students to use in conjunction with their diagrams.

Nancy Ostereich Lurie (personal communication), formerly of the University of Wisconsin, Milwaukee, has made some interesting observations when she assigned kinship diagrams in her classes. She found that students emphasized their matrilineal line in terms of whom they were descended from and related to. The explanation may be that maternal relatives are more likely to keep genealogies (in the family Bible or in their heads) and pass them on to their children, thus making that ancestral line more known to the children. This observation is useful when students are in a quandary over bilateral descent in a society that traditionally takes the husband's last name after marriage. Impressions that students have of patrilineality in the United States are further eroded by asking students the simple question, "whom are you descended from?" The response is inevitably a variation of "my mom and my dad." Finally, estate disputes in the United States have established a legal precedence for bilateral descent. In a court of law, one is not denied nor awarded inheritance simply because of one's sex.

Conclusion

Most students opt to do this project rather than write a more conventional essay. I give them three weeks to prepare the diagram and they inevitably come to class with eager "what if...?" questions. Many diagrams are spectacular, show a great deal of sophistication, are beautifully drawn, and evidence much research and care. I get feedback about amusing and tender conversations with relatives. Students talk after class about an uncle they never knew who died in infancy, or the gratitude their grandmother expressed that they were interested in family history. Many students go beyond the three generation minimum. One student traced her maternal line back to the 1820s and now has a precious document to give her two young daughters someday. This is a satisfying assignment every time. A kinship diagram personalizes anthropology in ways unique and meaningful for students.

MY KINSHIP DIAGRAM

_____

(Name)

Instructions: draw part of your own kindred from either your mother's or your father's ancestral line. Chart this part of your family back at least to your grandparents. You should include affines and consanguines, cousins, siblings. Birth, death, marriage, and divorce dates should be noted. If anything is unusual, such as remarriages, half siblings, or adoptions, mention it in accompanying notes, but the diagram and notes together should constitute one line of your entire kindred. Treat yourself as Ego, do the following activities, and answer the following questions:

1. Why did you choose your mother's or your father's side of the family for this exercise?

2. Identify your cross and parallel cousins on the diagram.

3. Explain your family's formal and/or informal rules of endogamy and exogamy as illustrated on the diagram.

4. Where would you live today if your family came from a culture with strict patrilocal or matrilocal residence rules?

5. If your family were Trobriand Islanders, whom would you live with and why?

6. What lineage system does the diagramed family use?

7. How did you gather the necessary information on your family? Were there any surprises?

MUSEUM VISITS IN CULTURAL ANTHROPOLOGY COURSES*

Serena Nanda

I always try to include at least one museum visit in my cultural anthropology courses. These visits have many aims: to concretize and make vivid abstract anthropological concepts; to encourage social and intellectual interaction among the students; to encourage a cultural experience that students can share with their families and/or friends, and continue as part of their adult leisure experiences; to foster pride in diverse ethnic and national heritages; to provide a peaceful site in which the skills of observation, concentration, and description can be developed; to provide the basis of a short, written paper that enhances writing skills; to familiarize and make students comfortable with the diverse cultural and intellectual resources of their city; to expand particular anthropological topics; to raise questions about representation of our own and other cultures as an anthropological and political issue; to provoke discussions of ethnocentrism within the framework of aesthetics; to enhance the student's ability to discuss issues with regard to specifics rather than in vague generalities; and last, but certainly not least, to provide students with opportunities to experience the awe of encountering extraordinary creativity and beauty.

Museum visits are appropriate for any culturally-focused course from the introductory to the advanced level, and since they do not require an entire class physically going to the museum at the same time, such required visits are appropriate for any size class. While not every college and university city has the vast facilities of New York City, most cities of any size have several museums that would be appropriate for such an assignment. If in doubt, start with the Yellow Pages under "museums."

Four elements go into the successful museum visit as a teaching tool: planning, preparation, structure, and follow-up. Planning means thinking about the aims of a museum visit in connection with course goals, and specific syllabus topics. I have found museum visits are most successful when they are closely tied into a specific topic, and when the connection between the topic and the museum visit is clearly explained to the students beforehand. Planning also involves scheduling: for example, I never plan a visit just before an exam or when a paper is due.

Preparation involves both preparing myself and preparing my students, many of whom have never visited a museum. I always visit the exhibit before assigning it. (I use both permanent collections and special exhibits.) In order to qualify for a class visit, the exhibit must be visually dramatic, relevant to an anthropological topic or concept, and lend itself to several of the aims described above, particularly that of concretizing anthropological concepts. The exhibit displays should be well labeled; at the same time, the objects should "speak" for themselves (the whole point is to give the students a visual, as opposed to a "word" experience). The exhibit should not take more than 1 or 1 ½ hours to view, including time for selective observation and note taking. If a written brochure is available, I photocopy this for the class and distribute it before the visit.

Very early in the semester, I hand out a museum visit sheet, specifying the date and place of the visit, entrance fees (either free or "pay as you wish"); the reading assignment required prior to the visit (I try to keep this short -- two or three pages; it may be from the assigned text or a photocopied handout; it serves as background for the visit; in addition, I may give a brief handout on the exhibit itself); the follow up writing and discussion assignment; grading information (required or extra credit; how to make up a missed visit; % of the grade); how to reach the museum by public transportation, location of the exhibit within the museum; opening and closing hours. Sometimes, I have a museum expert visit the class beforehand with slides of the exhibit or related objects; sometimes I use my own slides. I usually try to work in at least a brief discussion by the students on their museum visiting experiences (many have never visited a museum or did so only as elementary school children), and try to convey to them my own enthusiasm for museums. In all cases, I encourage the students to visit the museum with friends or family, if we are not taking the visit as a class. Most of all, I encourage the students to use my questions/paper topics as a guide to their museum visiting, as I have found that focusing is essential to a successful visit. Otherwise, museums are often experienced by students as overwhelming.

What follows are four assignments that I have used in the past for different museum visits. Museums differ in permanent exhibits and special exhibits, but questions similar to the ones noted below can be assigned to students for any exhibit that has a cultural focus.

Four Museum Assignments

1. In my introductory Cultural Anthropology course, I assigned a visit to the Chinese and Indian exhibits in the Hall of Asian Peoples at the American Museum of Natural History in New York City. In addition to very artfully displayed and colorful dioramas, both of these exhibits display brief but accurate written information about patrilineal systems, arranged marriages, kinship and gender relations. The exhibit is particularly dramatic in displaying the elaborate wedding rituals and sumptuousness of the bride's clothing and jewelry, and yet through the informative labeling, accurately conveys the subordinate position she occupies in the traditional patrilineal extended family.

The students were required to visit the exhibit outside of class in connection with their text book reading assignment on the patrilineal extended family (approximately 3 pages). The follow-up assignment was a 500 word paper containing three elements: (1) a brief description of the forms and functions of the patrilineal extended family and its related marriage system; (2) a description of these systems as they are both similar and different in India and China, as indicated in the museum exhibit; and (3) a description of the student's personal reaction to the exhibits in terms of what they found most interesting and how the exhibit (or a particular section of it) extended their understanding of the patrilineal extended family and related marriage system beyond what was gained from their reading.

2. Another assignment on authority and African art is also assigned to the introductory Cultural Anthropology course. In this case, the class visited the hall of African Cultures at the American Museum of Natural History in connection with our reading of *Things Fall Apart* by Chinua Achebe. The intellectual theme of the museum visit was the relationship between power, social control, religion, and art, a prominent dimension of culture in the West African village where Achebe's story takes place. Achebe's descriptions of masquerades, for example, and in-class discussions of the relationships between art and power implied in the text formed the background of the visit.

The museum visit was structured by a writing assignment of approximately 600 words that required the student to focus on one object in the several rooms of the exhibit and its relationship to some aspect of power/social control. I did not guide the students through the exhibit but let them wander on their own. I made myself available for questions and guided them toward a particular display if they seemed to be having trouble responding to the exhibit.

The elements of the paper are: (1) a detailed description of one object or display that the student found most interesting, artistic, wonderful, or mysterious. This description had to include the object's form, materials, whether it was realistic or abstract, and its symbolic elements; (2) the function of the object in terms of power or control; for example it may have been used to express political status, to effect social control, to maintain links with ancestral spirits, to distance the king/chief from his subjects, or to legitimate the leader's powers. This information is sometimes on the labels, but sometimes implicit; (3) an analysis of the connection between the appearance (form, materials, symbolism) of the object and its function; and (4) a subjective analysis of the student's personal, emotional, response to the object.

Because African art often conforms to an aesthetic that is unfamiliar to our students, I preface this visit with a class session on art in Africa and show slides as a way of engaging the students in a discussion about their responses to unfamiliar art.

3. In an upper division course on Culture and Personality, I offered an extra credit assignment, based on a visit to the special exhibit "Facing History: The Black Image in American Art 1710-1940" at the Brooklyn Museum in New York City. One of the many topics discussed in this course is the effects of prejudice and discrimination on personality, specifically the effects of colonialism, slavery, and other forms of oppression and how dominant cultures use various media to convey their own view of superior and inferior peoples.

This special exhibit provided an opportunity for my students to focus on the political dimensions of art and to grapple in a concrete way with the relation between specific images and their effects, particularly regarding stereotyping. In the paper, students were required to discuss how the images of African Americans in American art from the colonial to the modern period furthered stereotyped images that reflected and intensified racial prejudice. The students began with a general statement discussing the images in the exhibit as a whole and then discussed the issue through description and analysis of any three specific images in the exhibit. I suggested that as one of the three examples, students might describe and analyze one image that ran counter to the exhibit theme, i.e., that did not further stereotypes, but undermined them. This last question, particularly, provided the basis for a very interesting class discussion.

4. In my introductory Cultural Anthropology class, I arranged for my students to view "The Art of India," a splendid special exhibit at the Metropolitan Museum of Art in New York City. Unlike the exhibits at the American Museum of Natural History and the Brooklyn Museum, the focus of this exhibit was the objects themselves rather than the cultural context, although the exhibit was loosely based on an important cultural theme in Indian history, that of unity in diversity. Other themes, implicit in the exhibit, were the relationship between art and religion, and the relationship between art and the state.

Prior to the field visit, a docent from the museum gave a slide lecture in class, emphasizing the "unity in diversity" theme, illustrated by objects in the exhibit. The follow-up paper asked the students to: (1) summarize the theme as lectured on by the docent; (2) analyze the exhibit in terms of how it realized this theme, citing specific examples; (3) write about the relationship of art and religion as exemplified by two objects in the museum; and (4) write about the relationship between art and the state as exemplified in two objects in the exhibit.

Conclusions

Museum visits enable students to concretize anthropological concepts, add additional information to text and lectures, enhance skills of observation and concentration, and improve student writing in ways that carry over to other classes. They also give students an opportunity to interact with their peers and family members around significant cultural issues. Research indicates that one of the most important factors in adult museum visiting is whether an individual has visited a museum prior to adulthood and enjoyed the experience. Visiting museums as children, with family members, has been found to be a key factor to continuing museum visits as an adult leisure time activity, and this activity is unevenly distributed among class and ethnic groups. None of my students major in anthropology, and many only take one, introductory, cultural anthropology course at our college. Most come from communities whose members are least likely to visit museums. The focus on the visual that is at the core of the museum experience, is congruent with the visual orientation of most of my students. The museum provides a learning experience not only different from the classroom, but for many of them, also exposes them to an environment of beauty and quiet that is different from their homes and neighborhoods. My students' responses to museum field trips indicate that not only do these visits provide a basis for future student visits, but also, through word of mouth, for visits with family and friends. Thus, the museum visit enables students to expand their horizons spatially and emotionally, and to help them feel more of a part of the potentially enriching city in which they live.

* Museum field trips are particularly appropriate for interdisciplinary classes. My deep thanks to Beth Pacheco, of the Developmental Skills Department at New York City Technical College,

for her invaluable contributions to my museum assignments and for the many happy hours we have spent together in visiting museums and planning student visits.

TEACHING THE POLITICAL ECONOMY OF SOCIALISM

Elizabeth Dunn

I developed a technique to teach the political economy of socialism as part of a course titled "The Collapse of Communism" and have also used it in introductory cultural anthropology classes and in classes on comparative economic systems and political economy. I developed it as a means of teaching the fundamental principles of the political economy of state socialism, that can then be used as a basis for explaining other social phenomena such as the gray market, the importance of social "connections," and problems of the transition from state socialism to capitalism. I have taught it to everyone from fifth-graders to graduate students and they all have been able to grasp the operating principles of state socialist economies in under 30 minutes.

There are two basic problems that the lesson tries to address. The first is the simple problem of explaining a tightly interconnected system in which one action has effects that ripple throughout the system. I focus on explaining the relationship between central planning and the problem of chronic shortages. The information could be delivered by assigned readings (and one is assigned), or by lecturing, but the experiential part of the lesson is extremely important. Unlike subjects in which students are fairly acutely aware of what they don't know, most students assume that they know quite a bit about the political economy of socialism, mostly based on Cold War era propaganda. So when I ask, for example, "Why did socialism fall?" students often answer "Because it is human nature to be free." By asking them to function within a shortage economy for even a brief moment, I can elicit the same kind of behaviors that socialist managers use. Having arrived at the same solutions, students are much more likely to see the logic of certain behaviors (like hoarding or stealing) and much less likely to condemn such behaviors out of hand. The lesson has a peculiar sort of emotional force that I find useful in overcoming preconceptions and getting on to the material I really want to teach.

Materials Needed

... plastic sandwich bags (at least one per student)
... toothpicks (17 per student plus 30 or so extra)
... gummi bears (a class of 25 students requires about 2 ½ pounds of mixed color gummis or gumdrops
... a large plastic bag or bucket
... wire ties

Preparation

The week before the session slated for this demonstration, assign parts of Janos Kornai's "The Political Economy of Shortage," or alternatively, the first chapter of Katherine Verderey's *What Was Socialism and What Comes Next?*

Before the class begins, take all the gummi bears and sort them by color. Then build a model house: take four gummi bears of different colors and join them into a square using toothpicks. Then, make another square, using gummi bears of assorted colors. Join the two squares together using toothpicks. Build a roof beam using a toothpick between two differently colored gummi bears. Join this to the cube with the toothpicks to make a roof. You should have a structure that looks like this (you may or may not follow the same color scheme as in the diagram, but you can use the same code: R=red; O=orange; W=white, Y=yellow, and G=green).

Draw yourself a map of the colors of each gummi and their positions in the house. Set the house aside.

Before class begins, count out the number of gummi bears of each color that the class would need if each student was going to build two houses (with gummis of the appropriate color in the appropriate place). So, if you have 25 students, each of whom is to build two houses that each use two red gummi bears, you would need 100 red gummi bears. Do this for each color. Don't worry if you run short of one color or another. Set the extras aside.

Now, create a nice socialist economy of shortage. Eat most of the red ones and some of the orange ones before class begins. Don't mention this until the discussion part of the session. I don't recommend eating the white ones as they taste revolting. Multiply the number of students times 17, count out that many toothpicks, and then take a handful of them and throw them in the wastebasket.

Make a note of which colors you will have a shortage of, and **make absolutely sure that you do not add enough of those colors into the surplus pile to rectify the shortage.** If you add too many of the "shortage" colors back into the overall "economy," the lesson will not work. Add some extras of "non-shortage colors" back into the surplus pile.

Prepare a plastic sandwich bag for each student. Each bag must contain some gummi bears and some toothpicks, but **no** bag should contain enough gummi bears of the right colors to make two houses. Some bags can contain extras of "non-shortage colors," and even surplus toothpicks, but each bag must have a shortage. These shortages are in addition to the overall shortage in the "economy."

Put the remaining gummi bears into a large plastic bag, and throw some toothpicks in as well. This large plastic bag is yours since you are the "State." Isn't it great to be in power?

The Lesson

The lecture/lesson opens when I talk about images of economic hardship and corruption, and try to give students a feel for the experience of living in a shortage economy. If your students are politically well informed, you might ask them to describe their images of life under socialism. If not, you might show pictures (*Life Magazine* had some nice ones) or videos of long lines outside of shops, people queuing for bread, or stores with empty shelves. Slavenka Drakulic has a well-written description of life under an economy of shortage in her book *How We Survived Communism and Even Laughed* that you might also read from. You might query students as to their ideas about the relationship between shortages and the fall of communism, and talk briefly about economic collapse in the Eastern Bloc.

Announce: "Welcome to the People's Republic of Hopkins!" (or wherever you are teaching). Tell students that they are to imagine they are the managers of a state socialist construction firm. The state has just sent them their plan that includes their production quotas. If they are to fulfill the plan, they must finish building two houses in the next fifteen minutes. There will be severe penalties for those who fail to meet their quotas.

Hand out the plastic sandwich bags filled with "shortage" gummi bears and toothpicks, one to each student. Tell them to start building. On the chalkboard, reproduce your diagram of the house, specifically which color gummi bears go where. Basically, you have a cube with a roof beam on it that is supported by toothpicks going diagonally from the top corners to the end points of the beam. Tell the students that the plan specifies that each house should follow this "blueprint" exactly. Do **not** give them any more rules. If they ask you for clarification about rules, do not answer. Put your big plastic bag with extra supplies on the table or podium so it is in full view.

About thirty seconds later, the first student will announce: "I don't have enough red ones." Respond by saying something like "Well, you do have a problem, don't you? I'd love to help, but I've already allocated all my resources. Sorry." The next student will whine similarly. Tell him or her "Well, work it out." When the third student whines (of if they are all discouraged, when you note the next student having a shortage problem), go up to her or him with your big bag of gummies and announce loudly "You need red ones? Sure you can have them! You can have whatever you need."

This will provoke more students to ask for things. Vary your response by (a) giving nothing; (b) giving what they ask for, but only rarely; or (c) give them something else entirely. Try to announce what you are doing so the rest of the class can hear "No, you can't have any red ones, but you can have three green ones."

At the same time, students who get their requests denied should have figured out one of several alternative strategies. They are either (a) trading, (b) stealing from other students, (c) using the wrong colors, biting gummis in half and using halves or breaking toothpicks, or (d) making themselves into teams. If you see two or three people getting together to make two houses, you should announce loudly, "I see you are trying to make one house apiece! OK, since you asked, you can have your quota lowered." Then grant a few more requests and deny the rest. Be completely arbitrary -- it is more fun that way.

As you walk around the class holding your bag of gummis and doling a few out here and there, be sure to grab a few off the student desks (I usually just pop them into my mouth). Make up some completely spurious reason for seizing their allocation: "Whoops, having a war! Need more material!" or "Sorry! Socialist brothers in Cuba need some help building ghetto settlements!" or "Where were you at last night's Party meeting?" Or my favorite, "Did I mention that I needed some repairs done to my house? I'm giving these to the contractor who does the work at my place after hours!" Be sure and pick on whomever is closest to being finished.

At fifteen minutes, call time. Ask the students to put their houses on their desks and leave them alone. Then ask everyone who met the quota to raise their hands. In a class of 25, only four or five should make it. These are often the people who did the reading, since they grasped the analogy more quickly, traded for the red gummis (the color in short supply) and toothpicks (also in short supply) before the other students figured out what was going on, and then hoarded their materials.

Discussion

Begin by asking students what the basic problem was here. ("Too few red ones and too few toothpicks.") Tell them that you ate most of the red ones last night. (I like to cackle here and shout "I love having absolute power!") and emphasize that there were both individual and an overall shortage of red gummis in the economy.

Ask them to brainstorm about the strategies that they, the "managers" of this "enterprise," used to overcome shortages. They will usually list the following strategies:

... exchange with other managers
... hoard
... use substandard quality production (here is where I hold up one of the twisted, ugly houses that someone made by cutting gummis in half or breaking toothpicks, and I say "Whoo! Would you want to live in THAT?"
... stealing
... asking the state for more resources
... asking the state to lower the quota

Write these on the board as they are mentioned, as they will be the basis of your talk.

Using the strategies that students have listed, begin making analogies to the real functioning of the socialist system. You might begin by talking about the ways managers exchange with one another even though the state was supposed to allocate all resources. Then talk about why managers hoard surplus supplies (since they might need to trade them for the things they do need later on). Explain how this "freezes" supplies in places where they aren't needed, thereby making the overall demand for that input greater and exacerbating shortage.

From there, you might move into items (e) and (f) that together make up the institution of "plan bargaining." Tell students about how managers inflate their requests for materials at every level, which means that by the time the aggregated requests reach the center, they are wildly inflated. (I often introduce the concept of "investment hunger" or unconstrained demand here. I try and contrast this with capitalism's problem of supply constraint and crises of overproduction, showing how the two systems are opposites of one another.) Mention that plan bargaining also involves having quotas reduced. Emphasize the importance of personal relationships to the process of plan bargaining, and connect that to the need for personal relationships in interfirm barter. Contrast this with the impersonal sales mechanisms of capitalism.

You might want to talk about the problem of sub-standard production that was due to "storming," the need to assemble all the material during the first part of the production and then work like crazy at the end of the period in order to meet the plan. Tie this to the need to hoard labor that was due to the fact that managers need enough labor to meet peak production periods, not average ones. Talk about the "we pretend to work and they pretend to pay us" problem. I like to throw in some anecdotes about substandard production from my own fieldwork in Rzeszow, Poland, like the story of the friend of mine who lived in an apartment building that had a three-foot gap along one wall because the construction firm ran out of bricks. A good resource for this part of the discussion is Haraszati's *A Worker in a Worker's State*.

And now a joke: a team of inspectors from the Ministry in Warsaw comes to the factory to see how things are going. While they are standing on the factory floor, they see a man run by with an empty wheelbarrow. A few seconds later, they see him run in the direction he came from, still pushing the empty wheelbarrow. When he runs past them the third time, the head of the inspection team stops him and asks, "Why are you running around pushing an empty wheelbarrow?" The man replies, "We're so busy trying to meet the plan that I don't have time to fill it up!"

Finally, talk about "stealing." I like to emphasize that "stealing" was not usually done between firms (although managers certainly "arranged" for under-the-table allocations from the center or from supplier firms), but by individuals. I mention that "stealing" was seen as the act of taking property from another person and was immoral, but that taking material from a work place or from the state was merely viewed as "organizing," and was not socially frowned upon.

Another joke: A factory worker went out the factory gates pushing a wheelbarrow full of sawdust. The guard stops him, and the worker says, "My boss said I could take this sawdust home." Of course the guard is suspicious, and he digs and digs through the sawdust to find whatever the worker is stealing. He finds nothing, though, and has to let the worker pass through. The next day, the same worker passes through the gate pushing a wheelbarrow of sawdust, and again the guard searches through it and finds nothing. This continues for a week. The next Monday, when the worker saunters through without a wheelbarrow, the guard stops him. "OK," he says, "Fess up. You got away with it and there's nothing I can do. But I know you were stealing something, so tell me what it was." The worker looks at him and smiles. "Wheelbarrows, of course."

Finally, I try to give students a sense of how all these phenomena are tied together, so that while they helped individual people and firms to cope with shortages, they made the shortages worse and worse. I talk about the downward spiral of state socialist economies, briefly discuss some of the reform strategies that were devised to deal with them, and end by talking about the economic collapse of state socialism. In subsequent sessions, I talk about problems of economic and industrial restructuring, but here I end by flagging the fact that the production problems, social structures and habits, and relationships that this economic system engendered were legacies that affected postsocialist reform.

References Cited

Drakulic, Slavenka
    1993 *We Survived Communism and Even Laughed.* New York: W.W. Norton and Co.

Haraszati, Miklos
    1977 *A Worker in a Worker's State: Piece Rates in Hungary.* New York: Penguin.

Kornai, Janos
    1992 *The Socialist System: The Political Economy of Shortage.* Princeton: Princeton University Press.

Verdery, Katherine
    1996 *What Was Socialism and What Comes Next?* Princeton: Princeton University Press.

BUILDING STUDENT INTEREST, INPUT, AND ENGAGEMENT: ORGANIZING SMALL GROUP PROJECTS IN LARGE LECTURE CLASSES

Marilynne Diggs-Thompson

The Problem

Some departmental faculty said it couldn't be done, or shouldn't be done, that the logistics were just too complex to ultimately be feasible. If one wanted to conserve time and preserve sanity, then using small groups, giving two exams, and assigning two written papers is simply out of the question. My teaching experiences elsewhere were with class size set at a maximum of 50 students. At Hunter, with a combined enrollment of 380 students in two introductory sections of cultural anthropology, it would seem that common sense and crowd management mandates multiple-choice exams, straightforward, and relatively simple assignments. Yet, given the tendency for large classes to be sterile, uninspiring, and often confusing to first year and even upper level students, I felt the need for a different approach.

Without engagement and personal connection with the instructor and with each other, the drop out rate (both on a temporary and permanent basis) for large enrollment courses can be quite high. And when I first developed this more intensive, interactive approach, I had an additional problem to overcome, the complication of teaching two different sections at opposite times of the academic day. In the early section (9-10 am), students were just waking up, if they made it to class at all. The later section (3:45-5) fell at the end of the day for most day students and often the temptation was to cut that last late class and start the evening or weekend a little early. Thus the challenges (in addition to the obvious ones) became how to keep the masses awake, impart knowledge, engage their interest, get to know them at least a little, and encourage directed dialogue among each other. Given that its New York City location makes the Hunter College student body one of the most culturally and ethnically diverse in the country, and that student activism and extracurricular involvement continues to reach new heights, I felt that Hunter was an ideal setting for my experiment.

A Solution

My first tasks were to select a relatively straightforward user-friendly but comprehensive text and to construct a clear, direct yet flexible, syllabus to keep us all on track. I use Haviland's *Cultural Anthropology,* 9th edition. It also seemed important to distribute a separate one-page summary of guidelines for writing assignments that included the due dates and the expectations for each specific assignment. The text, covering traditional introductory cultural anthropology material, is supplemented with two small contemporary studies of ethnic groups (from the Allyn and Bacon New Immigrant Series) to be tackled at the end of the term. The syllabus mandates the reading of the *New York Times* at least three times a week with the specific charge that the first written assignment would be a one page summary of a newspaper article that discusses a contemporary social, cultural, economic, or scientific issue. This assignment is designed to drive home the fact that anthropology is not just the study of ancient, extinct, primitive, or remote peoples. The secondary purpose of this assignment is to identify group project topics that are related to specific topics in the assigned text. The other one page assignment requires that students provide follow-up on the initial topic and critique the way the article is presented. Both papers also serve the purpose of getting students accustomed to writing academic papers early in the term; this in turn serves my own covert agenda which is to get students to develop the habit of reading a "national focused" newspaper.

Ultimately, I select approximately 60 topics and then classify them into 20-22 broad themes that correspond roughly to chapters in the basic text. Next, I randomly divide the class into 20-22 groups; in order to achieve maximum participation and to prevent some students from being left out or overlooked, I refuse to allow them to pick their own group or topic. (In a class of 190 students, this makes the groups of 9-10 students quite manageable.) Each group selects one of the 20-22 topics (a representative from each group randomly draws a topic from a hat) for which they are to give group presentations at the end of the term. Members of each group are encouraged to exchange telephone numbers, and in addition to the fifteen minute get-together allowed in class each week, are encouraged to meet informally whenever possible. The group project is worth 10% of their final grade and students are told that an evaluation will be made of their final presentation and the demonstrable level of involvement of each group member. Predictably, the endeavor is not a bed of roses and requires a certain amount of time, patience, and persistence on the part of all. Complaints and problems are expected: for example, some students complain that other students fail to appear for group meetings, or do not contribute to discussion or preparation. However, in the end, a clear division of labor did emerge and each group finally settled into a regular working pattern.

Results

I have used this approach for four semesters and am happy to report that the process gets easier and the logistics now run fairly smoothly. Because it is interactive, I find that both morning and evening students respond well to this approach. The process of preparation animates the morning students and keeps the late-afternoon students awake and involved. More importantly, the results have been astounding and certainly have surpassed my expectations. My students and I have enjoyed imaginative, insightful, thoughtful, and thought-provoking, highly creative presentations on topics such as: prevention and treatment of HIV and AIDS; the declining effectiveness of antibiotics (biological anthropology); gay and lesbian marriage and parenthood, arranged marriage versus "romantic" marriage (sex and marriage); bilingualism and linguistic nationalism (language and communication); homelessness and "street people" (patterns of subsistence); global capital, global music, the power and abuses of multinational corporations, computer technology and its discriminatory effects, sweat-shop labor (globalism and culture change); welfare and workfare, unemployment and underemployment, Russian capitalism, dismantling the U.S. welfare system, and a topic that we are locally fond of, the socio-economic foundations of anti-CUNY attacks (economics).

To date, students have been attentive, involved, and more importantly, responsive and supportive of each other's presentations. They have utilized poster formats as well as video and audio-taped media to make their points. This allows students who are extremely shy, uncomfortable with English, and/or creatively talented to showcase their contributions. Despite the size of the groups, students have divided the labor so that each member is able to demonstrate a specific participatory task. For example, some students have introduced the presentations while others have summarized their group's presentation in a concluding statement. When students within a group have found themselves at opposites ends of an issue, they have taken sides and presented the material in the form of a debate. Some students have prepared class handouts, while others have created slides, transparencies, or charts. Certainly students have added to their body of knowledge well beyond the boundaries of introductory course materials. They have connected anthropology with real and contemporary local and world issues and have added their own interdisciplinary dimension to the subject.

Three other tactics prove to be helpful and supportive of the end of term group project approach: (1) the "mid-term" and "final" exams are replaced by "Exam 1" and "Exam 2," each covering different material, the latter taking place at the end of the completion of the textbook assignments, approximately three weeks before the end of term; (2) the final 3-4 page final take-home essay/paper is based on the short ethnographies of particular ethnic groups and due the last week of class; (3) while several groups (approximately half) who select projects corresponding to "formal anthropological" topics make their fifteen minute group presentations during the week in which the "formal" topic is covered in class, the final three weeks of class are given over to the remaining presentations. Students are instructed that their group presentations must in some way enhance, expand, or debate material obtained from their reading of the *New York Times* and/or issues covered formally in the text. For example, I notice that many groups introduce their presentations with either the formal definition of a term or concept, or with "ethnographic" examples cited in the textbook. They then proceed to elaborate or to debate the text readings with information they have assembled from library and Internet sources, and with information that they have obtained from the *New York Times*.

The timing of exams and student's preoccupation with preparing for the final presentation are tactics that combine to significantly reduce stress. In addition, the elimination of the traditional end-of-semester final has resulted in a significant reduction (about 80%) in the number of students who are absent from exams. The reduction of exam-associated stress allows students to concentrate on writing final papers and to become actively involved in preparing for the final group presentation. I am rigorous about taking attendance during the final three weeks of presentations (by way of sign-in sheets), particularly since I have told students that grading of their final presentation is also contingent upon their attending the presentations of other groups.

Granted, not all colleges and universities around the country have as culturally diverse a student body as Hunter College, nor is the *New York Times* easily available in large numbers outside of New York City. However, you could either make a deal with your local newspaper stand to get multiple copies of the *Times* for the term and place them in an establish place (such at the reserve desk in the library and/or in folders placed in your departmental office) or assign another "national focused" newspaper that is more readily available.

Conclusions

What about those skeptical faculty who said it couldn't be done? Some faculty argue that the process involves too much grading and is too time consuming; I certainly won't argue with that. But this approach lends itself very nicely to the excellent use of a teaching assistant to help in grading the writing assignments and in organizing the group topics. And I must admit that I derive a great deal of pleasure from watching students (mostly nervous freshmen) who start the semester as disconnected strangers begin to enter and exit class animatedly chattering in groups. Another advantage of using small groups is that they provide a venue for students to pose at least some questions and or queries to each other, exchange missed lecture notes and materials, and build support for informal study groups. In short, using the small group approach in large classes allows me to turn a demanding teaching situation into a process of mutual learning, personal satisfaction, and to generate excitement among initially resistant student participants.

MNEMONICS, QUOTATIONS, CARTOONS, AND A NOTEBOOK: "TRICKS" FOR APPRECIATING CULTURAL DIVERSITY

Charles F. Urbanowicz

A number of teaching "tricks" can be woven together to encourage students to appreciate cultural diversity wherever it exists. In my introductory Cultural Anthropology course, I use various quotations, selected mnemonics, appropriate transparencies, and as much current information as possible. All can be interwoven into a single course, or one "trick" can be used alone, as instructors see the fit with their own courses.

Introduction

"Remember, Jim [Michener]. Writing a book or a dozen books [or giving a lecture or dozens of lectures] doesn't remake you or create miracles. Next morning, when you wake up, you're the same horse's ass you were yesterday. Writing [or teaching] is a job. Do it well, it's a great life. Mess around, its disappointments will kill you." James A. Michener, 1992, *The World is My Home: A Memoir*, p. 323.

The courses I regularly teach (and some for over 25 years) include a lower division Introduction to Cultural Anthropology (that briefly mentions archaeology, physical anthropology, and language), an upper division course on Peoples and Cultures of the Pacific, and the History of Anthropological Thought. Although I use the "tricks" described here in all of these courses, I will concentrate on their use in the term-long introductory Cultural Anthropology course that ranges in size from 40-125 students. Most, if not all of the students in these classes are taking the course as part of their General Education requirements.

Introductory Cultural Anthropology is designated a lecture-discussion course and it is heavily mediated. There are writing assignments, examinations, and as many discussions in class that can be generated in a large lecture hall (filled at times with some students who haven't an idea of what cultural anthropology is all about). Students are required to purchase a Notebook (that I developed) that includes lecture outlines, film notes, and terminology.

Quotations

Throughout the term, I incorporate various "quotes" from anthropologists and non-anthropologists to get certain ideas across; these include ideas from various authors of fiction that students may have read at some point in time.

"Travel is fatal to prejudice, bigotry, and narrow-mindedness." Samuel Langhorn Clemens, also known as Mark Twain (1835-1910).

"Prejudices, it is well known, are most difficult to eradicate from the heart whose soil has never been loosened or fertilized by education; they grow there, as weeds among stones." Charlotte Bronte (1816-1855).

Students may not have read Marcus, Mead, or Malinowski (yet), but perhaps they have been exposed to Twain and Bronte. As an anthropology instructor, you might consider incorporating your favorite authors into class lectures. Students do read for leisure at times and I am willing to draw on any author to get an idea across, be they historical authors or contemporary writers of fiction:

"Okay, class -- what you see at the scene of a homicide is frozen in time, it is no longer a moving, living dynamic. You can create several stories about this still life, but these are only theories. **A detective, like an archaeologist, can assemble hard facts and solid scientific evidence, and still draw the wrong conclusions.** Add to this, a few lies and red herrings and people who are trying to help but make mistakes. Plus people who tell you what you want to hear consistent with your theory, and people with hidden agendas, and the murderer himself, who may have planted false clues. Through all this mess of contradictions, inconsistencies, and lies is the truth [**stress** added]." (Nelson DeMille, 1997 *Plum Island*, p. 215.)

Perhaps students have read DeMille, perhaps not, but if students read that what the archaeologist or biological anthropologist does is similar to what a homicide detective does (someone who might be more familiar to them because of their television "cultural knowledge"), perhaps they will see some value in anthropological approaches.

Mnemonics

"What Bosch had were just parts of the whole. What he needed was the glue that would correctly hold them together. When he had first received his gold shield, he had a partner on the robbery table in Van Nuys who told him that facts weren't the most important part of an investigation, the glue was. He said the glue was made of instinct, imagination, sometimes guesswork and most times just plain luck." (Michael Connelly, 1996 *The Black Ice*, p. 163.)

Anthropology is obviously an exciting subject and for the introductory courses, I utilize a **KISfS** idea: Keeping It Simple for Students. Most of my students in these introductory classes range from 17 to 19 years old (with a few "older" seniors finishing their general education requirements and at times, a few older reentry students) and one of my personal problems is how to **not** share everything I know in a single term: the choice of material to be covered and "distillation" of ideas is essential. I have created various mnemonics that I incorporate into lectures and that summarize my vision of anthropology; **KISfS** is one of them.

134

ABCDE is another mnemonic that summarizes my vision of cultural anthropology: to me, anthropology is the Appreciation of Basic Cultural Diversity Everywhere. I stress in lectures, as well as in readings and films, that in order to "appreciate" basic cultural diversity, one must first acknowledge cultural diversity as well as accept it. The ABCs seem to get the idea across for me. I often combine quotations and mnemonics in an attempt to summarize a great deal of information into a single tight phrase. I share these quotes with students in their Notebook (and on the Web) or on large transparencies:

"The unit of survival [or adaptation] is organism plus environment. We are learning by bitter experience that the organism which destroys its environment destroys itself." (Gregory Bateson, 1972, *Steps to an Ecology of the Mind*, p. 483.)

"...descriptions vary with the conceptual or theoretical framework within which they are couched. To evaluate a description properly one must know something about the theoretical framework that brought it into being." (D. Kaplan, and R. Manners, 1972, *Culture Theory*, p. 22.)

Another alphabetical mnemonic I use, building on Bateson, is simply FGHI, which (in my mind) stands for Foraging, Gathering, Hunting, and Invention. While "true inventions" take place in foraging, gathering, and hunting societies, I use my definition of "inventions" to discuss continuing adaptation to the environment and the development of agriculture and eventually the industrial revolution. FGHI builds upon ABCDE and it seems to work in getting ideas across to students and having them think about anthropology and retain information about various people and how those people adapted to their environments. With my quotes, I continue to weave fact and fiction together when appropriate: "Don't fall in love with the theory of the case. It was, in fact, one of [Butch] Karp's sacred maxims." (Robert Tanenbaum, 1996, *Falsely Accused*, p. 316.)

A final mnemonic that seems to work (and I have "created" these to allow me to easily recall a great deal of information) occurs when I get students to think about "research" and their own research and writing projects: here I use PQRSTU, standing for (again in my mind): Problems, Question(s), Research, Solution(s), Temporary Understanding (and possibly Verisimilitude). Every researcher is faced with a "problem" and the research that we do is generated by the questions that we ask; we come up with solutions and temporary understanding, and perhaps we even approach verisimilitude or truth in our research. I argue that PQRSTU is what all scientists do and it seems to work. At this point, I point out to the class:

"In the field of observation, chance only favors those who are prepared." Louis Pasteur (1822-1895).

"We were getting close to the answer and I was beginning to fly. I could feel my brain cells doing a little tap dance of delight. I was half-skipping, excitement bubbling out of me as we crossed the street. 'I love information. I love information. Isn't this great? God, it's fun....'" (The character Kinsey Milhone in Sue Grafton, 1990, *"G" is For Gumshoe*, p. 277.)

"Research is the key. You can never do enough research. This is so vital I'll repeat it. You can never do enough research... Research can either lower the odds or tell you it's hopeless." (Clive Cussler, and Craig Dirgo, 1996, *The Sea Hunters*, p. xxxi.)

By now, students have read some anthropologists and perhaps they are also familiar with the novels of Sue Grafton or Clive Cussler's action pieces: anything to get them to read and think! Of course, when one uses novels to get certain ideas across, one must also be prepared to explain the following to the audience: "The structural engineers and the marine scientists huddled around in small circles, mumbling to themselves as they **frantically shoved their slide rules back and forth [stress** added]." (Clive Cussler, 1976, *Raise the Titanic*, p. 219.) The instructor must always remember the age of the students: what may have been "real things," such as the slide rule, for the instructor are but wisps of "memory culture" or "ancient history" or unknown to the undergraduate student of today.

A final way to incorporate these verbal "tricks" into lectures is to associate the mnemonics or quotes with one "master" transparency that I begin the class with: the passage of time in a given term along one axis *versus* the increase of knowledge or information shared/obtained during the term along the other axis. A hard copy of this transparency can be found at the end of this article; it can be turned into a transparency to use in class. With this cumulative and temporal approach, I then use a "building block" approach to develop various ideas and theories, such as the following for **FGHI** and **PQRSTU.** (See end of article for these two figures.) Using these and other visuals as a constant template, the semester flows smoothly. Incidentally, **RSTU** is used to encourage the following in their assigned readings: **R**eading, **S**tudying, **T**hinking, and **U**nderstanding. Merely reading an article is not the same as studying it, thinking about it, or even understanding it; unfortunately, too many students think just "reading" is sufficient, and it is not.

Cartoons (and newspaper articles)

In order to make anthropology "relevant" to today's students, I feel we must point out that what anthropologists "do" does have an impact in the "real world" (or the non-academic world) and information from the real world can be interpreted in an anthropological context. I use, as I know many of us do, cartoons of an anthropological nature (not only Gary Larson's but Watterson's "Calvin and Hobbes" and Thaves' "Frank and Ernest"); they provide ample topics for classroom discussion and getting things started.

Aware that many of my students do not spend a great deal of time reading newspapers, I attempt to incorporate as many newspaper articles (and headlines) as possible in the classroom, making transparencies as large as possible of various contemporary events: whenever the

American Anthropological Association meetings are held, or the Association for the Advancement of Sciences meetings are occurring, I look for articles in the local paper and use them in class. I also tell students that I use "these references" as a jumping off point to go to scholarly publications such as in *Science* or *Nature*. Indeed, other disciplines use this approach and one can substitute the word "anthropology" for "mathematics" in the following phrase and it makes perfect sense:

> "It's time to let the secret out: Mathematics [or Anthropology] is not primarily a matter of plugging numbers into formulas and performing rote computations. **It is a way of thinking and questioning that may be unfamiliar to many of us, but is available to almost all of us [stress** added]." (John Allen Paulos, 1995, *A Mathematician Reads the Newspaper*, p. 3.)

In addition to cartoons and newspapers, I keep a blank videotape in my home/office VCR at all times and when something pops up that appears appropriate, I tape it (archive it) and use it in class when appropriate. I also use segments of various videotapes to get certain ideas across and I find the opening segment from *Fiddler on the Roof* a great introduction for certain points in the course. Other small segments of contemporary culture would work well in introductory-level courses as well.

> "Myth and rumor come first. People don't believe it until they see it with their own eyes. Then suddenly there it is, and afterward nobody even remembers we disbelieved it. It seems ridiculous to have discounted it. It's all hubris. We think ourselves as the chosen ones, the supreme beings on the whole planet. We think we own the place, but we don't know the first thing about it." (John Darnton, 1996, *Neandertal*, p. 51.)

Once again, perhaps they have read Darnton's *Neandertal*, or perhaps I can encourage them to read Trinkhaus and Shipman's 1993 publication entitled *The Neanderthals: Changing The Image of Mankind*. Perhaps they can read the scholarly works and compare the established scholarship with the "fiction" woven into the following novel by Clive Cussler:

> "'*Sinanthropis pekinensis*,' Sandecker spoke the words almost reverently. 'Chinese man of Peking, a very ancient and primitive human who walked upright on two feet. In nineteen twenty-nine the discovery of his skull was announced by a Canadian anatomist Dr. Davidson Black, who directed the excavation and was funded by the Rockefeller Foundation. Over the next several years, digging in a quarry that had once been a hill with limestone caves near the village of Choukoutien, Black found thousands of chipped-stone tools and evidence of hearths, which indicated Peking man had mastered fire. Excavations carried out over the next ten years found the partial remains of another forty individuals, both juveniles and adults, and what has been acknowledged as the largest hominid fossil collection ever assembled.'" (Clive Cussler, 1997, *Flood Tide*, p. 483.)

For the past few years I have also been placing my introductory syllabus as a Notebook on the World Wide Web ("For the fall 1998 syllabus, please see http://www. ...etc." and "For the spring 1999 syllabus, please see http://www...etc") with lecture outlines and appropriate websites. The copyrighted Notebook is available for purchase at the student bookstore and I update the notebook every Monday with new websites and appropriate course information; this keeps the course current for me and for the students and seems to work well. Web pages for particular courses and email communications with students are becoming more and more common and will continue to be an important vehicle for communication in the future.

Conclusions

"Anthropologists are highly individual and specialized people. Each of them [or us] is marked by the kind of work he or she prefers and has done, which in time becomes an aspect of that individual's personality." (Margaret Mead [1901-1978] as cited in Isaac Asimov and Jason Shulman, eds., 1988, *Isaac Asimov's Book of Science and Nature Quotations*, p. 20.)

All in all, anthropology is fun! I enjoy what I do and I honestly believe that teaching should be fun. I will use any "hard" anthropological data available to get the anthropological message across as well as appropriate "soft" fictional data (or ideas). When I first came to California State University, Chico in 1973, some geography faculty were using a 1949 publication entitled *Earth Abides* by George R. Stewart (1895-1980). I had never read the novel before but once I did, I have used it in my introductory classes ever since. The book is most appropriate for a northern California setting: the opening scenes take place a few miles outside of Chico in the foothills of the community of Oroville. The story quickly moves to the San Francisco Bay area (where approximately 50% of our student body come from) and the students can readily identify with the imagery; it is a "classic" novel and the best summary comes from the anthropologist Leon Stover who wrote the following in *Cultural Anthropology* in 1973:

"Anthropological science fiction enjoys the philosophical luxury of providing answers to the question "What is man? while anthropology the science is still learning how to frame it. ...Perhaps the most persuasive answer to the question is *Earth Abides* (Stewart 1949). The novel reverses the story of Ishi, which Kroeber (1962) has recorded as the "biography of the last wild Indian in North America." Ishi, the last member of the Yahi Indians of northern California, stepped out of an isolated Stone Age existence into a world of trolley cars and electric lights in early 20th century California. Ishi's name in the Yahi language means "man." Ish [in *Earth Abides*] survives a pandemic disease to see civilization collapse and his children and grandchildren return to the life of Stone Age hunters. Ish is the last of the civilized Americans, Ishi the last of the aboriginal Americans. The one fiction, the other biography, both have the same moral: man is man, be he civilized or tribal. Stewart shows us that a tribal hunting culture is just as valid and real to its members as civilization is to us." (Leon E. Stover, 1973,

138

Anthropology and Science Fiction. *Current Anthropology* Vol 14(4): pp. 471-474, p. 472.)

There are other pieces of fiction that are based on particular locales that can be exploited for use in introductory-level courses.

I firmly believe that learning should be fun but teaching **is** work and the words of the French essayist Joseph Joubert (1754-1824) couldn't be more truthful: "enseigner, c'est apprendre deux fois," or "to teach is to learn twice." (In George W. Seldes, compiler, 1985, *The Great Thoughts,* p. 215.)

References Cited

Asimov, Isaac, and Jason Shulman, eds
  1988 *Isaac Asimov's Book of Science and Nature Quotations.* New York: Weidenfeid & Nicholson.

Bateson, Gregory
  1972 *Steps to an Ecology of Mind.* San Francisco: Chandler Publishing Co.

Connelly, Michael
  1996 *The Black Ice.* New York: St. Martins.

Cussler, Clive
  1976 *Raise the Titanic.* New York: Pocket Books.

Cussler, Clive
  1997 *Flood Tide.* New York: Pocket Star Books.

Cussler, Clive, and Craig Dirgo
  1996 *The Sea Hunters.* New York: Pocket Star Books.

Darnton, John
  1996 *Neandertal.* New York: St. Martin's Press.

DeMille, Nelson
  1997 *Plum Island.* New York: Warner Books.

Grafton, Sue
  1990 *"G" is for Gumshoe.* New York: Bantam Books.

Kaplan, D., and R. Manners
  1972 *Culture Theory.* Clifton Hills, New Jersey: Prentice Hall.

Kroeber, Theodora
1962 *Ishi in Two Worlds.* Berkeley: University of California Press.

Michener, James
1992 *The World is my Home: a Memoir.* New York: Fawcett.

Paulos, John Allen
1995 *A Mathematician Reads the Newspaper.* New York: Doubleday.

Seldes, George W. compiler.
1985 *The Great Thoughts.* New York: Ballantine Books.

Stewart, George R.
1949 *Earth Abides.* New York: Fawcett

Stover, Leon E.
1973 Anthropology and Science Fiction. *Current Anthropology* Vol 14 (4): Pp 471-474.

Tanenbaum, Robert K.
1996 *Falsely Accused.* New York: Signet.

Trinkhaus, Erik, and Pat Shipman
1993 *The Neanderthals: Changing the Image of Mankind.* New York: Knopf.

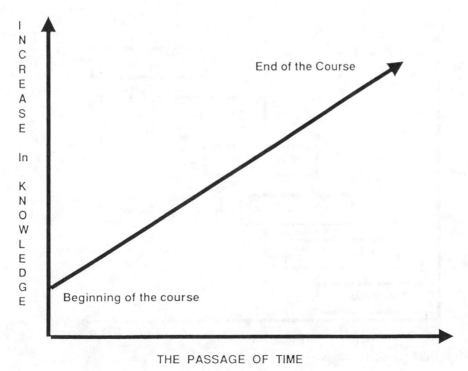

THE PASSAGE OF TIME

Figure 1: Increase in Knowledge Over The Passage of Time

140

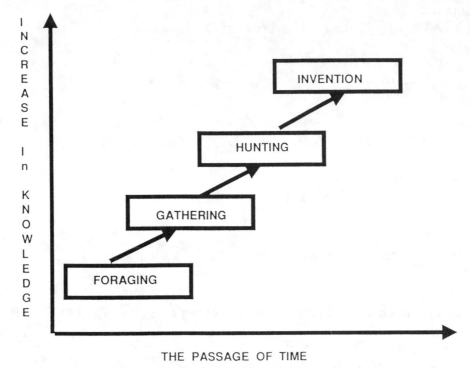

THE PASSAGE OF TIME

Figure 2: Foraging, Gathering, Hunting, and Into Invention and the Industrial Revolution

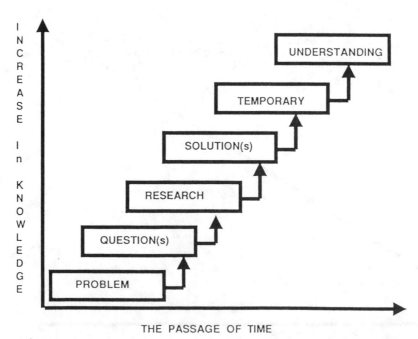

THE PASSAGE OF TIME

Figure 3: PQRSTU (Problem, Question[s], Research, Solution[s], Temporary Understanding)

FIELD TRIPS AND STUDENT INVOLVEMENT:
HANDS-ON LEARNING COMPONENTS

Ruth M. Krulfeld

The object of adding a field component to introductory-level courses is to give beginning anthropology students direct experience with a culture different from their own (or presenting some aspect of the student's own society that they are unlikely to directly experience), and to offer them the opportunity of directly participating in events in that culture in an organized way under professional anthropological guidance. This allows students to relate their knowledge from class work to what they experience themselves on a field trip, to formulate their own questions about the experience in relation to what they are studying in a course, and to learn how to observe and interview in the field to obtain answers to their questions.

I designed the field trips because I felt the lack in my own education as an undergraduate of anything that related the ideas that were being taught in lectures or readings to real world hands-on experience. I, therefore, felt the need to incorporate some experiential field component in my classes. I want students to feel some of the excitement anthropologists have when they go into the field, and to undergo some of the same learning experiences we ourselves have. The inclusion of a field trip met with great enthusiasm by the students, many of whom mention it as the high point not only of the class, but often of their undergraduate experience.

Structured Field Trips

The structured student field trip was originally an added component of an Honors Introduction to Sociocultural Anthropology. Granted, this was designed to a class limited to 22 students, but with some foresight and planning, field trips can easily accommodate a much larger introductory class. And, although I designed the field trip to visit an ethnic group with which I am conducting my own research -- the Lao community -- it could easily be done with any ethnic community, religious sect, or enclave group in the instructor's immediate area, such as the Hari Krishnas, a Wiccan coven, any religious cult, or an immigrant group's "event." Any one of these would allow students the hands-on, direct experience of participant observation of people with whom they do not usually associate. Any group selected will afford an important learning experience since students, with the help of the instructor, will approach this field trip analytically, with new ways (that they are learning in class) of looking at and understanding what they observe. The trip is meant to offer students an opportunity to apply many of the anthropological concepts and ideas they are learning in class through lectures and readings.

Field trips should only be undertaken after the instructor contacts the group to be studied, makes appropriate arrangements, and gets appropriate permission. I explain to the group my wish that students be able to learn about them. Some preparation of students will also be necessary, with the instructor explaining the reason for the trip, proper field etiquette, the need for respect of those being observed, some background information on the culture, and suggestions for specific things they are to look for. I provide much of this in a handout "Tips for the Field Trip" that includes directions to the site, proper dress and etiquette, and information on the event they are about to observe. Background information has already been provided through reading assignments on the group -- in my particular case, of my own work -- but articles by others on similar groups may also be used. The choice of a time for the field trip will obviously depend on when the event you want to attend is scheduled. I have found that weekends are most convenient for both students and myself, since there is no conflict with other classes. And weekends are also likely to be the times many groups will schedule their significant events, since their membership also works. I have found it useful to make the field trip a required part of the course, announced as such on the syllabus[1] and in class, and to have students sign up for their choice of field trips, since I offer two or more, with one being required. If at all possible, two or more field trips -- although more work for the instructor -- allows students a choice and evens out the attendance, making the trip more manageable for the instructor and less overpowering for the studied group.

Why can't students simply go out on their own and get the same thing from the experience, thereby saving part of a Saturday or whenever other time the event you want to observe is scheduled and that is most convenient for the instructor and class members?[2] The structured field trip offers two things of major importance that cannot be easily obtained through sending introductory level students out to individually conduct their own field studies:

(1) The group field trip offers a safe and secure environment for learning in which the inevitable experience of culture shock (which is, after all, an important part of this experience) is made more manageable so students can get beyond it relatively quickly in order to go on and make their observations on religious practices, gender relations, economic transactions, use of material culture, or whatever is assigned. Your presence and that of their fellow classmates eases their feelings of insecurity, of not knowing what is expected of them, of shock in encountering different behavior, values, and views of the world. Of course, their shock will continue to some extent throughout the field experience, but I have found that they become more aware of their own culture and their own cultural biases through experiencing it. Student notes in their journals or response papers are often quite explicit about this point.

The field trip enables students to directly encounter what they are learning in class, but in class it is likely to be more distancing and much less engaging of their feelings. Therefore, as they read case studies or examples of major anthropological issues, or hear someone else talk about them, they are likely to have less impact and be less memorable than the field experience offered to them.

---

[1] Many colleagues and I have noticed an increasing tendency for students to regard syllabi as contracts and to abide by the requirements stated in them.

[2] I do not try to negotiate this with the whole class, but rather schedule the trips on weekends when events are being held by the group I have selected for study.

(2) You, as the instructor, are there to explain some of the things that students should be noticing, to answer some questions that they feel are important (and that might otherwise be lost in the interim between the field trip and the next class) and to raise other questions, to make sure that students do not do anything that might offend the group being observed, and to resolve any problems in the unlikely event that any occur, to help them put much of what is being studied in the class in context of the culture they are studying on the field trip, and also to offer a setting in which all members of your class have the opportunity to observe the same things.

This latter point can be used in several ways in the classroom based on this field experience. First, the shared field experience provides a commonality for students from which they can explore for their different observations and interpretations of what they observed in the same setting during the same time frame. The point can be made here that no field researcher can observe everything at once, that each one is likely to pick up different things even when observing the same event at the same time. The roles of hypothesis formation in the field and of inference can be explored with the class as students discuss various things they have observed. Although excellent for upper division students, for introductory-level students, the student-designed, individual, one-time field experience is much less likely to yield these benefits.

Case Study: Field Trip to a Ceremony at Wat Lao Buddhavong, a Lao Temple in the Greater Washington Metropolitan area

To facilitate student in-depth encounters with another culture, I not only take students on the required field trip, but add two additional components. All three are described:

(1) The required field trip. I schedule from one to three field trips on Saturdays because this is when major Lao ceremonies are usually held. One field trip is required but students may take the option to go on more than one, pending room in the van.

(2) Guest speakers. I invite guest speakers from the same ethnic community the students have visited to talk about aspects of Lao culture, following the lecture and readings on that particular subject. This might include Lao kinship and marriage, Lao values and value conflicts with American culture, or Lao religion. Students often ask questions directly of the speaker. This raises issues about what anthropologists do that makes them different from members of studied communities and how and why their knowledge differs from those they research. It also aids students in forming hypotheses and checking them out.

(3) Assigned readings. I assign readings (my own and other authors) appropriate to the topic so students see the range of what anthropologists do, how anthropologists address current issues in anthropology when working with the very people the students have met and observed. Being able to use one's own work introduces the excitement of research and discovery that I feel, as well as introduces the application of research to help the group studied. Students feel they can ask questions of the person who did the research they are reading about.

144

Most of us use our own research on some level in our classes and include the rich case material in our lectures as well as more theoretical ideas of our research experiences and how these relate to the methods we have used to obtain our data. However, if the instructor has not researched the group used for the field trip, other articles may be substituted, with differences between these and what is observed in the field being discussed in class or addressed by students in short response papers.

Conclusions

Field trips take advanced planning to organize students into groups, order vans, and get permission from the studied group for each visit. In addition, a handout describing the "rules" for behavior in the field culture is of value. Students must bring their journals on the trip to record their observations and interviews. They have already been instructed on how to take good field notes and are asked to record their feelings and responses to their field experiences. At the conclusion of the trip, they are required to submit their journals as well as a four-page response paper relating their observations from the trip to major concepts studied in the course. Student evaluations of the field trip experience have been excellent and enthusiastic.

GROWING UP PINK OR BLUE: USING CHILDREN'S TELEVISION COMMERCIALS TO ANALYZE GENDER ENCULTURATION

S. Elizabeth Bird

The Issue

The notion of gender as a cultural construction is sometimes hard for introductory students to accept, but obviously a key to an anthropological understanding of gender roles. I find a good way to jump-start my unit on gender in introductory Cultural Anthropology classes is to use material that students find instantly striking and recognizable, but may not have actually thought about much -- contemporary TV commercials. The exercise can be done in a 45-minute to one-hour in-class segment, using previously videotaped materials. It can also be used in upper division courses that focus on cross-cultural gender issues, and at least one of my colleagues has used it in an introductory four-field class. I have also used the exercise in a graduate seminar on Media in Contemporary Culture, although in a less structured way. It has worked well in classes that range from 10 to 150 students, so the size of the class does not seem to be an issue.

I begin with discussion of the basic idea of gender construction through enculturation (later I return to consider some more biologically-based explanations of gender difference), inviting students to think about what elements in culture teach children "how to be male" or "how to be female." Of course they usually list such staples as family, education, religion, and traditional stories, and someone eventually suggests that the media may play an important role.

The Exercise

At this point, I show a tape I have compiled of TV commercials aimed at children, which strings together commercials arranged by gender. It includes around six commercials aimed at boys, a similar number aimed at girls, and a small group supposedly selling gender-neutral products, such as fast food and breakfast cereals. The whole tape lasts only about five minutes.

The discussion that follows is usually lively. I try to start broadly, with a question such as "OK, what do you see?" before focusing into specific areas. By the time the discussion is over, the students are usually marveling at the way they have taken the gender coding in these commercials so much for granted. Regardless of the specific commercials used, we find that masculinity and femininity are indeed coded in very specific ways, which leads naturally into consideration of the clear cultural implications of those differences.

At this point, the results of the discussion can be summarized in a variety of ways. One way is for the class to generate a chart, which I write on the chalkboard or on a blank overhead using the categories suggested below ("grooming, behavior, etc.") as guiding questions. A faster way is to use a prepared overhead listing the categories but leaving the information blank for the students' suggestions. Fastest of all is to show a prepared overhead, copied from or based on the chart below which summarizes the usual results. While this obviously saves time and is most efficient in larger classes, it tends to have the effect of discounting quite valid responses that may have been overlooked in my analysis. The appeal of this exercise is that students feel genuinely involved in generating the conclusions rather than simply being told the "right" responses by the teacher. Thus, whenever circumstances permit, I prefer to use a more spontaneous approach.

	[Male]	[Female]
Grooming:	boys dress casually and look unkempt	girls dress up, with carefully coifed hair and noticeable make-up
Behavior:	boys rush around shouting	girls sit quietly and play, often giggling with delight
	boys are competitive, only banding together against adults	girls play in cooperative groups and nurture each other and their dolls
Location:	boys play outside, apparently roaming freely	girls play indoors
Sound:	boys have a soundtrack of thumping music, loud voices, screeching tires	girls' music is quiet, gentle, soothing, with quiet sound effects
	boys' commercials often feature adult male voices, spoken in loud commanding tones	girls' commercials more often feature children's voices
Color:	"male" colors are black, red, deep blue, and other strong, primary colors	"female" colors are pink, mauve, and pastels
Language:	Masculinity is expressed in words like "power," strong," "win"	femininity is expressed in words like "love," "soft," "pretty"

Gender Asymmetry:

in commercials aimed at both genders, boys predominate overwhelmingly. This illustrates what has been called the "Smurfette principle, whereby boys are differentiated by activities or interests, while girls are simply girls. It also stems from advertisers' belief that girls will identify with a boy principal character, but not vice versa, raising the issue of the male as norm, the female as "other."

I find that all these issues are raised by the students themselves, sometimes prompted by such questions as "what does femininity/masculinity look (or sound) like?" Occasionally, students accuse me of picking the commercials deliberately, but I explain that they were all drawn from two-hour blocks of cartoons, and no special selection was necessary. [Note: I have compiled a tape that includes both the current 1999 commercials and some from the early 1960s. Interested readers who would like copies of this may send a blank tape and I will copy it for them.]

There are, of course, several well-done educational videos available that focus on gender coding in advertising, such as Jean Kilbourne's "Killing Us Softly" series, but I have found that using the "raw data" of the commercials themselves is much more useful (and more anthropological), allowing students to reach the answers themselves through observation and discussion. The brevity of the tape also allows more time for in-class analysis.

Supplemental Activities

(1) Depending on time available and the focus of the class, the discussion can be fairly brief or more developed. If time allows, and especially in classes centered on media or popular culture, I like to show another series of clips from 1960s toy commercials. What is especially striking about these is how little basic coding has changed, with boys roaming the countryside on bikes, and girls rocking dolls at home.

Many students do notice, however, the clear difference between the eras in terms of the role of parents. In the earlier ads, parents, especially fathers, are frequently present, acting as good-humored supervisors and mentors, while in the contemporary ads, parents are either absent, or are buffoons whose authority must be subverted at all times. This can lead to interesting discussions about changes in family structures and value systems. In addition, students notice the almost complete absence of racial and ethnic minorities in the earlier ads. Contemporary commercials carefully represent minorities, although rarely as central characters, except for ads focused on sports. This point often provokes a lively discussion about how media depictions of race both reflect and reinforce cultural attitudes.

(2) This exercise can also become a chance for students to do some data gathering of their own, and in fact I have done this with students in media-focused classes. In this case, I ask them to choose a two-hour block of children's programming, and watch the commercials on their own time. They then come to class prepared to discuss their findings, and the exercise progresses as described. Sometimes I have them share their observations in small groups before we move to generating the chart. This tends to work well in smaller classes. In addition to its usefulness in analyzing content, it can also lead to discussion of how one draws meaningful conclusions from raw data by looking for common themes, and how careful observation of everyday, taken-for granted culture can yield important anthropological insights.

After the Discussion

This exercise then takes us into a more comparative discussion of gender roles in other cultures, and the various cultural, biological, and economic explanations offered for these differences. During the gender unit as a whole, and after we move on to other topics, I find that the TV commercials usually become frequent points of reference (initiated by students) when we discuss such issues as:

(1) cross cultural differences in the incidence of rape. When males are socialized to be aggressive and competitive, rape rates are high.

(2) the biological basis for gender differences. Are women "naturally" programmed to be nurturing and caring, and men to be aggressive?

(3) the impact of media images on cultural values in other societies. Many readings and texts on globalization and social change point to the replacement of traditional values by attitudes stressing consumerism. Part of this is often a new idealization of impossible Western standards of beauty that are inculcated in children from an early age.

(4) the power of language. From looking closely at the distilled language of commercials, students gain a new awareness of linguistic codes that carry gendered and racialized meanings. What does it mean that boys' commercials ring with the language of "power" while girls' ads speak of "love and caring?"

HOW TO TEACH SELF ETHNOGRAPHY

John L. Caughey

Introduction

Anthropology shows us how culture influences the lives of people in other societies; turned back on ourselves, it also sheds light on the cultural dimensions of our own experience. A useful teaching trick is to take ethnographic techniques for studying others and systematically apply them to our own lives. Techniques of "autoethnography" or "self ethnography" are effective tools for engaging students' interest in introductory anthropology courses, in special topics courses, and in advanced fieldwork courses. Here, I will briefly discuss the theory of self ethnography and then show how its perspectives and practices can be used in conjunction with other teaching methods.

The Theory of Self Ethnography

Ethnography has always been oriented toward the study of "other cultures" but the idea of self ethnography lurks just below the surface. As Agar (1986, 1994) and others suggest, the paradigmatic ethnographic situation has been understood as the encounter between an ethnographer operating with one cultural tradition and a set of informants operating with an alternative tradition -- a different system for thinking, feeling, and acting in the world. As Agar suggests, it is the creative tension between the ethnographer's tradition and that of his or her subjects that provides the medium for understanding. One sees the other culture through contrast, because its beliefs and practices differ in multiple ways from the tradition the ethnographer thinks with. A key opening involves "breakdowns" or "rich points," moments when our own expectations are violated. When your informant mentions that "sharks are people," that "the world is flat," or that a particular young person is "obviously more attractive" than another, one is alerted to the fact that the informant classifies sea creatures, understands cosmology, and operates with standards of beauty drastically different from your own. Instead of glossing over such statements, we need to cultivate them as key entry points into the orientations of other cultures. Awareness of difference reveals cultural construction that can then be systematically explored through interviews, observations, and the analysis of conceptual domains.

But rich points are not only entry points into the **other**, they are also the moments that raise our consciousness of our own cultural conditioning. To learn how others orient differently to animals, cosmology, and attractiveness raises all sorts of interesting questions about how these previously taken for granted matters are conceptualized in our own culture.[1] Called to

---

[1] Behar (1996) provides a good review of the issues involved in investigating our own "intellectual and emotional baggage" as these have developed in the reflexive tradition of anthropological writing.

Called to awareness, these cultural domains can now be investigated carefully. Providing students with this "ah hah" experience about their own cultural conditioning forms the basis for teaching self ethnography.

Turning the systematic questioning and analysis of ethnography back on ourselves requires another modification of ordinary procedure. Many anthropologists still speak as if people operate with one single culture or cultural tradition. This is not useful in getting students to think about the cultural dimensions of their own lives. Most students, like other contemporary humans, are multicultural. They operate with a diverse and often conflicting set of cultural traditions. This is obviously true of "halfies" and other classically bicultural individuals but even students who have never left the United States are still likely to be influenced by a diverse set of religious traditions, work traditions, leisure traditions, music traditions, or political traditions. Often people know a minority tradition, a dominant tradition, and more than one ethnic, religious, or class tradition. It is also useful to get students thinking about the particular **relationship** they have with each tradition; ask them: "Do you have a dominant relation with the tradition, generally accepting its beliefs and practices? Do you have an oppositional relationship with the tradition, resisting and seeking to evade its orientation? Or do you have a 'negotiated' or critical relationship with the tradition, selectively accepting some aspects but modifying, resisting, or evading others?"[2] Much more than a mono-cultural approach, such questions can productively fuel the use of self ethnography in anthropology courses.

Because the issues of self ethnography are clearest in fieldwork courses, I will begin with a discussion of how self ethnographic techniques can be used in teaching ethnography and then move to how they can be adapted for exercises in special topics and introductory courses.

Using Self Ethnography in the Fieldwork Course

The undergraduate fieldwork course is the best way to give students a feel for the interest and power of the ethnographic experience including its self ethnographic dimension. While useful in many ways, guides to teaching this course do not adequately address self ethnography.[3] However, this dimension can be added by getting students to turn the methods presented back on themselves as well as on their informants. What follows is a way to do this.

---

[2] This approach to different "relationships" to cultural traditions has been adapted from a formulation on different "readings" of media ideologies as developed in British cultural studies (Fiske 1987:260).

[3] How-to-do-it texts like Spradley (1979) or Emerson, et al (1995) typically advocate keeping a fieldwork journal and discuss the importance of being wary about the influence of one's own cultural perspectives in doing fieldwork -- but these directives are typically presented as methodological suggestions for studying others; they are not developed as ways of systematically raising one's consciousness of one's own cultural conditioning.

Teach the fieldwork course as a life history class and require students to locate an individual whose cultural background is significantly different from their own. Tell students it is to be a dual or double life history since it is about the other's cultural experience in comparison with the student's own. The student's main assignment is to:

(1) identify the student's own and the other person's several cultural traditions;
(2) determine each person's "relationship" to each tradition;
(3) discover how each manages or juggles multiple traditions;
(4) consider how all of this has shaped past and current experience.

Ask students to keep this general inquiry in mind but direct them to focus on a particular theme or issue, such as how an individual's diverse traditions affect his or her experience of family or work or leisure or how the person negotiates two particularly contradictory traditions, such as evolutionary biology and fundamentalist Christianity, or how each person constructs a meaningful sense of life from disparate traditions. Suggest that all of an individual's traditions are likely to impinge on such focal issues, though some more than others.

The following exercises are useful in self ethnography. Before the students ask their informants about a given area of life, have them ask the question of themselves and write out the answers. Then, after interviewing the other person, have students reanalyze their own initial answers in light of and in contrast with the informant's responses. Usually they will find that the responses of the other, used as leverage for self inquiry, reveal new aspects of their own cultural conditioning and deepen self understanding.

Exercise 1: "Chapters of Your Life." The first task is to get an overview of each individual's life and to seek to identify how and in what context the person learned the various cultural traditions that were influential. Ask students: "If you were going to write your own autobiography, what would be the chapters or phases of your life so far? Label each chapter and then explore what was going on in each phase, particularly what cultural traditions you encountered and learned. For example, in a given phase were you introduced to a new occupational tradition, switched to a new school, or more deeply involved in a religious tradition?" Use class discussion of student self ethnographic exercises to show how people are introduced to new traditions at many different stages of life and how they incorporate them in relation to other traditions.

Exercise 2: "Who am I?" Ask students to think about the question "Who am I?" or "What kind of a person am I?" and write out a series of words and phrases as answers: "I am...." "I am a person who...." Locate each response in its particular language concept system. Is it a term from a work tradition ("waitress"), a psychological tradition ("adult child of an alcoholic"), a religious tradition ("lapsed Catholic"), a media tradition ("a John Wayne fan"), a large bureaucratic tradition ("224-55-9867")? Use class discussion of self ethnographic responses to help students see how their very sense of self is constituted by the concepts for kinds of persons available in the traditions they have learned to think with.

Exercise 3: Roles, Dramas, and Social Worlds. Ask students: "What social scenes, institutions, or groups do you move through over the course of a given day, week, month, and year? What are the work worlds, school worlds, clubs, commercial establishments, religious institutions, and entertainment worlds you move through? Take one or more of these worlds and explore it further. What is the dominant cultural tradition at play here? What role do you play here in relation to what sets of others playing complementary roles? What expectations and obligations do you have as an actor in this role? What are the problems, strains, and successes in role play? Discuss the cultural structure of a current drama, a particular story about social interaction in this world." Use class discussion of self ethnographic exercises to help students see how each of us moves through different roles with different cultures and different expectations. Help them learn to analyze their own and other people's worlds as culturally constructed dramas.

Special Topics Courses

In virtually any special topics anthropology course, self ethnography assignments can be developed that require students to systematically map out their own cultural experience with the topic at hand. Since teaching self ethnography is especially effective when used in conjunction with interviews, consider having students pair up and do a series of interviews with each other while they are also doing self ethnography. If this is not feasible, you can still set up self ethnography exercises by using class readings about other cultures, including case studies of individual experience, as comparative leverage to get students to defamiliarize and then systematically investigate how religion or economics or aspects of social organization, such as gender or kinship or friendship or courtship, work in the cultural traditions they operate with.

Anthropology of the Mass Media

Since contemporary students are extremely involved in mass media, it is useful to tap this interest as part of such courses. A good format is to use readings that illustrate other cultural constructions of mass media and then to ask students to use this as a starting point for exploring the cultural dimensions of their own experience.

Exercise 4: Relationships with Media Figures. Give students the following assignment: "Make a list of at least 20 figures (e.g., actors, sports figures, politicians, musicians, fictional characters) you know about through the mass media (TV, film, radio, books, magazines, newspapers) and describe in a sentence or two how you feel about them. Pick one figure who has been significant to you. Consider how you conceptualize and emotionally orient to this figure. Do you like him or her or not? What real relationship would you say is most analogous to the imaginal mediated relationship you have to this figure (do you see the person as a hero, a role model, a friend, a lover, an enemy)? Through what media do you relate to the individual and what are these experiences like? How and to what extent does the person affect your consciousness, do you dream about him or her, recall past performances, or construct daydreams? How and to what extent does the individual affect your actual interactions (e.g., do you discuss the person with others, participate in fan clubs or listservs, use the individual as a model or anti-model in deciding how to behave)? How and to what extent does your interest in this figure connect to your particular social and cultural location in contemporary American society?"

Using this exercise helps students see how media figures are a pervasive and powerful part of our social experience. In class discussion, compare American orientations to mass media with those of other societies, or with traditional cultural orientations to spirits and gods, and show how a person's social location (age, class, gender, race, ethnic, or sexual orientation, including complex aspects of individual and group acceptance of and resistance to these cultural categories) affects orientations to mass media figures.

Psychological Anthropology

Many aspects of such courses including the study of emotions, ethnopsychology, identity, deviance, and dreams lend themselves to self ethnographic exercises.

Exercise 5: The Culture of Dreams. Tell students about their assignment: "For the next ten days, keep a pencil and paper by your bedside and try to record a dream or two immediately upon awakening. Try to record the narrative of the dream from the inside as exactly as possible. Pick one (or more) dreams for cultural analysis. What was the dream like as an alternative world? What were the characteristics of the dream self, dream settings, other dream figures, and dream action? How is the dream world similar to and different from your culturally constructed experience in the waking world? How does the dream reflect your particular mix of cultural traditions and roles? Can it be read as a commentary on the stresses and strains of your waking social world? How might the dream be interpreted in the culture we read about last week? What meaning do you see in it? In our dominant American culture, dreams are often dismissed as meaningless, yet there is a lurking suspicion that they may be significant, e.g., psychologically revealing or even premonitions of the future. How do you read your dreams given these prevailing notions? How have dreams been interpreted in the religious, ethnic, or psychological traditions you know? To what extent do you use such traditions in thinking about your own dreams?

Use class discussion to show how dreams are composed of culturally relative materials available in the individual's waking experience and how types of dreams can be systematically linked to the strains of particular roles (e.g., student dreams, waitress dreams, nurse's dreams) and how variously dreams have been interpreted in the multicultural traditions that prevail in different sectors of American society.

Introductory Anthropology Courses

In introductory classes, self ethnography helps students realize that the cultural

154

perspectives, analytic concepts, and methods being introduced can not only illuminate other cultures but that they can also help us understand our own cultural conditioning. Simplified versions of all the above exercises are suitable for introductory courses as well as other relatively less complex exercises, such as the following:

Exercise 6: Greeting Rituals. Tell students: "As you walk around campus tomorrow, try the following exercise. What thought process do you use as you see someone you know approaching you on a campus sidewalk? What are the cultural categories you use to classify different kinds of persons on campus. What kinds of options do you have as you approach the other person (greet, avoid, or wait and see what the other person does) and how do you decide which option to use? What would happen if you chose to violate these rules, such as looking at people you know but not greeting them?"

Use class discussion to describe how different cultures use different kinds of greeting rituals and how our rules reflect the pervasive power of our own culturally constituted system for social interaction. Discussion can help students see the struggles we all go through in accepting and resisting the ways our cultures sort people out into kinds of persons and the profound influence this has on our social experience.

Conclusions

Self ethnography helps students understand the cultural structuring of human experience and it helps them grasp the tools we anthropologists use for investigating cultures. Self ethnography raises student's interest in anthropology because they find that learning more about their own cultural conditioning is an engaging as well as important part of anthropological education.

Self ethnography works for us as teachers too. First, there are several ethical aspects to teaching self ethnography. To ask students to discuss their own lives and cultures in class or in homework papers is not a typical practice and may be initially strange or even threatening to a few students.[4] Clearly we do not want to push people into making revelations they are uncomfortable with. We need to make sure students know that they have permission to avoid areas of life that they do not want to reveal and we need to create a classroom climate that is accepting and respectful of difference. It is also important for us as teachers to model self ethnography for the students. If we are asking students to analyze and discuss their own cultural experience, we need to offer examples of **our** experience and to model ways of talking about them in class. It is useful to adopt a perspective of curious, interested self inquiry, to show amusement with one's self, to be critical of aspects of traditions one uses but feels critical of, but

---

[4] While a few instructors seem to fear that asking students to investigate their own cultural traditions risks jeopardizing their faith or loyalty in them, I have not found this to be the case. To know that something we do is culturally constructed and relative does not mean it is not valuable and important.

also to show respect for one's own sense of the value of cultural traditions one believes in whether these be anthropological traditions, ethnic traditions, or religious traditions. I think it is good to be relativistic about one's own beliefs but not cynical about them.

Finally, in my experience, teaching self ethnography is not only good for students, it is good for the instructor. For me, it makes the effort to teach more interesting because it is more like collaborative ethnographic research than "just" teaching. To ask myself and my students to use self ethnography to dig into the ways cultures influence some aspect of our experience -- whether this be friendship, dreams, or greeting rituals -- and then to come together in class to discuss our efforts and compare our findings is surprisingly satisfying. By doing this together, students always teach me something new and interesting about how cultures structure our individual lives.

References Cited

Agar, Michael
   1986 *Speaking of Ethnography*. Beverly Hills, CA: Sage.

   1994 *Language Shock*. New York: Morrow.

Behar, Ruth
   1996 *The Vulnerable Observer*. Boston: Beacon Press.

Emerson, Robert M., Rachel I. Fretz, and Linda L. Shaw
   1995 *Writing Ethnographic Fieldnotes*. Chicago: University of Chicago Press.

Fiske, John
   1987 British Cultural Studies and Television. In *Channels of Discourse*. Robert C. Allen,
   ed. Chapel Hill, NC: University of North Carolina Press.

Spradley, James P.
   1979 *The Ethnographic Interview*. New York: Holt, Rinehart, and Winston.

Additional Reading

Caughey, John L.
   1982 Ethnography, Introspection, and Reflexive Culture Studies. *Prospects: An Annual of
   American Culture Studies* 7:116-139.

   1985 *On the Anthropology of America. Epilogue to Symbolizing America*. Herve Varenne,
   Ed. Lincoln, NE: University of Nebraska Press.

156

1994   Gina as Steven: The Social and Cultural Dimensions of a Media Relationship. *Visual Anthropology Review* 10(1):126-136.

1999   *American Selves: A Life History Approach to the Study of Identity.* Scholarly Resources Press, forthcoming.

Ellis, Carolyn, and Arthur P. Bochner, eds.
    1996   *Composing Ethnography: Alternative Forms of Qualitative Writing.* Walnut Creek, CA: Altamira Press.

PRE-CLASS FIELDWORK: ETHNOGRAPHIC INTRODUCTIONS

Dickie Wallace

For the first class meeting of every cultural anthropology course I have taught, I always begin with my "doing ethnography" demonstration. I find it to be a novel way to introduce both myself and the idea of ethnography to a classroom full of students who are accustomed to having a boring first class session. Although this "trick" may be more suitable for cultural anthropology courses, it could be used at the beginning of a four-field introductory-level course as well. Class size is no obstacle as it works equally well in small or large classes. It does not work well in upper-division classes, however, if students know you from a previous experience. And, given the nature of the "trick," at a certain age, the instructor will probably not be able to "get away with it."

For each first class meeting, I come to the classroom well ahead of time. I leave a pile of syllabi on the front desk and a few notes on the chalkboard. One note asks students to take a syllabus and to read through it.

Then I sit in the back of the classroom as if I am a student, usually with the college newspaper in front of me or some innocuous reading material. I always have a copy of the syllabus with me. Then I wait and watch as the students come in. I take "field notes" during this time, observing seating patterns, interactions, mode of dress, cognizance of my syllabus note on the chalkboard or whatever occurs at that time and place. I record the passing time, "map" the classroom, and generally record the type of things I would record in the "field."

After a minute or two into official class time, a few people start getting edgy as they begin wondering if the teacher is going to show up. At that point I get up and walk to the front of the classroom. I quickly make it plain that I am the instructor and immediately launch into an explanation about participant observation and qualitative social science research. (I like to watch students come to realize that I am already teaching in the first five minutes and that they should be taking notes instead of sleeping through the usual introductory spiel and syllabus overview.)

I explain that I was doing an "ethnographic experiment" as they were coming into the room. I tell them that this has been the one point in the semester when I am able to see what my classroom might look like before the instructor has entered the room; once the presence of the teacher is known, the classroom power dynamic changes and students are likely to act differently. As I explain this, I summarize some of my "field notes" and pull out interesting details. Usually I can find some pattern in student seating: for instance, students who do not know each other will not sit next to each other until the class is more than half full. Or female students are more likely to read the chalkboard instructions and take a syllabus than are male students. And if the males take the syllabus, they usually don't read it. Unacquainted students are likely to speak to each other only if they sit next to each other in the five minutes immediately preceding class. Sometimes I can use the field notes to put the class at ease, inject some humor, and tease the males who didn't take a syllabus.

I ask students to compare the participant observation method with a questionnaire or an interview: "If I had asked you what students do before the instructor arrives, would you have been able to give me those details? Would you have observed these different behaviors? Would direct questions have elicited as full a picture as an ethnographic method?"

We also question whether my participant observation was ethical. Was I not spying by "misrepresenting" myself as students walked in? Could my data now be used against anyone? I mention, teasingly, that the best students are the ones who read the syllabus right away (as I hand out syllabi to the students who did not heed my chalkboard instructions). I talk about the second time that I did this pre-class fieldwork and how, just as I was about to identify myself, two students, who happened to know each other vaguely, sat down on either side of me and proceeded to talk about how they hoped the "instructor in this class wouldn't suck." I explain that if I were truly doing ethnographic research, that for ethical reasons, I would have had to introduce myself at the beginning of the observation. Doing pre-class fieldwork allows me to discuss participant observation and ethics in an ethnographic context beyond the classroom situation, one that all field anthropologists find themselves in at one time or another. I conclude this subject, for the first session anyway, by talking about the difficulties of doing research when one is up front about research objectives.

Only later in the first session do I worry about attendance and rosters, the syllabus, and where to buy the textbooks. At the end of the class period, I hand out the first assignment, in which students must work together to write "mini-ethnographies."

I have often worn a baseball cap and a baggy T-shirt the first day of class in order to blend in with students, though to be honest, as I get further away from the "traditional student" age, I am not sure how much longer I will be able to use this "trick." Most recently, I have had two students insist that they found me very suspicious because I did not "look right" and I was "way too busy writing stuff" to even be a non-traditional student!

Hopefully, however, I will be able to continue doing some form of this "Pre-class Fieldwork" because it catches student attention and helps establish rapport quickly. And, best of all, it shows students that ethnographic methods are really part of our everyday world, making cultural anthropology immediately relevant.

FAMILIARIZING THE EXOTIC IN ETHNOGRAPHIC FILM

Sam Pack

The Problem

Ethnographic films are now a common component of many introductory anthropology courses. Since most students enrolled in these courses are not anthropology majors, but rather are taking the course because it fulfills general education requirements, this is the one and only chance most students have to see the cultural "other." Generations of students have become acquainted with people from all over the world through such classic ethnographic films as Robert Flaherty's *Nanook of the North* (1922), John Marshall's *The Hunters* (1958), Robert Gardner's *Dead Birds* (1963), and the Timothy Asch/ Napoleon Chagnon corpus on the Yanomamo. Although for some instructors, films provide a needed respite from lecturing duties, for the vast majority, films are shown in a serious attempt to convey anthropological knowledge in a way not possible through a written medium.

In a highly heralded project, Wilton Martinez conducted a reception study of ethnographic films among undergraduate anthropology students at the University of Southern California and found that instead of challenging stereotypic perceptions, these films confirmed and reinforced prejudices that audience members held toward foreign cultures (1990, 1992, 1994, 1995). Martinez's study has sounded a panic alarm in anthropological circles because of its subversive implications: "These 'symptomatic' readings indicate more than a pedagogical problem; they suggest that the use of film has powerfully catalyzed the crisis of representation in the classroom" (1992:132). His conclusions suggest that anthropology instructors may be unintentionally perpetuating the devaluing of other cultures by screening ethnographic films to their students.

Martinez calls the interpretive gap between the intentions of the film makers and student responses "aberrant readings" (1992:132). However, a key weakness of Martinez's study is that he does not address where these so-called "aberrant readings" come from, presents no explanations for their causes, and offers no suggestions for solving the problem.

Why do ethnographic film representations reinforce negative stereotypes? Once we begin to understand the answer to this question, we might be able to help solve the problem. I contend that negative stereotypes of the "primitive" are inherited by and perpetuated through popular media representations. After a lifetime of exposure to television programs, feature films, music videos, video games, and the like, how can consumers of the electronic age view the "exotic other" in any way other than negatively? Based on the breadth and depth of this inculcation, there is nothing "aberrant" about these readings at all. They are, in fact, perfectly normal readings.

So it should not be surprising that students watch ethnographic films from an inherently ethnocentric perspective. One of the students I interviewed in my own reception study (Pack 1997) eloquently states:

> We're going to watch the things and look out for the important things to us. That's the most fundamental problem about learning things when it comes to different cultures. We, through media, through television, through advertising, through personal experience, through what we learn from our parents, we grow up our entire lives looking at -- and I'll be real general -- the world in a very certain way, other people in a very certain way. And to suddenly alter things that have been ingrained in our brains for our whole lives is exceptionally difficult. (Male senior, age 25.)

What a picture means to the viewer is strongly dependent on his or her past experience and knowledge. The reading of an image, like the reception of any other text, is dependent on a prior knowledge of possibilities. As anthropologist and film maker, Allison Jablonko points out, "people only 'see' what they already have in mind" (1988:175). In this interpretive setting, viewers construct their own meaning of images based on previously acquired knowledge.

Invariably, the viewer will interpret a film according to existing stereotypes from his or her own culture. Despite a film maker's best intentions, ingrained viewing habits encourage viewers to attribute to footage whatever stereotypic explanations they may believe to be accurate (Biella 1995:243). Research indicates that when the intended message conflicts with viewers' world view, the viewers' attributions will likely dominate (Ruby 1994:195). In the contested space between the power of the film maker and the power of the viewer, the latter will always win.

Different kinds of visual texts require different strategies of interpretation. Unfortunately, these are lacking for the majority of the viewing population. Most of our viewing socialization has resulted in a rather narrow or restricted set of viewing instructions and habits that have produced a meager repertoire of interpretive skills (Chalfen 1988:179). It is my contention that viewers of ethnographic film rely on viewing habits and interpretive strategies more appropriate to popular modes of representation. Simply stated, most viewers attribute to these films what they already know, or think they know, regardless of what the producer intended (Ruby 1994:195).

Indeed, both negative and positive stereotypes of the "primitive" are shaped by mass mediated images that influence how viewers interpret ethnographic films. But the reverse is also true: ethnographic, or that which purports to be ethnographic, representations reinforce popular ones. Thus, the process is circular rather than linear as the "reel" and the "real" are mutually perpetuating. To the undiscerning eye, the antics of the "Uta Bagee" (Professor Krippendorf's penis sheath-clad alter ego in *Krippendorf's Tribe)* is given credibility because of his similarity to a Yanomamo headman on "The Discovery Channel" or to Tim Asch and Napoleon Chagnon's portrayal of another Yanomamo headman in *The Ax Fight*. All of these images meld together into a homogenous, nameless, indistinguishable mass called "the primitive."

Solving the Problem: Pedagogical Pointers

Devising ways to combat ethnocentrism in film spectatorship in introductory level anthropology courses is certainly a formidable challenge. Ruby wonders how many instructors even recognize the need to deal with students' visual naivete: "In order to teach anthropology with film, teachers have to first instruct students on how to critically examine what they see" (1995:28).

The majority of introductory anthropology courses survey a wide variety of cultures around the world. This form of "ethnic snacking" is hazardous to the goals of cultural understanding. One week it is the Dani, next the Yanomamo, followed by the Kayapo, and so on. Ethnographic film maker John Marshall asserts that "we shouldn't be surprised to hear that after a quick trip on the ethnographic Love Boat most students remain ethnocentric, oblivious and self satisfied" (1993:129). Even the most serious student has trouble remembering all of the exotic names, much less anything substantive about the culture of the given week.

As a pedagogical model to remedy some of these deficiencies, I offer my own experiences in teaching cultural anthropology through film. The introductory course I teach operates from an underlying premise that most students bring certain preconceived notions of "primitive" peoples that have been shaped by media representations of alien cultures. I designed the course to explore this relationship between ethnographic and popular constructions of the "exotic other" with the ultimate goal of utilizing the former to help dispel the latter. Therefore, I show *Krippendorf's Tribe*, a feature film starring Richard Dreyfus as anthropologist James Krippendorf in conjunction with *A Man Called "Bee,"* an ethnographic film about anthropologist Napoleon Chagnon, to compare and contrast the depiction of anthropology and its practitioners. In a similar capacity, we, as a class, juxtapose the African villagers in *The Hunters* with their fictional counterpart in *Ace Ventura 2*. This can be accomplished with any feature film that depicts "exotic" people in tandem with an ethnographic film about a comparable "looking" culture.

The class assignments further compel students into confronting their own ethnocentrisms. For their final papers, students select a feature film that describes some component of their own culture and relate its treatment by an ethnographic film. Paper topics include investigating kinship in *The Brothers McMullen* and *Jaguar*, culture change in *Hoosiers* and *Trobriand Cricket*, warfare in *Braveheart* and *Dead Birds*, and social control in *Good Fellas* and *The Ax Fight*. Feature films provide a wonderful spring board for class discussion and paper writing precisely because students feel a sense of competence and expertise when asked to comment on mass mediated forms of information that are so familiar to their media-saturated visual environment (Chalfen and Pack 1998:104).

In order for this assignment to be successful, the instructor must possess some degree of familiarity with a variety of ethnographic films to make adequate suggestions. Either in the absence of such knowledge or as a supplement to limited knowledge, I highly recommend *Films for Anthropological Teaching* (Heider and Hermer 1995). The book organizes anthropologically relevant films and videos alphabetically as well as by topic and geographical area. It also provides brief summaries of each entry and includes the necessary distribution information in the event that the college/university where the instructor teaches does not own a copy of the desired film or video.

Another assignment that I have found to work extremely well is asking students to analyze one of their home movies as if it were an ethnographic film about a culture different from their own. In a style similar to Horace Miner's Nacirema work, one of my students described a video of her wedding from a surprisingly detached perspective while another commented in detail about all of the exotic rituals involved in footage of a friend's 21st birthday party. By turning the tables, students were able to see and feel what it is like to be on the other side of the anthropological gaze. In the process, the us/them dichotomy begins to blur. Thus, one path to familiarizing the exotic – which is the expressed goal of all ethnographic films – is by first exoticizing the familiar.

References Cited

Biella, Peter
   1995   Academic Hypermedia: A Reply and Update. In *Visual Anthropology* 7(3):240-248.

Chalfen, Richard
   1988   Navajo Filmmaking Revisited: Problematic Interactions. In *Native North American Interaction Patterns*, Regna Darnell and Michael K. Foster, eds. Quebec: Canadian Museum of Civilization, Pp. 168-185.

Chalfen, Richard and Sam Pack
   1998 Why Krippendorf's Tribe is Good for Teaching Anthropology. In *Visual Anthropology Review* 14(1): 103-105.

Heider, Karl and Carol Hermer
   1995 *Films for Anthropological Teaching*, 8th ed. Arlington VA: American Anthropological Association.

Jablonko, Allison
   1988   New Guinea in Italy: An Analysis of the Making of an Italian Television Series from Research Footage of the Maring People of Papua New Guinea. In *Anthropological Filmmaking: Anthropological Perspectives on the Production of Film and Video for*

General Public Audiences, Jack Rollwagen, ed. Chur Switzerland: Harwood Academic Press, Pp. 169-196.

Marshall, John
1993   Filming and Learning. In *The Cinema of John Marshall*, Jay Ruby, ed. Chur Switzerland: Harwood Academic Press, Pp. 1-133.

Martinez, Wilton
1990   The Ethnographic Film Spectator and the Crisis of Representation in Visual Anthropology. MA Thesis, University of Southern California.

Martinez, Wilton
1992   Who Constructs Anthropological Knowledge? Toward a Theory of Ethnographic Film Spectatorship. In *Film as Ethnography*, Peter Crawford and D. Turton, eds. Manchester: University of Manchester Press, Pp. 130-161.

Martinez, Wilton
1994   Deconstructing the 'Viewer': From Ethnography of the Visual to Critique of the Occult. In *The Construction of the Viewer*, Peter Crawford and Sigurjon B. Hafsteinsson, eds. Aarhus: Intervention Press, Pp. 69-100.

Martinez, Wilton
1995   The Challenges of a Pioneer: Tim Asch, Otherness, and Film, Reception. In *Visual Anthropology Review* 11(1): 53-82.

Pack, Sam
1997   Beauty and the Beast: Imagining the Primitive in Ethnographic Film and Indigenous Media. Temple University. Unpublished paper.

Ruby, Jay
1994   The Viewer Viewed: The Reception of Ethnographic Films. In *The Construction of the Viewer*, Peter Crawford and Sigurjon B. Hafsteinsson, eds. Aarhus: Intervention Press, Pp. 193-206.

Ruby, Jay
1995 Out of Sinc: The Cinema of Tim Asch. In *Visual Anthropology Review* 11(1): 19-35.

DOING ETHNOGRAPHIC RESEARCH IN THE CLASSROOM: A SIMPLE EXERCISE FOR ENGAGING INTRODUCTORY STUDENTS

Grace Keyes

I use the following exercise early in the term in introductory Cultural Anthropology, a survey course taught to non-majors. It has a two-fold purpose that is generally achieved quite successfully: it is meant to be an ice-breaker and it illustrates a number of points and generalizations regarding anthropological research.

The exercise allows students to meet each other and get used to the idea that in this particular class, they are expected to be active participants. It also helps us all learn each other's names. The results of the exercise are used to illustrate various research activities such as interview experiences, collecting data, and interpreting data. In addition, students come to appreciate culturally patterned behavior and the power of culture. Thus the exercise serves as a good introduction into cultural anthropology. While I use the exercise early in the term, during the second or third class session, it could be adapted to any other appropriate time frame. Since its topic is field methods, it can be used in conjunction with any introductory text, as most of them have a chapter or section devoted to research methods, and often it is covered very early.

Setting Up The Scenario

The scenario can be set up in only a few minutes by telling students that they will pretend to be foreign or "alien" anthropologists visiting or studying the United States with a major interest in the eating habits of Americans. Foreigners quickly notice that the hot dog (or potato salad) seems to be a very common American food. It is the task of the student, as an anthropologist, to "interview a native informant" and ask three very simple questions:

(1) What is your name?
(2) Are you a native of the state?
(3) Do you eat hot dogs for breakfast?

The first two questions are meant to just get the conversation going and for students to actually meet or get acquainted with one of their classmates. The third question is the one for which the "anthropologist" is trying to get data. Students are paired up, preferably with someone they do not know, and each then takes his or her turn being the anthropologist and being the informant. In the event of an odd number of students in the class, the instructor can pair up with the remaining student. If students want clarification on what is meant by "hot dogs," you might suggest that they are the hot dogs eaten at ball parks, a hot dog in a bun with mustard or relish. If no one asks for clarification, students can assume what they will and later discuss such assumptions. I find that foods like hot dogs or potato salad work very well because not many Americans think of these as breakfast foods and so students find it amusing. (Using pizza would not work nearly as well as many students do think pizza is acceptable breakfast food.)

Only a few minutes are needed for each student to play both roles; I generally allow about 5-7 minutes, which is usually plenty of time for them to ask and answer the questions with a bit of spare time to chat. Once they are done, I ask one student to begin describing his or her findings so the whole class can hear: the name of the informant, whether the informant is a native of the state or not, and whether the informant eats hot dogs for breakfast. This will take a while, depending on class size, but it is important to have full participation. Students seem to find it easier to say something about someone else than about themselves, so "reporting" their findings goes rather smoothly. This portion is also beneficial for learning names. As each student reports, it often is the case that they have collected more information than required, such as "Mary is not from California, but from Texas;" or "Mary doesn't eat hot dogs for breakfast but one time she cut one up and put it into her scrambled eggs." I generally encourage these extra bits of information because they are useful for the next part of the exercise.

Data, Interpretation, and Implications

As each student reports, keep track of the information on the chalkboard or on an overhead transparency in a simple table format. You don't have to write the names of each student, but keep track of answers for questions 2 and 3 since these can be easily tabulated.

	Yes	No
Q. 2: Are you a native of the state?		
Q. 3: Do you eat hot dogs for breakfast?		

Once the data are collected as above, students are asked to discuss:

(1) the interview process itself;

(2) the interpretation of the data;

(3) some possible implications.

The interview process is generally enjoyable and leads to small insights about doing fieldwork. For instance, students find that a single research question can lead to all sorts of other information that perhaps they had not thought about. Some of this extra information may lead to further and possibly more interesting questions. This is, of course, what happens in real ethnographic interviewing.

General patterns are easy to see and thus a quick generalization is that Americans do not typically eat hot dogs for breakfast. Another observation may be that there are some Americans who do eat hot dogs for breakfast. Other generalizations may have to do with how many students are native to the state and how many were born in other states, but these can be put aside as not really relevant to our research interest on eating behavior of Americans. As students make generalizations, the instructor has the opportunity to clarify methodological issues, such as when a generalization or conclusion is or is not valid. Can such a generalization or conclusion be drawn from the given evidence? What other variables would be needed?

Getting at some **implications** and **meanings** behind the results is important because it reveals to students a number of things about culture and human behavior. For instance, one possible implication is that Americans tend to be conformist when it comes to eating patterns. Furthermore, it shows how foods are culturally defined in terms of when they are to be eaten and how. Hot dogs are certainly not seen as appropriate breakfast food even though it can be pointed out that the basic ingredients are rather similar to sausage, which **is** an acceptable breakfast food. And the ingredients that make the hot dog bun are certainly similar to that of breakfast "biscuits" or other acceptable breakfast breads. How these associations and meanings come about can lead to the articulation of taken-for-granted beliefs or values. And clearly, it reveals to students the importance and power of cultural rules (norms). The exercise clearly illustrates to students that much behavior is predictable once aspects of the culture are explored and understood.

Conclusions

Generally, the discussion that follows this simple exercise provides an opportunity to raise a number of further questions and observations about doing research as well as about interpreting and analyzing cultural data.

MOIETY EXOGAMY, SIBLING EXCHANGE, AND CROSS-COUSIN MARRIAGE

Ernest L. Schusky

The Problem

Long ago, anthropologists recorded exotic rules of behavior that made little sense to them or to their readers. For example, they found that many people around the world had norms saying a man should marry his mother's brother's daughter or his father's sister's daughter, but never his other cousins. From the female perspective, the same rule would find a woman marrying her father's sister's son or her mother's brother's son. Other people said a man should exchange his sister for a wife. (This is really sibling exchange because a brother-sister pair exchange with another brother-sister pair to form two married couples.) Still others divided themselves into two and only two groups, called moieties and say people must marry someone from the opposite moiety (moiety exogamy).

Anthropologists gave complicated reasons to explain these norms that made little sense while they came to agree that determining how rules of behavior originated was akin to discovering how species originated. Taking these descriptions of exotic rules into the classroom and trying to explain to naive students why they exist is a formidable task. This in-class exercise makes students not only aware of three exotic behaviors -- moiety exogamy, sibling exchange, and cross-cousin marriage -- but suggests that the rules will occur together in societies under certain circumstances. Just telling a class that this is so does not work, but once they have completed the exercise, they see what happens in certain societies and why it is almost inevitable that the three exotic behaviors will occur together. It also provides feedback into the nature of the rules and demonstrates the interrelationships among social rules.

The Exercise

The exercise has worked with as few as 15 and as many as 60 students. It is suitable for any introductory-level course or in an advanced course on social organization. The only equipment needed is as many red and white poker chips as there are students in the class and a black magic marker. Draw a triangle or a circle randomly on each chip. Two envelopes are needed to hold the chips.

To begin the exercise, the instructor should tell the class that to understand three exotic norms of marriage, namely moiety exogamy, sibling exchange, and cross-cousin marriage, that they should pretend they are stranded on a desert island with no contact with other people. Point out that resources are never distributed evenly even on an island. On this particular island, there is a spring located at each end along with nearby fishing lagoons. You might map such an island on the chalkboard. Suggest that the group will obviously want to settle in two villages around the resources. Then tell them that the front half of the classroom will settle the east end of the island and the back half will settle the west end. (The two groups do not have to be equal in number.) Suggest that since communities are often represented by symbols, and often colors, that in this case, red is the symbol of the east village and white is the symbol for the west village. When you know how many students will "live" in the Red Village, put that number of red chips (drawn with male and female symbols) in the Red Village envelope; do the same with the white chips in the White Village envelope. If your class space allows, move the red/east people to one side of the room and the white/west people to the other side of the room.

Then point out that people who live in close contact with each other become **like** brothers and sisters to each other. So, people in the east village are like siblings to each other and people in the west village are like siblings to each other. The first step is for students to have actual brothers and sisters so have either your male students choose one or two female students to be their **actual** sisters or have your female students choose one or two male students to be their **actual** brothers. Either way, ask them to sit next to their chosen siblings. You will probably have to prompt students to actually move.

While students are getting used to their new siblings, suggest that women on this island can net fish in the lagoons and tend edible plants around the springs. Men, by contrast, fish the open ocean. Make sure that it sinks in that the resources worked by women are fixed in place, while men's canoes can and do go anywhere and no one can own the ocean. Give them a few minutes to absorb this information and continue adding detail to the chalkboard map, marking the two villages with red and white symbols, and marking the springs, lagoons, and open sea.

Next suggest to students what happens when people begin to look for spouses. Since people in the east (red) village are like brothers and sisters to each other, they must find spouses in the white (west) village and vice versa; this is termed **moiety exogamy**. Since men can fish the ocean from any place while women tend gardens fixed in place, it makes sense that men go to live with their wives, a custom called **matrilocal residence.** Since daughters remain with their mothers, the resources will be inherited by females (garden plots, digging sticks). By contrast, males cannot inherit the ocean. They might inherit a canoe, but canoes don't last more than a few years. Thus, this society will be **matrilineal** as well as matrilocal. Instruct the males in the class to go to the opposite village to find a spouse. The males will resist and be embarrassed, but you must insist that the males get up and go to the other side of the room and sit with a woman (his wife). The female students are pretty good at getting the males to cooperate. Males should be able to remember which females are their sisters and which are their wives; at the same time females should be able to remember which males are their brothers and which are their husbands.

All of the newly married couples are going to have babies. You can suggest that since you don't have nine months to wait, they will draw a poker chip to see if they have a son or a daughter. (Married couples in the Red Village draw from the envelope with the red poker chips; married couples in the White Village draw from the envelope with the white chips.) Since there is one chip per person, in most cases couples can pick two chips each. If there are more females than males in the class, explain **polygyny** and match up the extra women; if there are more males than females, explain **polyandry** and match up the extra males. Unless your class is evenly divided into males and females, you will have to use one or the other principle.

Take the time to point out that the Red Village is now half red (the non moving women) and half white (their husbands) but everyone still thinks of it as the Red Village. The same is true of the White Village.

Twenty years have now passed, and the children of the original couples are looking for spouses. Tell your students, who are the parents, to help their children find spouses, just as parents do everywhere, by going to the opposite village and finding a wife or husband (represented by poker chips) for their sons or daughters (also poker chips). Instructors will have to push students to do this. Have students keep their daughters at home (poker chips with circles on them) and leave their sons (poker chips with triangles) in the other village. Have them note the distribution of poker chips: red females will all be in the Red Village with white husbands and white females will all be in the White Village with red husbands. (What will often happen is that male students will go to the women they had chosen as sisters -- or were chosen as brothers.) Instructors should point out that just as students practiced sister/brother exchange (or **sibling exchange**), their children are now exchanging siblings. But from the parent's perspective, the children are **cross-cousins** to each other and from their perspective, people are practicing cross-cousin marriage. From the perspective of the spouses, it looks like sibling exchange. Allow students to soak up what has happened. Make sure they understand that sibling exchange and cross-cousin marriage are parts of the same phenomenon and that both are a reflection of exogamous moieties.

Some student is certain to ask about the person who does not have any different-sex siblings. This is an ideal time to consider **parallel cousins**. You might answer the query using the format of the hypothetical island and the two villages. Suggest that there is another kind of structural cousin, the parallel cousin who is the mother's sister's children and the father's brother's children. Relative to this island situation, all the red women are essentially sisters to each other because they identify with the Red Village; all the men in the Red Village consider themselves to be brothers. When they had children, all the red daughters remained at home and were equivalents in people's thinking; they were all sisters and all related to each other as mother's sister's daughters. The sons who were sent to the other village were equivalent brothers and were related to each other as father's brother's sons. If you are a "red" (of either sex), your father's brother's children are all red. So too are your mother's sister's children. But your father's sister's children and your mother's brother's children are all whites. So your kinship term for cross-cousin is something like "potential spouse" (and often the same term as spouse) while your kinship term for parallel cousin is the same as you use for "brother" or sister." The same situation applies to "whites."

Another student might ask what would happen if environmental factors led to major resources being in the hands of males. Suppose a society herded cattle. Males must protect the cows from being raided so brothers stay together and own herds. Their sons will inherit the

170

herds from them. Women will process the milk and farm small plots, which they can do after they marry and move to their husbands' households (patrilocal residence). Now the Red Village will be composed of red men and their white wives, with children being born into the red descent group. The White Village will be composed of white men and their red wives, with children being born into the white descent group. People find spouses in the opposite group (moiety exogamy), and siblings will exchange spouses, and in the next generation, the pattern will appear to be cross-cousin marriage.

Epilogue

If there is time at the end of the class session, encourage students to think about the distribution of reds and whites and cross and parallel cousins. If they have been introduced to kinship diagraming, have them diagram what has happened in the exercise. Be prepared to review why cross cousins are always different from parallel cousins. And most of all, spell out how the exotic norms probably originated as an adaptation to resource strategies while the two groups maintained close ties through marriage. If time permits, this is a good place to explain how kinship serves as the basis for politics and economics in all small, personalized, communities.

SHORT WRITING ASSIGNMENTS IN LARGE CLASSES

David F. Lancy

Assigning writing in anthropology classes is an article of faith, but it is daunting to contemplate grading 50 or more essays two or more times a semester. One approach that has been successful (Lancy, Rhees, and Kinkead 1994) is to organize students into teams of four to five students each, so only 10-15 essays have to be evaluated instead of 50-100. Here, I describe two mini writing assignments that have been successful.

Design Parameters

The design parameters for a writing assignment in a medium to large class includes the incorporation of careful library research, adherence to a model, and revision to improve the writing and the grade. But, the final product should be no more than 2 to 2 ½ pages. I developed this technique for mini writing assignments as part of my assignment to teach Civilization where I focus primarily on Egypt and Egyptology. The technique could work equally well in introductory classes or advanced classes using other subjects and examples.

In the Civilization class, I alternate between (1) process, i.e., the development of Egyptology from the early "raiders" days to modern scientific archaeology, and (2) the history of Egypt. The mini writing assignments grew out of these two related foci.

(1) For this assignment, students are given a list of historical figures from the field of Egyptology (Herodotus to Belzoni to Reisner) and told to research them, including, if available, finding samples of their writing. They then write two or three simulated letters/telegrams from their assigned character to others such as colleagues or family members. These are evaluated by me on historical accuracy, writing style, and flare. One student "aged" his letters.

(2) Later in the term, students are given a second list of Egyptian historical figures (Narmer to Hadrian) to research. They then prepare a commemorative stele for their figure, complete with the name in hieroglyphics.

Preparation

Preparing these assignments took a good bit of time. To avoid chaos, I have gathered together a critical source library, including Breasted's translations of a broad sampling of stelae, anthologies of writing by visitors to Egypt in the 17th and 18th centuries, and profiles from the journal KMT. Students report searching through 4 to 8 sources and ultimately I set up a special computer station with a hieroglyphic font and "stele paper." But, the payoffs are worth it. Students are very enthusiastic about the assignment: if the research doesn't excitement them, the simulation does. They particularly enjoy playing with the bombastic language found on the typical stele. Student papers have been very good and I do not have to wrestle with a host of grammatical and style problems because the writing is relatively formulaic. Most importantly, students experience a thorough research essay experience while the final products, the one and two page papers I grade, represent only the essence of their work, minus the usual jargon and padding.

Putting the best examples of letters and stelae on a webpage for the course is a boon to student researchers and they work to forestall queries from students who wonder why they got a low grade.

Reference Cited

Lancy, D.F., A. Rhees, and J. Kinkead
    1994. A sense of community: Collaboration in a large Anthropology class. *College Teaching* 42(3): 102-106.

INTERVIEWING TRICKS FOR STUDENT ETHNOGRAPHERS

David W. McCurdy

The Problem

I first sent undergraduates out to do ethnographic research in 1968. I asked them to identify subgroups or settings for action at Macalester College where I taught, and through observation and interviews, to describe the culture that organized them. As preparation, I had students read about interviewing and look at some ethnographies. There was little else they could do since systematic material on ethnographic field methods was scarce at the time.

As they undertook their research, students began to run into problems. Although they tried hard, they often complained about lack of direction. They didn't really know what to ask or look for. Field notes seemed scattered and unorganized. What should they ask next? How could they make sense of their field notes? Classroom advice didn't seem to help much, and in the end, I didn't feel the experience taught students enough about culture and its power to organize people's behavior and perceptions.

It was easy to believe that undergraduate students could not succeed in the field because they lacked anthropological training that only graduate students and faculty would have. Lack of time was also a problem. Their fieldwork had to be short-term, unlike the "total immersion so you can't help but learn something about a culture" ideology governing doctoral research during the 1960s. It was also more difficult to identify cultural groups to study within complex U.S. society where almost everyone speaks English.

The Solution

What was needed was a method of ethnographic research that would provide structure and direction for inexperienced field workers. The method should define what culture and ethnography are and identify the culturally organized groups or culturally defined situations that students could study. It should suggest questions that student ethnographers could ask and define ways for students to transcribe and analyze field notes. Finally, it should enable students to draw conclusions about the cultures they studied without having to rely on an extensive theoretical knowledge.

Such a method was first suggested by James Spradley, who joined the Macalester faculty in 1969. He had learned and used an approach called "ethnoscience" to study tramps in Seattle and he and I set about adapting it to guide undergraduate field research for our students at Macalester. Ethnoscience uses a cognitive definition of culture and argues that ethnographers can acquire the cultural knowledge of a group by discovering the words and their meaning its members use when they talk with each other. It stresses the idea that researchers are students, their informants, teachers, and that ethnographers seek to understand the world through the eyes of their informants. Interviewing is the focus of ethnoscience but we quickly learned to include some field observation as part of the research, especially after a study had progressed for a few weeks. (As a side note, most of you know that ethnoscience had a short life in anthropology and had largely disappeared by the late 1970s. Despite that fact and the limitations of the approach, I continue to argue that it represents an ideal framework for undergraduate research.)

Interviewing Tricks

The purpose of this article is not to lay out the whole student research process as we came to conceive of it. (Descriptions of the approach can be found in *The Cultural Experience* by Spradley and McCurdy and in Spradley's *The Ethnographic Interview* and *Participant Observation.*) Instead, several "tricks" have emerged over the years that seem useful to student interviewers no matter what approach they take. Let me state them here as a set of rules, although they might better be conceived of as guides or possibilities.

(1) Choose clearly structured, identifiable sub groups as the object of ethnographic study. (This rule assumes that the style of student research will be an open ended attempt to discover the culture of an organized group, not to answer specific research problems.) In today's postmodern world, interaction often occurs in less well defined situations where shared cultural understandings are constantly being negotiated. Although such situations can be studied, they make poor targets for undergraduate research because they lack shared culturally defined structure. For example, networks are difficult to study because they aren't usually culture-sharing groups. Friendship groups are difficult to investigate because they lack clear structure and purpose. On the other hand, occupational organizations, including "micro cultures" within larger companies, often make ideal research settings because they are clearly structured. So do recreational groups, fraternal organizations, and permanent political organizations and movements. Currently, my students are studying the inside cultural knowledge of TV anchors, fraternity members, physical rehabilitation workers, Civil War reenactors, hair stylists, parole officers, and environmental research team members among others. But there are hundreds more microcultures available to students on any campus.

(2) Don't lead informants by asking questions based on your preconceived notions. This rule is founded on the idea that ethnographers initially seek to elicit an **informant's** cultural knowledge, not impose their own ideas or views on the field data. Leading, or asking leading questions (sometimes I call these "leaders"), means asking questions based on your own interests or preconceived ideas, not your informant's responses. For example, you might start an interview with the member of a motorcycle club by asking whether most members are males or working class. This signals to your informant that *you* think riders have these backgrounds. If you lead this way you may not learn how how the motorcyclists identify themselves. Or you could ask a mortician if it is disgusting to embalm bodies, again signaling your own interests and feelings. In daily conversation it is natural to lead people with questions. For ethnographic interviews, try to avoid leaders.

(3) Ask informants to describe actions and things, not give feelings, overviews, opinions, evaluations, or meanings. A goal of ethnography is to learn enough about informant's cultures to actually be that person, to act in and interpret the world using the informant's culture. For example, if you were to interview stock brokers, could you discover the cultural rules they use as they arrive at work, pick up and evaluate their mail, and go to the appropriate office or cubical. Would you know where the "bull pen" is or what a "waffle" means? Could you talk about "rookies," "calls," "puts" and "dog and pony shows?" If you ask brokers what the business is "like" during an initial interview, they will give you a general characterization and may express what they think is most important about the business. This is fine information, but it is difficult to evaluate if you don't know the basic culture ruling day-to-day action and interpretation. So ask instead things such as "Could you describe what you do from the time you get to work until you leave?" or "Imagine I were blind and you were leading me around your office. What would I see?" "Describe" questions yield a bonus. They provide everyday context, and informants remember more and feel more comfortable about describing what they know and do every day (or when your informant's culture comes into play if it is not a daily scene.)

(4) Get lists of actions, things, times, people, feelings, or anything else that comes up in interviewing. Asking for lists helps produce exhaustive inventories of detailed information. Lists also help informants to remember what they know, since lists consist of categories that are associated with each other and association helps memory. If a used car salesperson you are interviewing says "We have lots of ways to classify ups," ask "What ways are there?" (Don't ask what "ups" are yet.) This should yield a list of "ways." If the sales person says, "We offer ups a long list of options," ask "What kinds of options do you offer?" Lists can be general, such as "dormitories at the college," or detailed, such as "things we don't tell Bob." (The latter list comes from a study of a ecological research crew.) Once you have a list, you can ask informants to describe particular items on the list or ask them to compare items, which will yield better detail as noted next.

(5) Get at meaning by comparing closely related things that contrast with each other. Most of us immediately ask what something is when we hear a word we don't understand. Don't. Wait until you have a list of things the word fits in before you find out what it means. For example, at Macalester College you might hear an informant say, "then I go over to Dupre." If you ask what Dupre is, the student will tell say it is a dormitory. This gives Dupre some meaning but you will learn much more if you contrast Dupre with Wallace, Kirk, New Dorm, and other dormitories. Then you will find out that it has narrow halls, very small singles, long thin windows that may not open, no sinks in the rooms, elevators, heating problems in winter, and cement block walls, all things that are important to students who must decide where they want to live. In short, if you want to find out what something means in detail, contrast it with closely related things.

(6) Collect stories that illustrate cultural categories and rules. Often the best stories are about mistakes. Most of us learn at least some cultural categories and rules by hearing

176

gossip or by making mistakes. If you make a mistake, you have probably broken a culture rule so mistakes reveal rules. For example, a new student said that when she arrived at Macalester College as a first year student and was eating in the dining hall, she said "This is really good food!" She went on to say, "There were three sophomores at the table with us and one of them said, 'you can't be serious,' and actually seemed annoyed. That was the last time I ever said the food was good." This student continued that she later learned to say, "the food is not all that bad today," or "well I see they aren't trying to poison us today," when she wanted to praise the food. Stories such as this also make useful illustrations when students ethnographers sit down to write their papers.

(7) Finally, it is helpful to understand culture as an adaptive response. People everywhere construct their culture, but I argue that they do so largely on the basis of what is important to them. Importance may stem from natural or social challenges or even requirements imposed by one's own values. For example, members of a local touring motorcycle association evaluate different brands of motorcycles on the basis of comfort, reliability, looks, power, ease of handling, and a host of other concerns that emanate from riding long distances in the open and from maintaining a respectable position in their club. Some Emergency Medical Technicians have three languages for the same set of conditions: one for responding to "calls," one for describing injuries over the radio to emergency room doctors, and one to use among themselves. Each style fits a different challenge or need. The advantage of this kind of analysis is that students can often discover functional causes for cultural categories without having a background in anthropological theory. "Problem analysis" provides a useful analytical structure that can make a paper into a significant contribution.

Conclusions

The rules stated above should not be thought of as rigid. Every student is different as is every informant and research situation. I use as clear a set of research rules and steps as possible when I send students out to do research. Clear expectations and instructions seem to answer some of the problems noted at the beginning of this article, but research also requires flexibility, so be ready to alter the rules to fit research conditions. Most of the points listed above can apply in any exploratory research situation.

Finally, I feel most of my students produce respectable ethnographic work these days. Most are more aware of the words people use when they talk. Most claim they find themselves asking "what are the rules for what is going on here" when they meet new situations. Most are able to set up field studies by themselves when they go on study abroad programs. Most claim anthropology and ethnography have been useful in their jobs once they have graduated. Most have gained a deeper understanding of what culture is from their mini field projects just as I learned about the concept from more intensive "sink or swim" fieldwork in India as a graduate student.

References Cited

Spradley, James P.
1979 *The Ethnographic Interview*. New York: Holt, Rinehart, and Winston.

1980 *Participant Observation*. New York: Holt, Rinehart, and Winston.

Spradley, James P., and David W. McCurdy
1972 *The Cultural Experience: Ethnography in Complex Society*. Chicago: SRA; Reissued in 1988 by Waveland Press, Prospect Heights, IL.

"SENSORY ANTHROPOLOGY:"
A SENSE-IBLE APPROACH TO TEACHING ANTHROPOLOGY

Ann Christine Frankowski

The whiff of the smoking brazier, the pious call to prayer at daybreak, the bite of hot buttered bread, the sight of a starving mother and her children asleep on the street corner, the touch of the beggar -- all of these phrases evoke images that rely on human senses. Cultural anthropologists do field work or ethnography and gather an extensive amount of data through observation (sense of sight) and interviewing (sense of hearing). Collecting responses and recording interactions provide the qualitative data that leads to theory. Ethnography is, however, more than mere data collection and analysis. Anthropologists do fieldwork because they enjoy interacting with villagers, sharing a church supper, laughing with colleagues, smelling damp earth, crying over a beer, seeing third graders smile; i.e., we use our senses when we are in out in the field.

"Sensory anthropology" focuses on the elements in the research process that are provoked by the senses. Even if the anthropologist ignores this aspect in the presentation of data, the senses -- sight, sound, smell, taste, and touch -- are still experienced. These sensory events are sources of data and add to ethnographic interpretation. Anthropologists can choose to include sensory data through description, demonstrate their effect on the research process, or even focus specifically on sensory stimuli. In teaching, sensory anthropology provides a way to help students learn concepts, and sensory experiences in the classroom, followed by appropriate discussion, reinforce this knowledge.

Sensory anthropology can be used in introductory cultural anthropology courses, or in more advanced cultural courses that are either topical or area. Ethnographic methods courses profit by a discussion of the senses in regard to the place of the researcher in the host/guest, insider/outsider, and backstage/frontstage dichotomies. Students studying fieldwork techniques should understand the use of the senses to gather various kinds of data. The role sensory anthropology plays in a course depends on class size as well as the course content; a class of 250 students would not be able to do the hands-on sensory exercises that a class of 25 could do. Some sensory projects can even result in term-long research-driven papers.

The Senses

The easiest way to demonstrate how sensory anthropology is applied to classroom teaching is by focusing on the senses themselves. We all have preferences in teaching relative to using our senses. Some of us take the whole body approach to teaching, using space, body language, and voice inflection to develop an academic persona in order to give a feel of the lesson, lecture, or exercise. Others are gourmands, tasting more than they eat. There are those who smell everything from the air to whatever is touched or consumed. And some are visual learners where seeing is believing. In using sensory examples in the classroom, I suggest starting with the most appealing sense and the one that is the most adaptable to teaching a particular course content. What follows are some examples of teaching sensory anthropology that I have developed over a number of years.

Taste. Everybody likes to eat. Students always seem to be hungry no matter what the time. In my introductory cultural anthropology courses, I assign "cultural snack" day. Every student must bring enough of a single "snack" for every classmate to have a "taste," not a portion. I do not give examples of what to bring nor will I define "snack;" students have been in class long enough to know what "culture" is all about. Before we partake of the snacks, students tell the class what they brought and why. Although some classes may be as large as 50 students, only twice have two students brought the same thing.

On "snack day," I ask the class to think about what a snack is and how it differs from a meal. Students eventually define snack as a food eaten to carry them over to mealtimes. I suggest that this implies a life with relative economic comfort and this leads to discussions of subsistence patterns, concepts of community, food gathering, sharing, stratification, and surplus.

In smaller classes where the focus is specifically on ethnicity or marriage and family, ethnic dinners or breakfasts are held with students bringing in ethnic food. At this time, the class discusses the role food plays in culture, the rules of eating and etiquette, and associated symbolism. The meal becomes a pleasant reminder that food is not just for eating but is tied to ethnohistory, gender, occupation, and socialization. Students report on how food and their specific dish reflect what has recently been covered in class.

Sometimes students need to be told that taste is culturally relative. The T-shirt slogan "Chocolate...not just for breakfast anymore," is meaningless in a society where chocolate is neither consumed nor valued. Americans eat their chocolate processed with sugar and milk, Mexicans mix it with chili and chicken, and pre-Columbian Aztecs drank it unsweetened. Popular foods like chocolate provide interesting examples of acculturation in historic contexts, and students are often surprised to discover how baking, i.e., unprocessed, cocoa actually smells and tastes when I offer samples in class. We also discuss what foods relished in other societies might be distasteful to Americans, such as dog and monkey. I pose the question: If roadkill is now offered to some of America's hungry, can dog and cat be far behind?

The absence of food is as important as its presence and this is a good time to remind students of the privilege of surplus. Some people have little food and are forced to scrounge for basic sustenance. In the United States, some individuals diet because they regard the cultural model of thinness as important. In this connection, it is important to note that dieting is a behavior that can only be practiced in a culture where there is an abundance of food from which to refrain.

Sight. Most people rely heavily on visual cues. The yardage and fabric of a sari conveys region, social position, and wealth in India. The particular style of a woman's veil portrays national identity, degree of religiosity, or age in some cultures in the Middle East and South Asia. Wearing indigenous dress can indicate a resurgence of ethnicity or traditionalism in parts of Africa and Latin America. I often bring Pakistani veils to class to show an example of gender identity. I also take large squares of cloth for students to see what life looks like through layers of darkly colored chiffon or open embroidery, to test their agility in wrapping themselves in fabric and still get household chores finished, and to hypothesize as to what cues children use to find a veiled mother or aunt amidst a sea of similarly veiled women; do they use jewelry (ankle, toe, wrist), height, stance, foot size, subtle veil design?

The Maori art of tattooing is discussed in connection with genealogy and mapping because here the facial design is divided into quadrants (maps) that represent parental lineages (genealogy) as well as occupations and status. After comparing several tattoos, students draw their own, keeping within Maori rules.

Using their sense of sight, students can view American culture in the recent past by watching "old" television shows like "I Love Lucy" to help analyze gender stereotypes and contemporary humor. The "March of Times" newsreel series can provide reference points from which students compare social data and glean America's world view of the 1940s. Juxtaposing two TV programs with a similar theme but two decades apart, such as the "Mary Tyler Moore Show" and "Murphy Brown," allows students to examine small scale social change.

Sound. Some students are surprised that not everyone uses a language that sounds similar to their own. I bring recordings to class of linguistic clicks, tonal languages, throat singing, and music that is both melodic and discordant to an American ear. The mixing of disparate sound and content is also interesting to students, such as bhangra (South Asian rock) and Christian salsa. Listening to the similarities in sound often elicits personal anecdotes such as the New Zealander who asked a bartender in Chicago for a book of matches and got a bowl of matzos.

Most campuses have International Student Centers of some sort, and often American students can be paired with exchange students for a session or two of conversational partnering that will be beneficial both to the international student learning colloquial English and anthropology students hearing language sounds that are very different from English. This pairing and resultant short papers can be assigned with a bit of planning.

Sometimes we neglect to inform students that silence is an important component of sound (or non-sound). There are times, for instance, in foraging societies when the absence of sound is crucial to the success of tracking, approaching, and killing hunted animals. In drawing on the subject of silence in class, students comment how they are trained from elementary school onward to jump right into a discussion and are judged by the quantity, not the quality, of what they say. They also report on how uncomfortable they feel with long periods of silence. This can lead to a discussion of cultural communication.

Smell. Because there is a physiological connection between smell and taste, it is difficult to separate these two senses. We have less control over smell than any other sense, since we can refuse to taste, cover our eyes, wear ear plugs, or put our hands in our pockets. But, it is almost impossible to avoid a smell. Few smells are neutral and when they are, we tend not to notice them, but most smells elicit positive or negative reactions. Students and I bring in "things" that have aromas or smells to show these reactions. While one student salivates at the odor of a Thai snack of dried cuttlefish, others are repelled and refuse to try it. Not being able to tolerate each other's odors has ended many a friendship.

As anthropologists, we rarely talk about odors of gasoline fires, garbage dumps, diesel exhaust, asafetida, unwashed bodies and tooth decay, but students verbally respond to the negative smells of trash-strewn streets, clogged sewer drains, bloody altars, garden privies, roasting captives, and industrial factories. These examples lead to recreating an olfactory history of Victorian England or pre-Columbian Mexico.

Touch. Most introductory anthropology texts include a section on a culture's use of space. This seems particularly relevant to business students who see hand shaking and back slapping as normal, at least among males, but close facial contact, hugging, and "fanny patting" as bizarre. Who can or cannot be touched is related to gender, class, religion, and kinship categories. Students are asked whom they can freely touch or not touch (and where) in each category. Different cross cultural examples can be brought into the discussion to show how cultural the sense of touch is.

Conclusions

The senses -- sight, sound, smell, taste, and touch -- provide an avenue to experience social phenomena, obtain data, and teach or reinforce concepts. Sensory anthropology focuses on the interaction of stimuli with culture and frames it within the context of ethnography, both in conducting research and analyzing results.

In the classroom, with relatively little effort or expense, teachers can integrate sensory-based activities with course content to teach ideas, illustrate facts, highlight qualitative methods, and lead interesting and relevant class discussions. Sensory anthropology offers a "sense-ible" approach to teaching that can be used in a variety of social science courses.